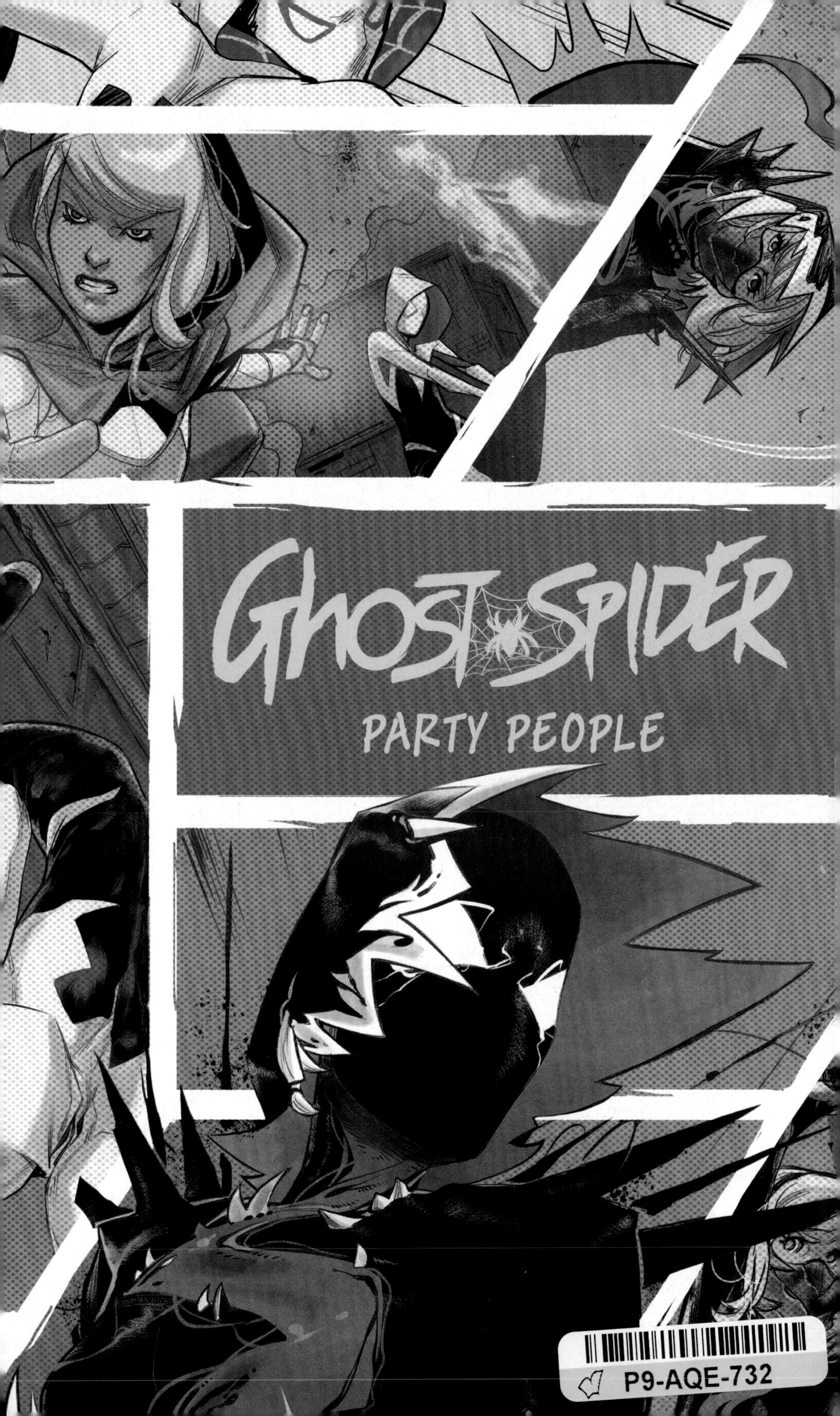
GHOST-SPIDER
PARTY PEOPLE

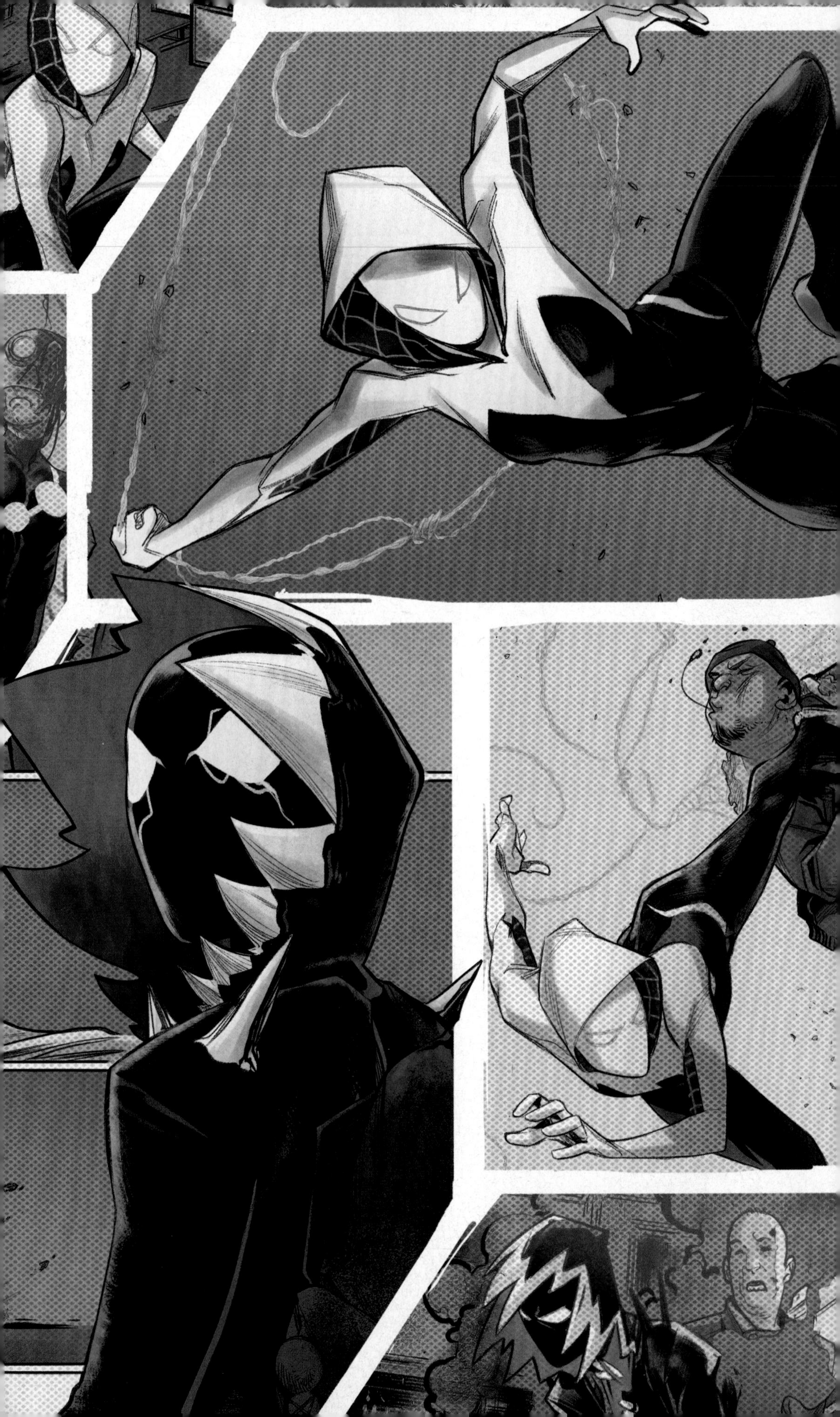

After an altercation with the Amazing Spider-Man's foe Miles Warren, A.K.A. the Jackal from Earth-616, which put her bandmates in peril, Gwen's trying to take it a bit easier.

GHOST-SPIDER

PARTY PEOPLE

Seanan McGuire
WRITER

Ig Guara
with Rosi Kämpe (#6)
ARTISTS

Ian Herring
COLOR ARTIST

VC's Clayton Cowles
LETTERER

Greg Land & Frank D'Armata (#6), Paul Pope & Bruno Seelig (#7)
and Takeshi Miyazawa & Ian Herring (#8-10)
COVER ART

Danny Khazem
ASSISTANT EDITOR

Devin Lewis
EDITOR

GWEN STACY CREATED BY **STAN LEE** & **STEVE DITKO**

COLLECTION EDITOR **JENNIFER GRÜNWALD** • ASSISTANT MANAGING EDITOR **MAIA LOY**
ASSISTANT MANAGING EDITOR **LISA MONTALBANO** • VP PRODUCTION & SPECIAL PROJECTS **JEFF YOUNGQUIST** • BOOK DESIGNER **STACIE ZUCKER**
SVP PRINT, SALES & MARKETING **DAVID GABRIEL** • EDITOR IN CHIEF **C.B. CEBULSKI**

GHOST-SPIDER VOL. 2: PARTY PEOPLE. Contains material originally published in magazine form as GHOST-SPIDER (2019) #6-10. First printing 2020. ISBN 978-1-302-92470-6. Published by MARVEL WORLDWIDE, INC., a subsidiary of MARVEL ENTERTAINMENT, LLC. OFFICE OF PUBLICATION: 1290 Avenue of the Americas, New York, NY 10104. © 2020 MARVEL No similarity between any of the names, characters, persons, and/or institutions in this magazine with those of any living or dead person or institution is intended, and any such similarity which may exist is purely coincidental. **Printed in Canada.** KEVIN FEIGE, Chief Creative Officer; DAN BUCKLEY, President, Marvel Entertainment; JOHN NEE, Publisher; JOE QUESADA, EVP & Creative Director; TOM BREVOORT, SVP of Publishing; DAVID BOGART, Associate Publisher & SVP of Talent Affairs; Publishing & Partnership; DAVID GABRIEL, VP of Print & Digital Publishing; JEFF YOUNGQUIST, VP of Production & Special Projects; DAN CARR, Executive Director of Publishing Technology; ALEX MORALES, Director of Publishing Operations; DAN EDINGTON, Managing Editor; RICKEY PURDIN, Director of Talent Relations; SUSAN CRESPI, Production Manager; STAN LEE, Chairman Emeritus. For information regarding advertising in Marvel Comics or on Marvel.com, please contact Vit DeBellis, Custom Solutions & Integrated Advertising Manager, at vdebellis@marvel.com. For Marvel subscription inquiries, please call 888-511-5480. **Manufactured between 10/23/2020 and 11/24/2020 by SOLISCO PRINTERS, SCOTT, QC, CANADA.**

10 9 8 7 6 5 4 3 2 1

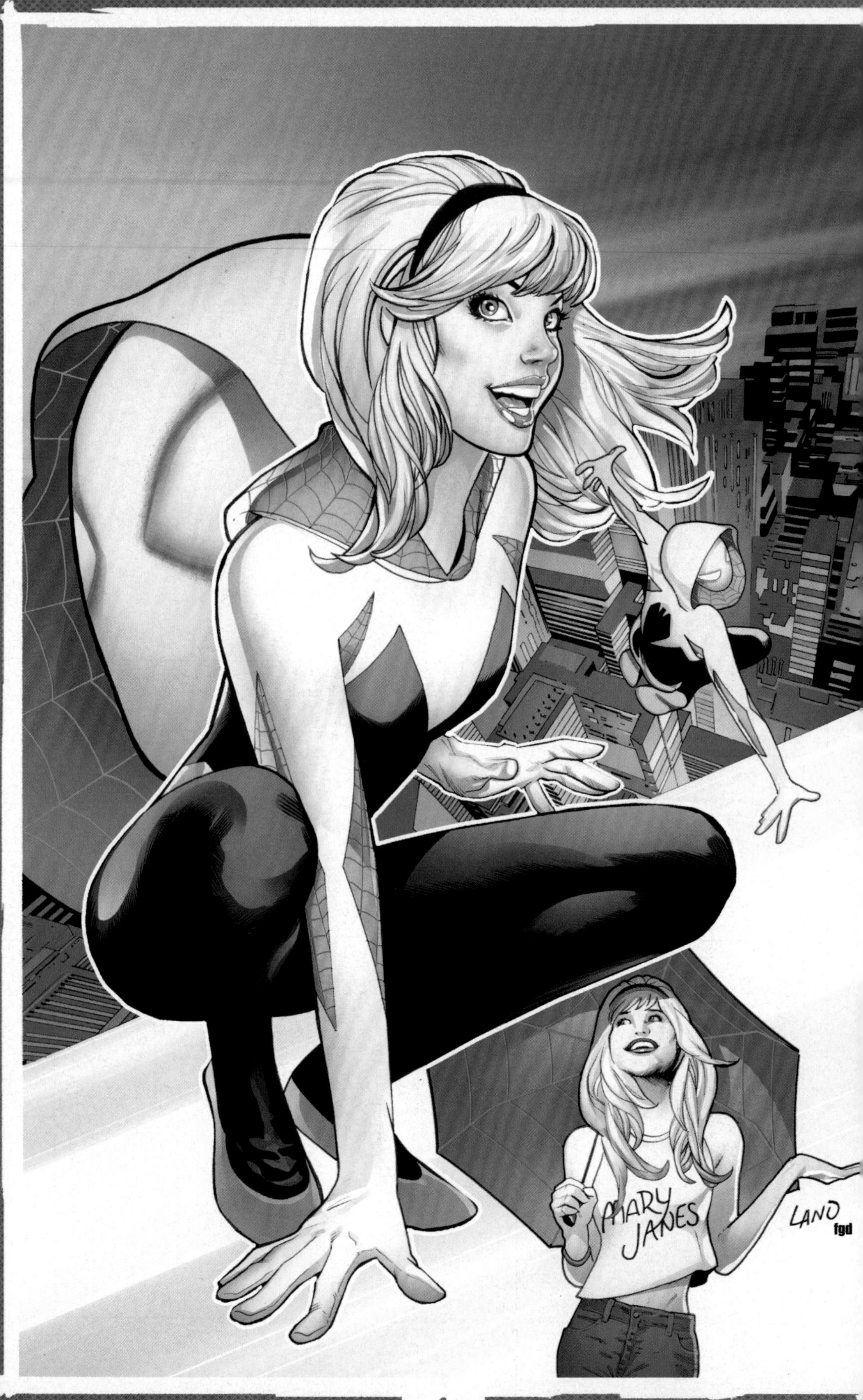
MARY
JANES
LANO
fgd

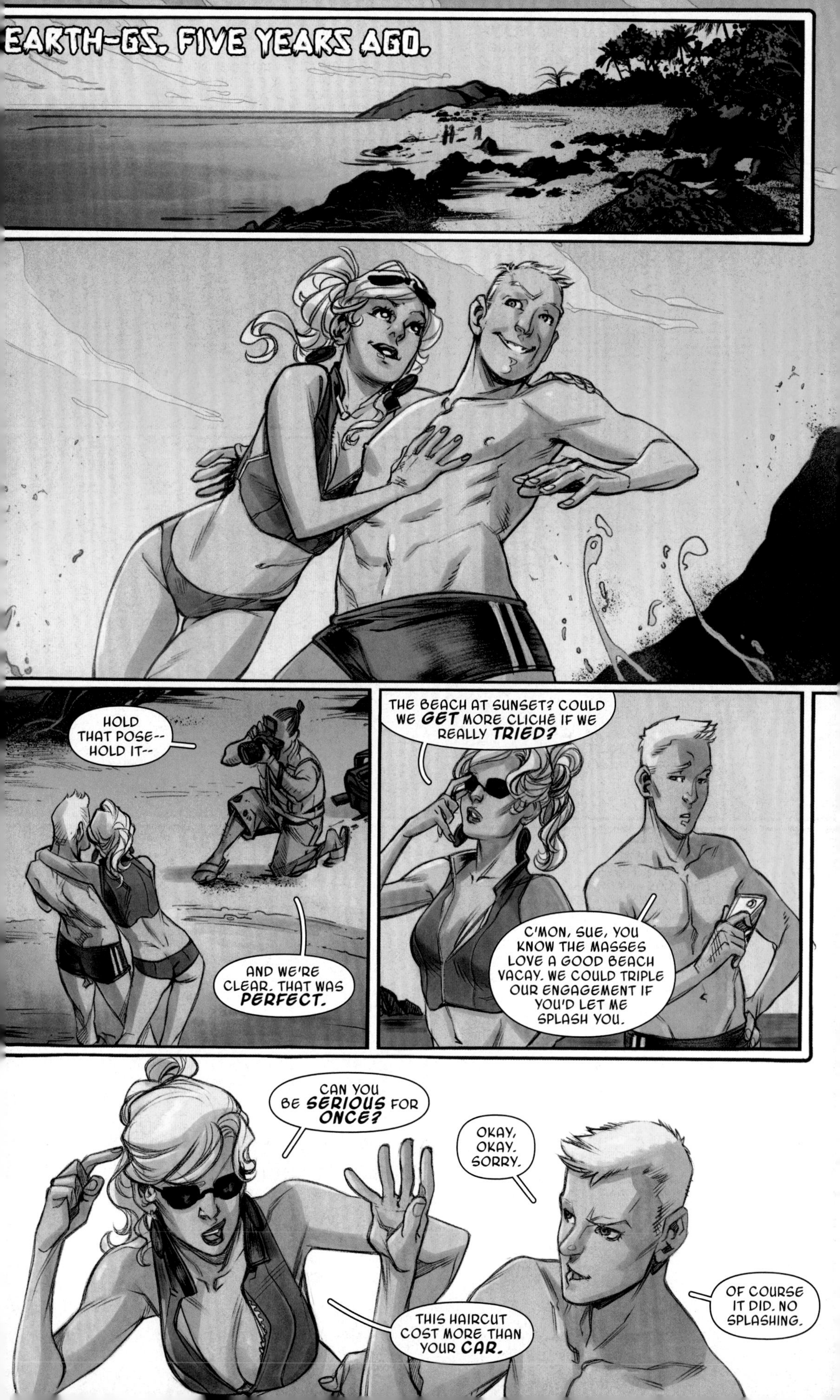
EARTH-GS. FIVE YEARS AGO.
HOLD THAT POSE-- HOLD IT--
AND WE'RE CLEAR. THAT WAS PERFECT.
THE BEACH AT SUNSET? COULD WE GET MORE CLICHÉ IF WE REALLY TRIED?
C'MON, SUE, YOU KNOW THE MASSES LOVE A GOOD BEACH VACAY. WE COULD TRIPLE OUR ENGAGEMENT IF YOU'D LET ME SPLASH YOU.
CAN YOU BE SERIOUS FOR ONCE?
OKAY, OKAY. SORRY.
THIS HAIRCUT COST MORE THAN YOUR CAR.
OF COURSE IT DID. NO SPLASHING.

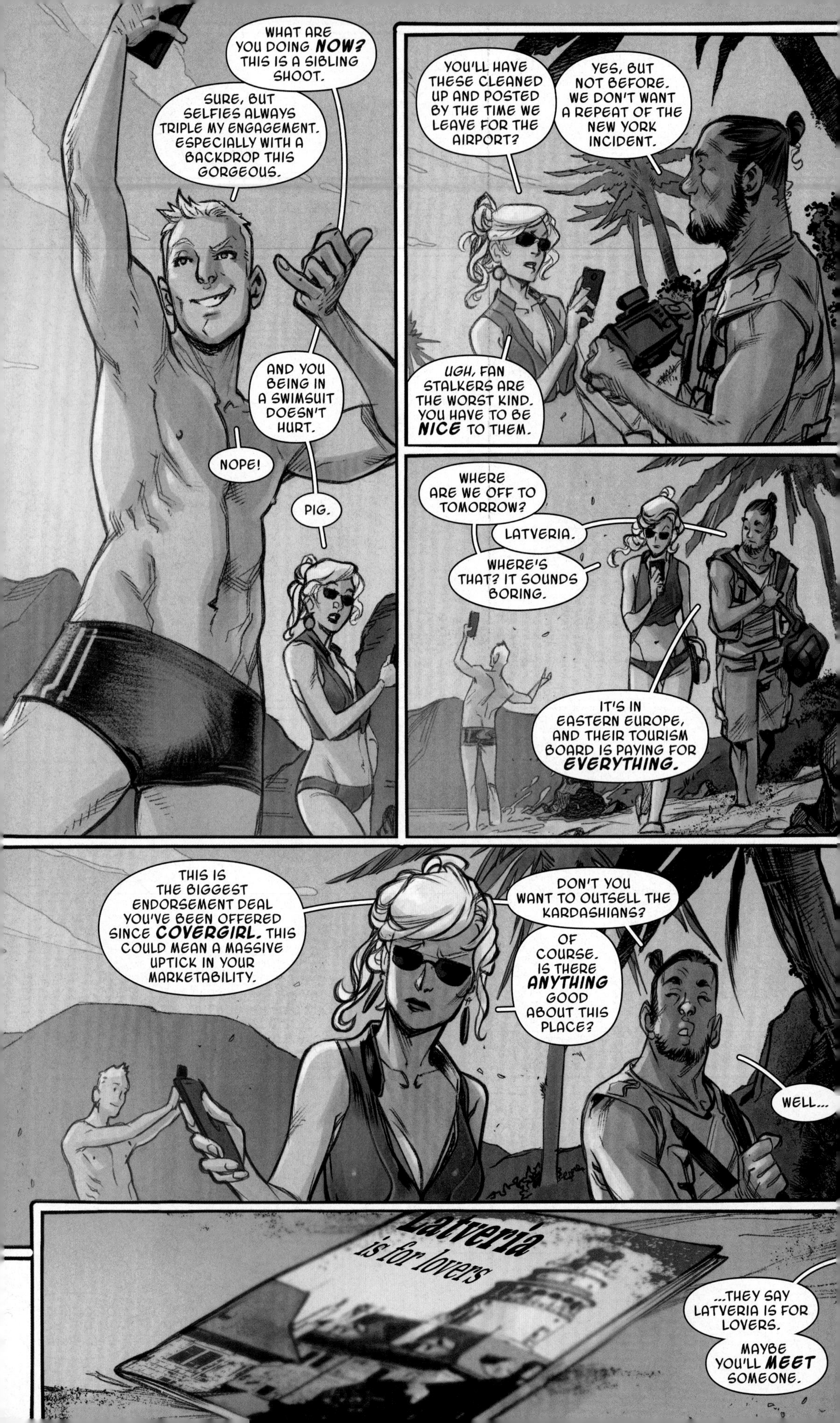
WHAT ARE YOU DOING NOW? THIS IS A SIBLING SHOOT.
SURE, BUT SELFIES ALWAYS TRIPLE MY ENGAGEMENT. ESPECIALLY WITH A BACKDROP THIS GORGEOUS.
AND YOU BEING IN A SWIMSUIT DOESN'T HURT.
NOPE!
PIG.
YOU'LL HAVE THESE CLEANED UP AND POSTED BY THE TIME WE LEAVE FOR THE AIRPORT?
YES, BUT NOT BEFORE. WE DON'T WANT A REPEAT OF THE NEW YORK INCIDENT.
UGH, FAN STALKERS ARE THE WORST KIND. YOU HAVE TO BE NICE TO THEM.
WHERE ARE WE OFF TO TOMORROW?
LATVERIA.
WHERE'S THAT? IT SOUNDS BORING.
IT'S IN EASTERN EUROPE, AND THEIR TOURISM BOARD IS PAYING FOR EVERYTHING.
THIS IS THE BIGGEST ENDORSEMENT DEAL YOU'VE BEEN OFFERED SINCE COVERGIRL. THIS COULD MEAN A MASSIVE UPTICK IN YOUR MARKETABILITY.
DON'T YOU WANT TO OUTSELL THE KARDASHIANS?
OF COURSE. IS THERE ANYTHING GOOD ABOUT THIS PLACE?
WELL...
Latveria is for lovers
...THEY SAY LATVERIA IS FOR LOVERS.
MAYBE YOU'LL MEET SOMEONE.

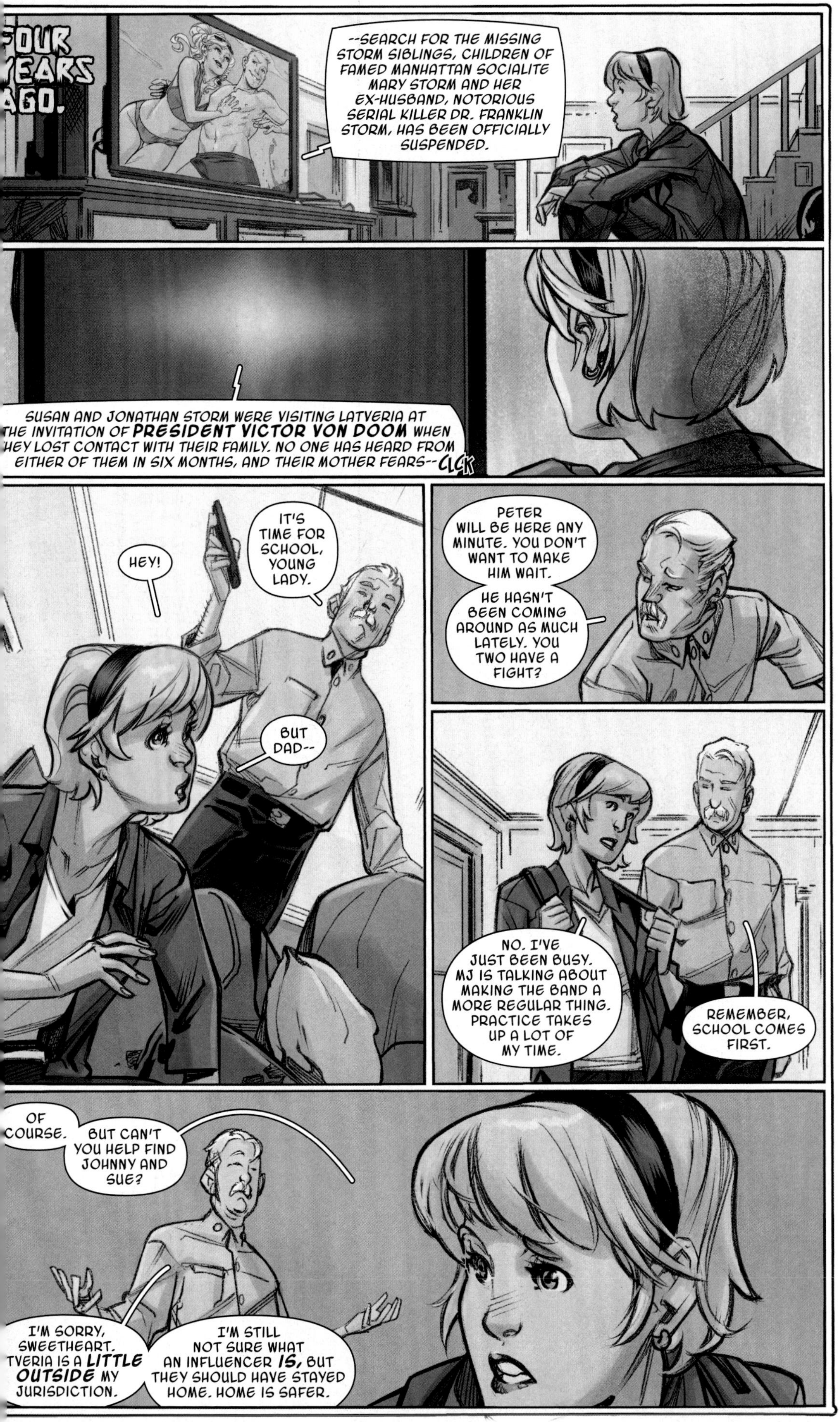
FOUR YEARS AGO.
--SEARCH FOR THE MISSING STORM SIBLINGS, CHILDREN OF FAMED MANHATTAN SOCIALITE MARY STORM AND HER EX-HUSBAND, NOTORIOUS SERIAL KILLER DR. FRANKLIN STORM, HAS BEEN OFFICIALLY SUSPENDED.
SUSAN AND JONATHAN STORM WERE VISITING LATVERIA AT THE INVITATION OF PRESIDENT VICTOR VON DOOM WHEN THEY LOST CONTACT WITH THEIR FAMILY. NO ONE HAS HEARD FROM EITHER OF THEM IN SIX MONTHS, AND THEIR MOTHER FEARS--
CLCK
HEY!
IT'S TIME FOR SCHOOL, YOUNG LADY.
BUT DAD--
PETER WILL BE HERE ANY MINUTE. YOU DON'T WANT TO MAKE HIM WAIT.
HE HASN'T BEEN COMING AROUND AS MUCH LATELY. YOU TWO HAVE A FIGHT?
NO. I'VE JUST BEEN BUSY. MJ IS TALKING ABOUT MAKING THE BAND A MORE REGULAR THING. PRACTICE TAKES UP A LOT OF MY TIME.
REMEMBER, SCHOOL COMES FIRST.
OF COURSE.
BUT CAN'T YOU HELP FIND JOHNNY AND SUE?
I'M SORRY, SWEETHEART. LATVERIA IS A LITTLE OUTSIDE MY JURISDICTION.
I'M STILL NOT SURE WHAT AN INFLUENCER IS, BUT THEY SHOULD HAVE STAYED HOME. HOME IS SAFER.

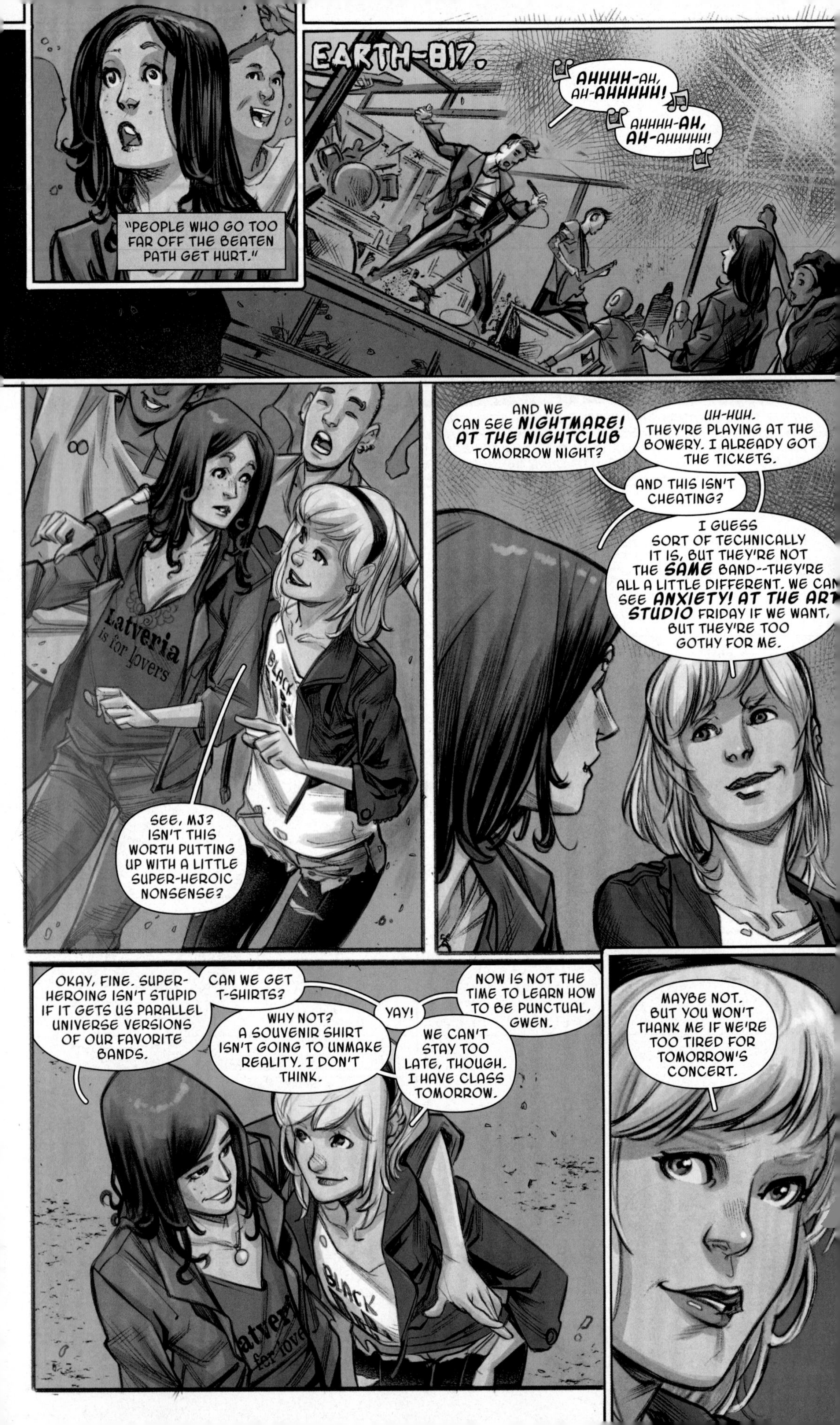
"PEOPLE WHO GO TOO FAR OFF THE BEATEN PATH GET HURT."
EARTH-817.
AHHHH-AH, AH-AHHHHH!
AHHHH-AH, AH-AHHHHH!
SEE, MJ? ISN'T THIS WORTH PUTTING UP WITH A LITTLE SUPER-HEROIC NONSENSE?
AND WE CAN SEE NIGHTMARE! AT THE NIGHTCLUB TOMORROW NIGHT?
UH-HUH. THEY'RE PLAYING AT THE BOWERY. I ALREADY GOT THE TICKETS.
AND THIS ISN'T CHEATING?
I GUESS SORT OF TECHNICALLY IT IS, BUT THEY'RE NOT THE SAME BAND--THEY'RE ALL A LITTLE DIFFERENT. WE CAN SEE ANXIETY! AT THE ART STUDIO FRIDAY IF WE WANT, BUT THEY'RE TOO GOTHY FOR ME.
OKAY, FINE. SUPER-HEROING ISN'T STUPID IF IT GETS US PARALLEL UNIVERSE VERSIONS OF OUR FAVORITE BANDS.
CAN WE GET T-SHIRTS?
WHY NOT? A SOUVENIR SHIRT ISN'T GOING TO UNMAKE REALITY. I DON'T THINK.
YAY!
WE CAN'T STAY TOO LATE, THOUGH. I HAVE CLASS TOMORROW.
NOW IS NOT THE TIME TO LEARN HOW TO BE PUNCTUAL, GWEN.
MAYBE NOT. BUT YOU WON'T THANK ME IF WE'RE TOO TIRED FOR TOMORROW'S CONCERT.

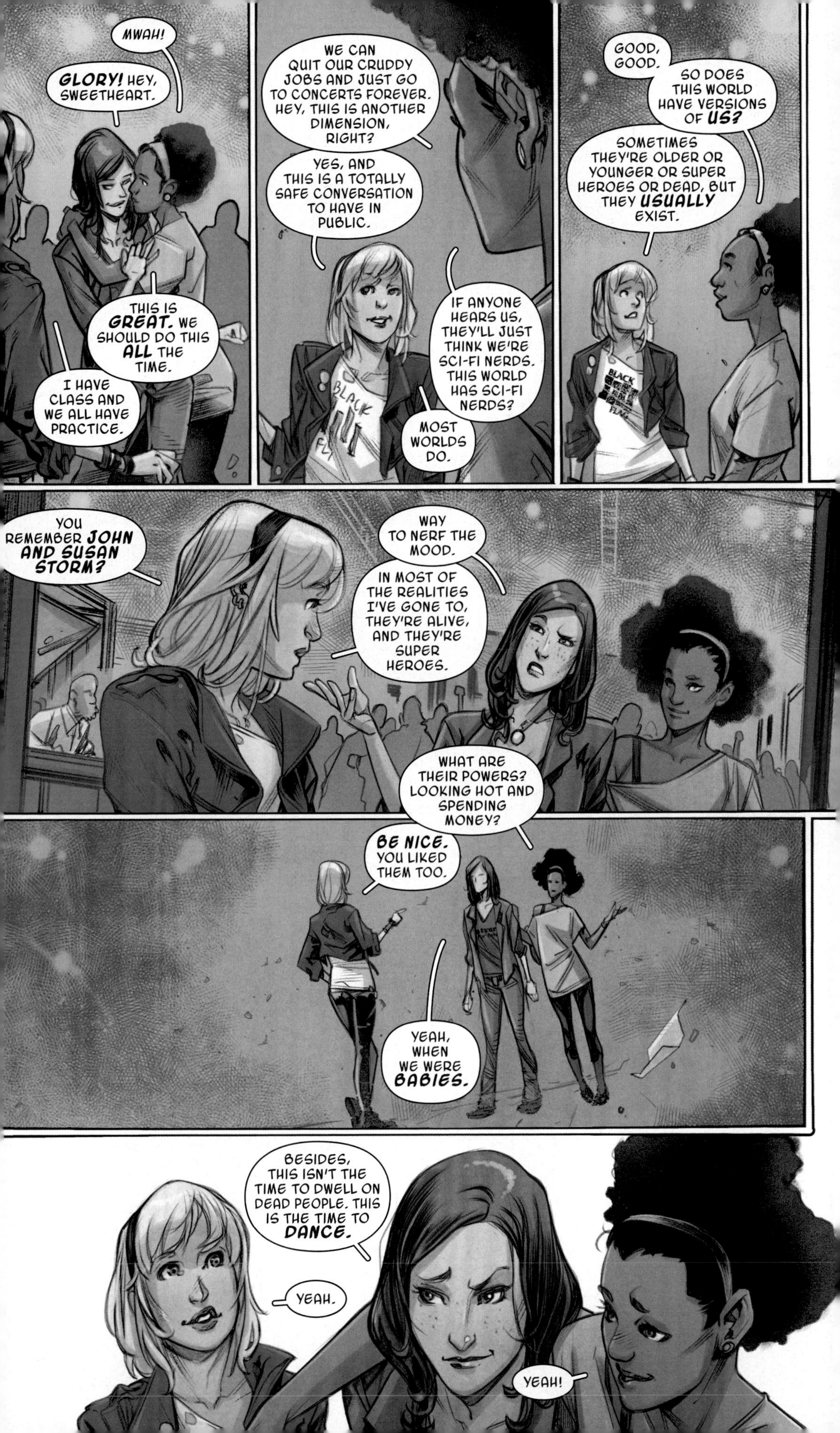
MWAH!
GLORY! HEY, SWEETHEART.
THIS IS GREAT. WE SHOULD DO THIS ALL THE TIME.
I HAVE CLASS AND WE ALL HAVE PRACTICE.
WE CAN QUIT OUR CRUDDY JOBS AND JUST GO TO CONCERTS FOREVER. HEY, THIS IS ANOTHER DIMENSION, RIGHT?
YES, AND THIS IS A TOTALLY SAFE CONVERSATION TO HAVE IN PUBLIC.
IF ANYONE HEARS US, THEY'LL JUST THINK WE'RE SCI-FI NERDS. THIS WORLD HAS SCI-FI NERDS?
MOST WORLDS DO.
GOOD, GOOD.
SO DOES THIS WORLD HAVE VERSIONS OF US?
SOMETIMES THEY'RE OLDER OR YOUNGER OR SUPER HEROES OR DEAD, BUT THEY USUALLY EXIST.
YOU REMEMBER JOHN AND SUSAN STORM?
WAY TO NERF THE MOOD.
IN MOST OF THE REALITIES I'VE GONE TO, THEY'RE ALIVE, AND THEY'RE SUPER HEROES.
WHAT ARE THEIR POWERS? LOOKING HOT AND SPENDING MONEY?
BE NICE. YOU LIKED THEM TOO.
YEAH, WHEN WE WERE BABIES.
BESIDES, THIS ISN'T THE TIME TO DWELL ON DEAD PEOPLE. THIS IS THE TIME TO DANCE.
YEAH.
YEAH!

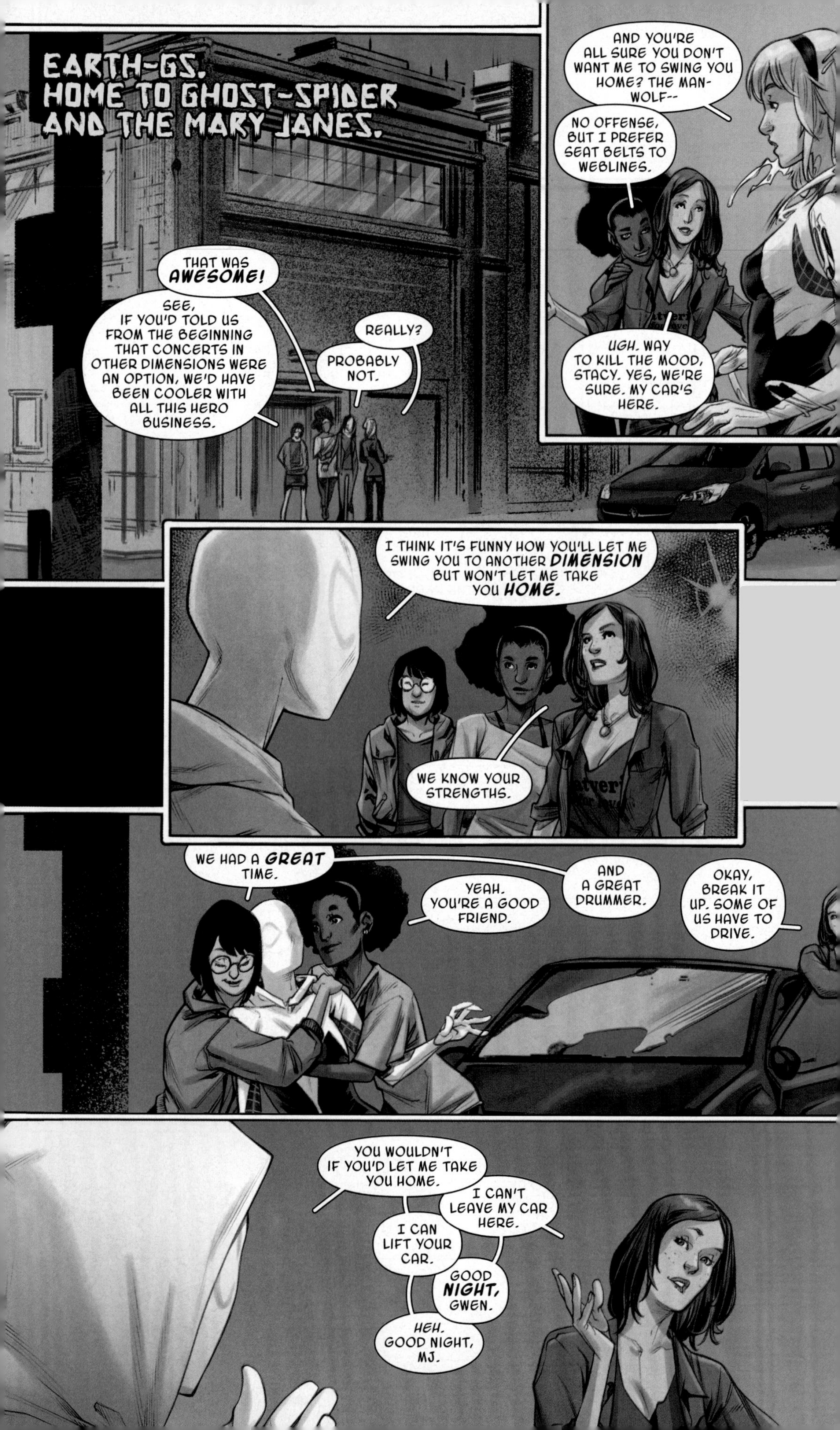
EARTH-65. HOME TO GHOST-SPIDER AND THE MARY JANES.
THAT WAS AWESOME!
SEE, IF YOU'D TOLD US FROM THE BEGINNING THAT CONCERTS IN OTHER DIMENSIONS WERE AN OPTION, WE'D HAVE BEEN COOLER WITH ALL THIS HERO BUSINESS.
REALLY?
PROBABLY NOT.
AND YOU'RE ALL SURE YOU DON'T WANT ME TO SWING YOU HOME? THE MAN-WOLF--
NO OFFENSE, BUT I PREFER SEAT BELTS TO WEBLINES.
UGH. WAY TO KILL THE MOOD, STACY. YES, WE'RE SURE. MY CAR'S HERE.
I THINK IT'S FUNNY HOW YOU'LL LET ME SWING YOU TO ANOTHER DIMENSION BUT WON'T LET ME TAKE YOU HOME.
WE KNOW YOUR STRENGTHS.
WE HAD A GREAT TIME.
YEAH. YOU'RE A GOOD FRIEND.
AND A GREAT DRUMMER.
OKAY, BREAK IT UP. SOME OF US HAVE TO DRIVE.
YOU WOULDN'T IF YOU'D LET ME TAKE YOU HOME.
I CAN'T LEAVE MY CAR HERE.
I CAN LIFT YOUR CAR.
GOOD NIGHT, GWEN.
HEH. GOOD NIGHT, MJ.

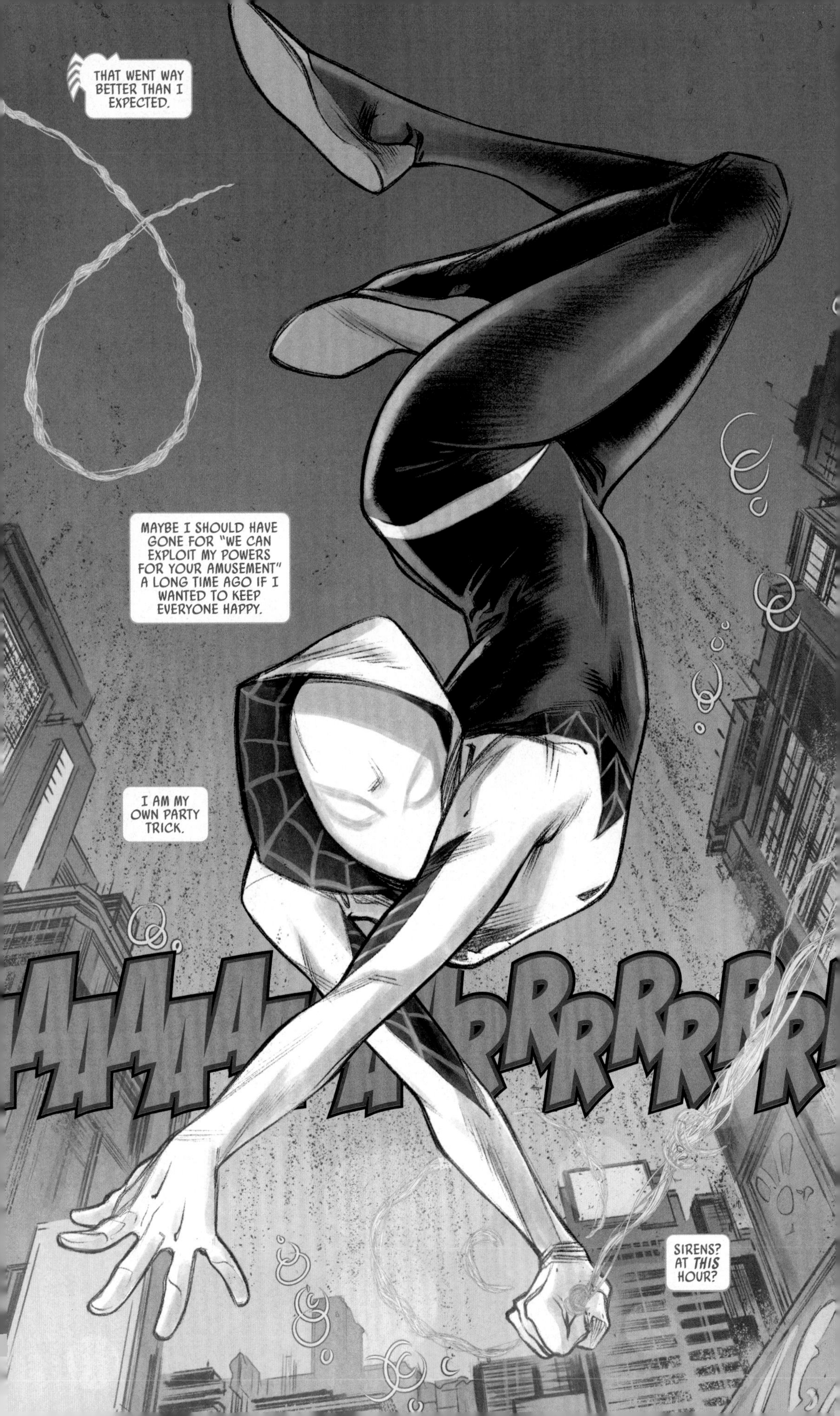
THAT WENT WAY BETTER THAN I EXPECTED.
MAYBE I SHOULD HAVE GONE FOR "WE CAN EXPLOIT MY POWERS FOR YOUR AMUSEMENT" A LONG TIME AGO IF I WANTED TO KEEP EVERYONE HAPPY.
I AM MY OWN PARTY TRICK.
SIRENS? AT *THIS* HOUR?

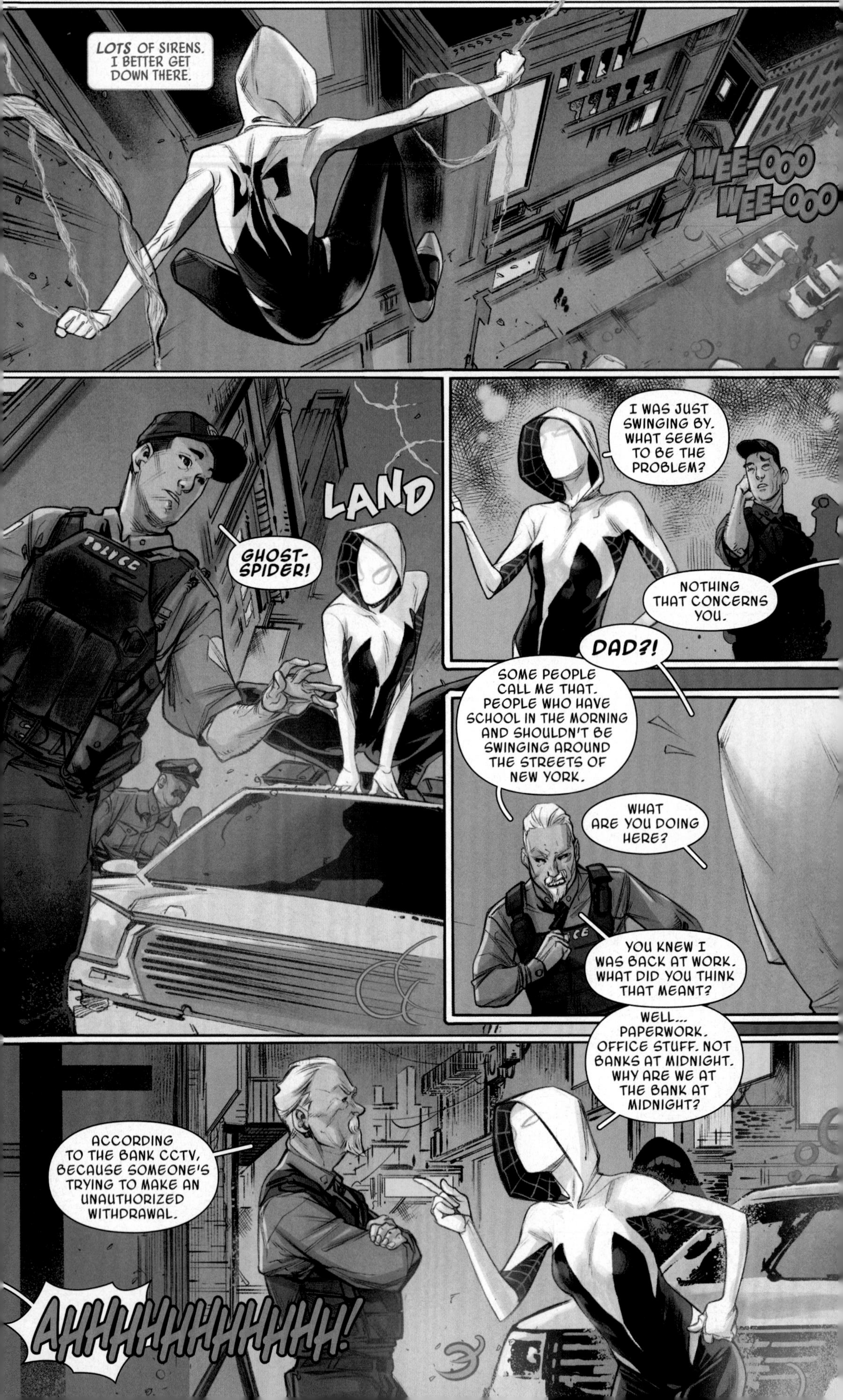

LOTS OF SIRENS. I BETTER GET DOWN THERE.
WEE-OOO WEE-OOO
LAND
GHOST-SPIDER!
I WAS JUST SWINGING BY. WHAT SEEMS TO BE THE PROBLEM?
NOTHING THAT CONCERNS YOU.
DAD?!
SOME PEOPLE CALL ME THAT. PEOPLE WHO HAVE SCHOOL IN THE MORNING AND SHOULDN'T BE SWINGING AROUND THE STREETS OF NEW YORK.
WHAT ARE YOU DOING HERE?
YOU KNEW I WAS BACK AT WORK. WHAT DID YOU THINK THAT MEANT?
WELL... PAPERWORK. OFFICE STUFF. NOT BANKS AT MIDNIGHT. WHY ARE WE AT THE BANK AT MIDNIGHT?
ACCORDING TO THE BANK CCTV, BECAUSE SOMEONE'S TRYING TO MAKE AN UNAUTHORIZED WITHDRAWAL.
AHHHHHHHHHHH!

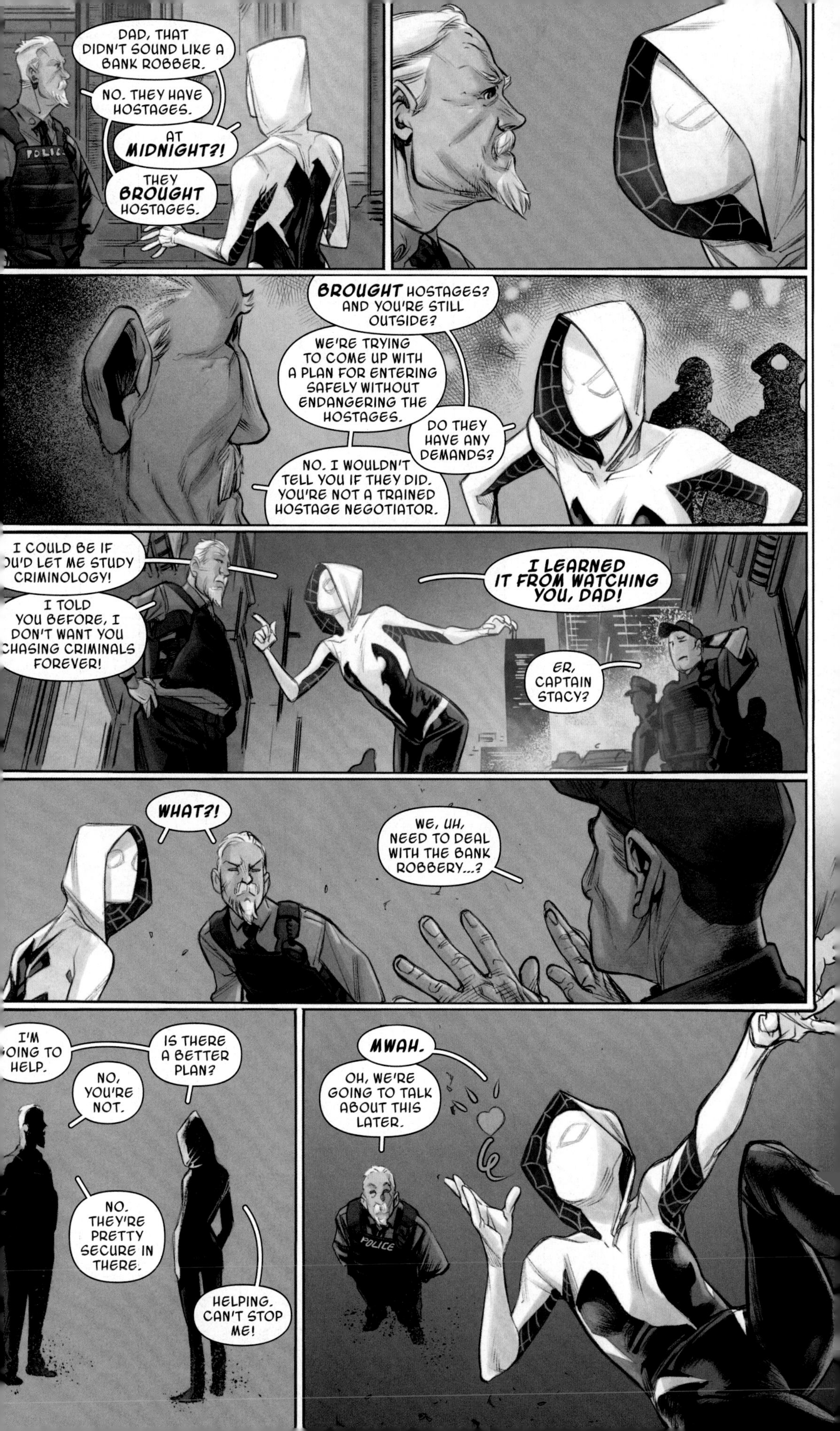
DAD, THAT DIDN'T SOUND LIKE A BANK ROBBER.
NO. THEY HAVE HOSTAGES.
AT MIDNIGHT?!
THEY BROUGHT HOSTAGES.
BROUGHT HOSTAGES? AND YOU'RE STILL OUTSIDE?
WE'RE TRYING TO COME UP WITH A PLAN FOR ENTERING SAFELY WITHOUT ENDANGERING THE HOSTAGES.
DO THEY HAVE ANY DEMANDS?
NO. I WOULDN'T TELL YOU IF THEY DID. YOU'RE NOT A TRAINED HOSTAGE NEGOTIATOR.
I COULD BE IF OU'D LET ME STUDY CRIMINOLOGY!
I TOLD YOU BEFORE, I DON'T WANT YOU CHASING CRIMINALS FOREVER!
I LEARNED IT FROM WATCHING YOU, DAD!
ER, CAPTAIN STACY?
WHAT?!
WE, UH, NEED TO DEAL WITH THE BANK ROBBERY...?
I'M OING TO HELP.
NO, YOU'RE NOT.
IS THERE A BETTER PLAN?
NO. THEY'RE PRETTY SECURE IN THERE.
HELPING. CAN'T STOP ME!
MWAH.
OH, WE'RE GOING TO TALK ABOUT THIS LATER.

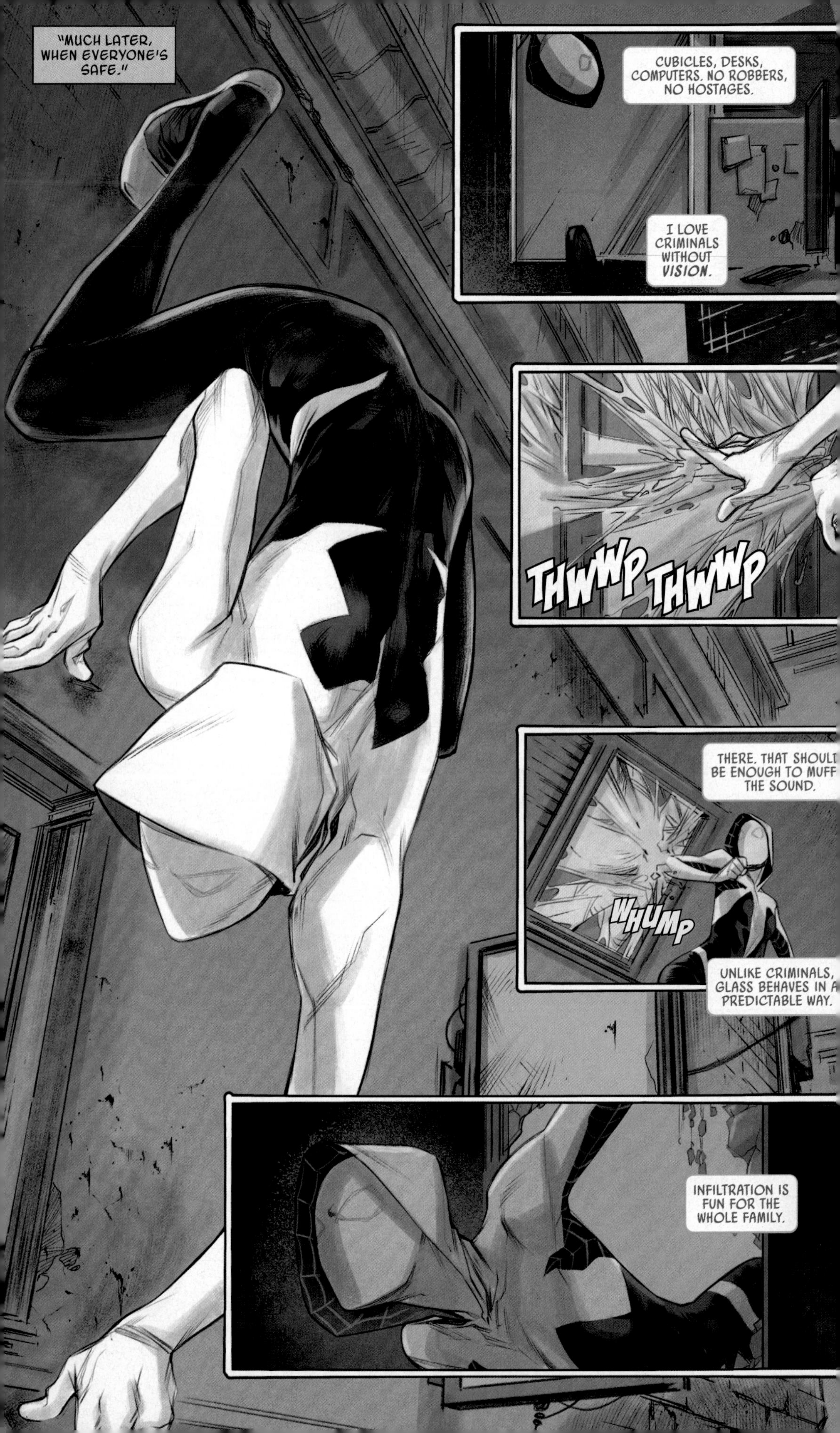
"MUCH LATER, WHEN EVERYONE'S SAFE."
CUBICLES, DESKS, COMPUTERS. NO ROBBERS, NO HOSTAGES.
I LOVE CRIMINALS WITHOUT VISION.
THWWP THWWP
THERE. THAT SHOULD BE ENOUGH TO MUFF THE SOUND.
WHUMP
UNLIKE CRIMINALS, GLASS BEHAVES IN A PREDICTABLE WAY.
INFILTRATION IS FUN FOR THE WHOLE FAMILY.

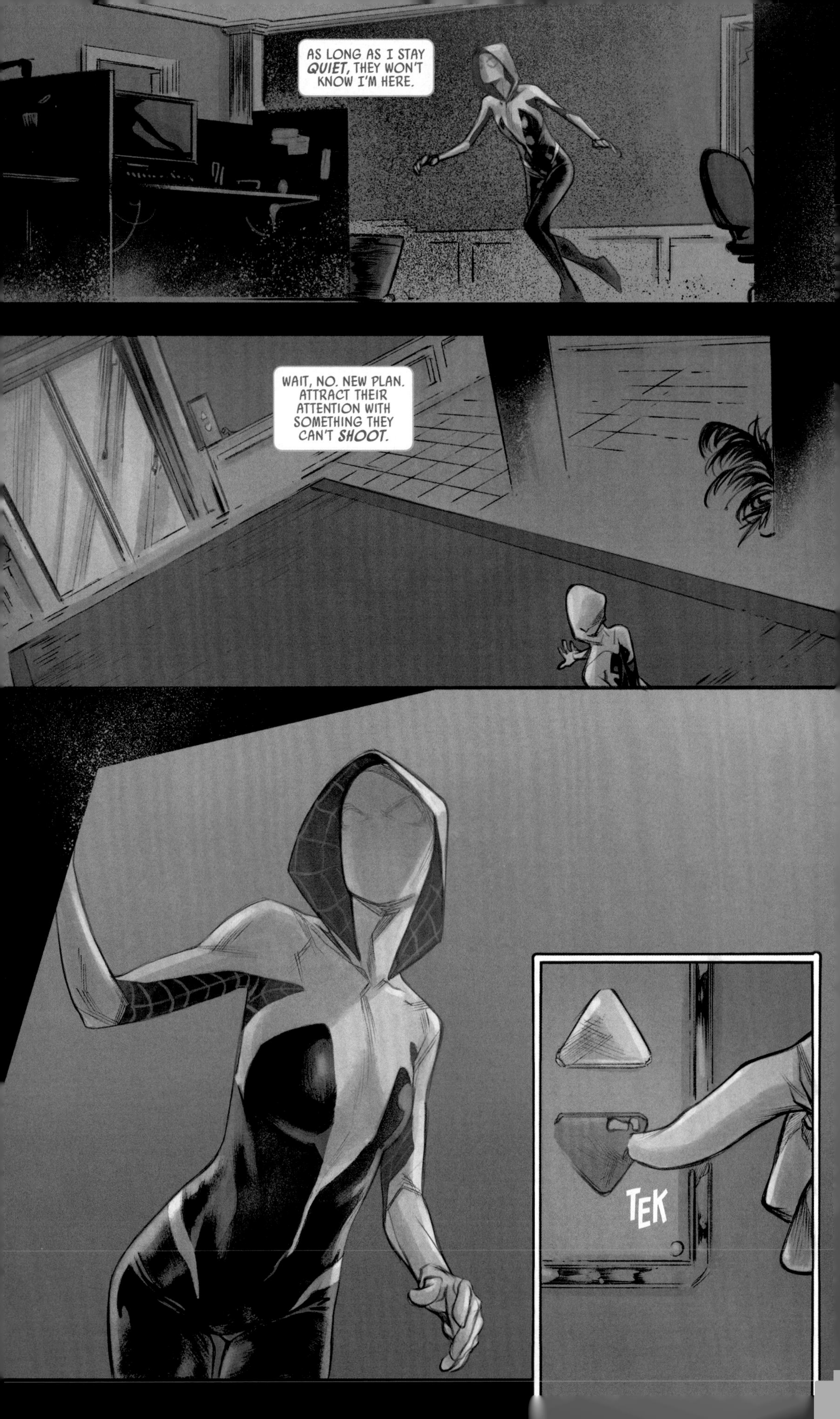
AS LONG AS I STAY QUIET, THEY WON'T KNOW I'M HERE.
WAIT, NO. NEW PLAN. ATTRACT THEIR ATTENTION WITH SOMETHING THEY CAN'T SHOOT.
TEK

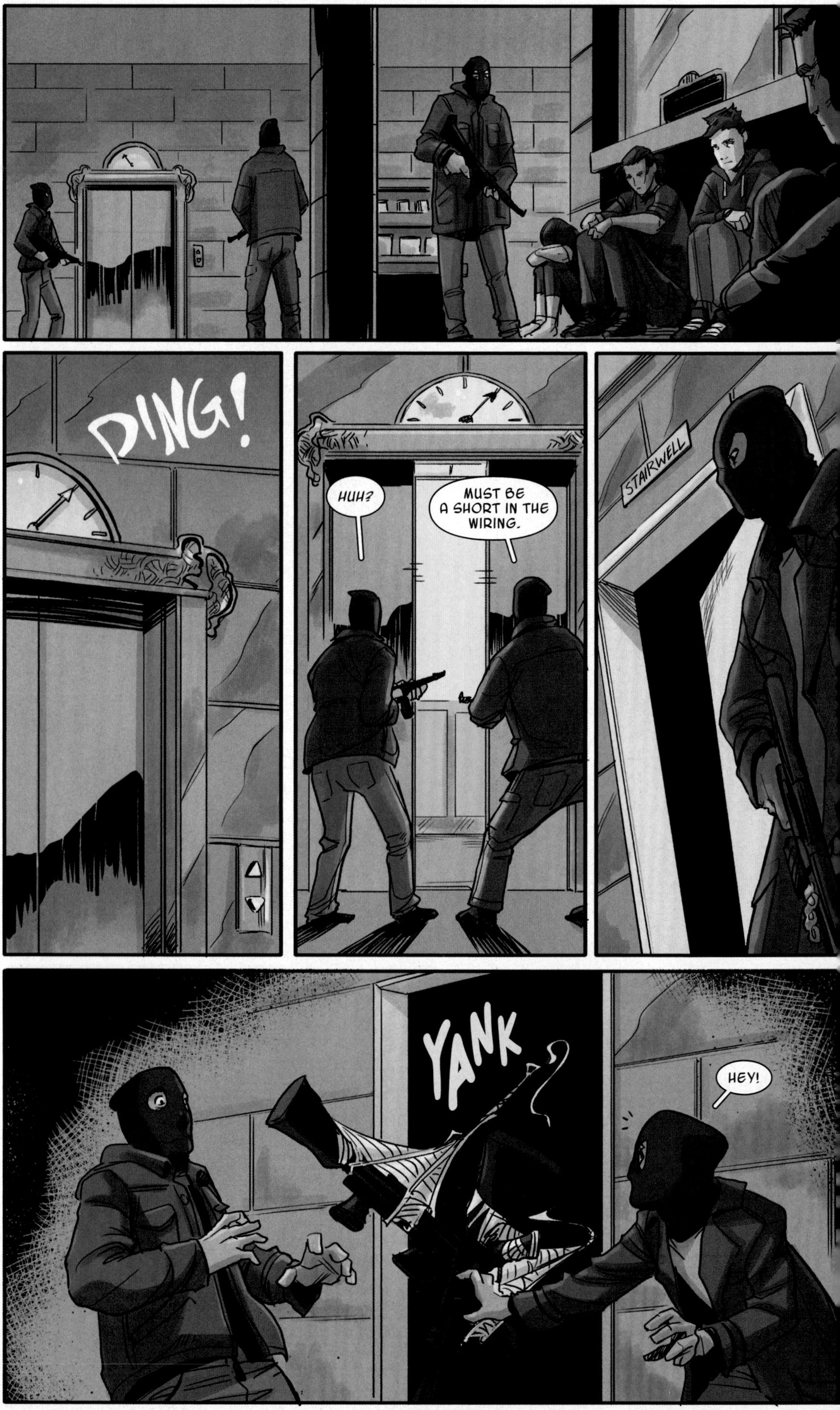
DING!
HUH?
MUST BE A SHORT IN THE WIRING.
STAIRWELL
YANK
HEY!

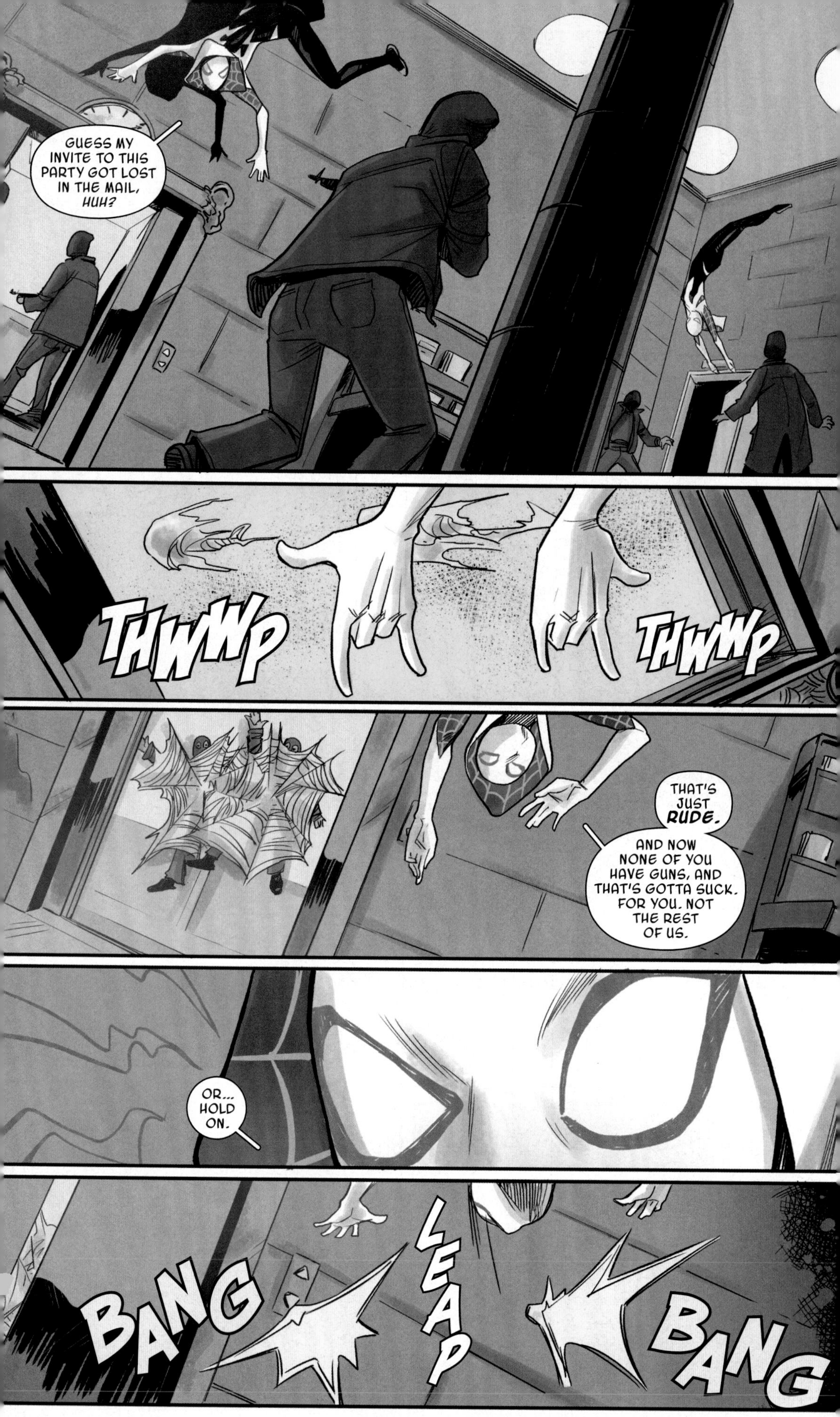
GUESS MY INVITE TO THIS PARTY GOT LOST IN THE MAIL, HUH?
THWWP
THWWP
THAT'S JUST RUDE.
AND NOW NONE OF YOU HAVE GUNS, AND THAT'S GOTTA SUCK. FOR YOU. NOT THE REST OF US.
OR... HOLD ON.
BANG
LEAP
BANG

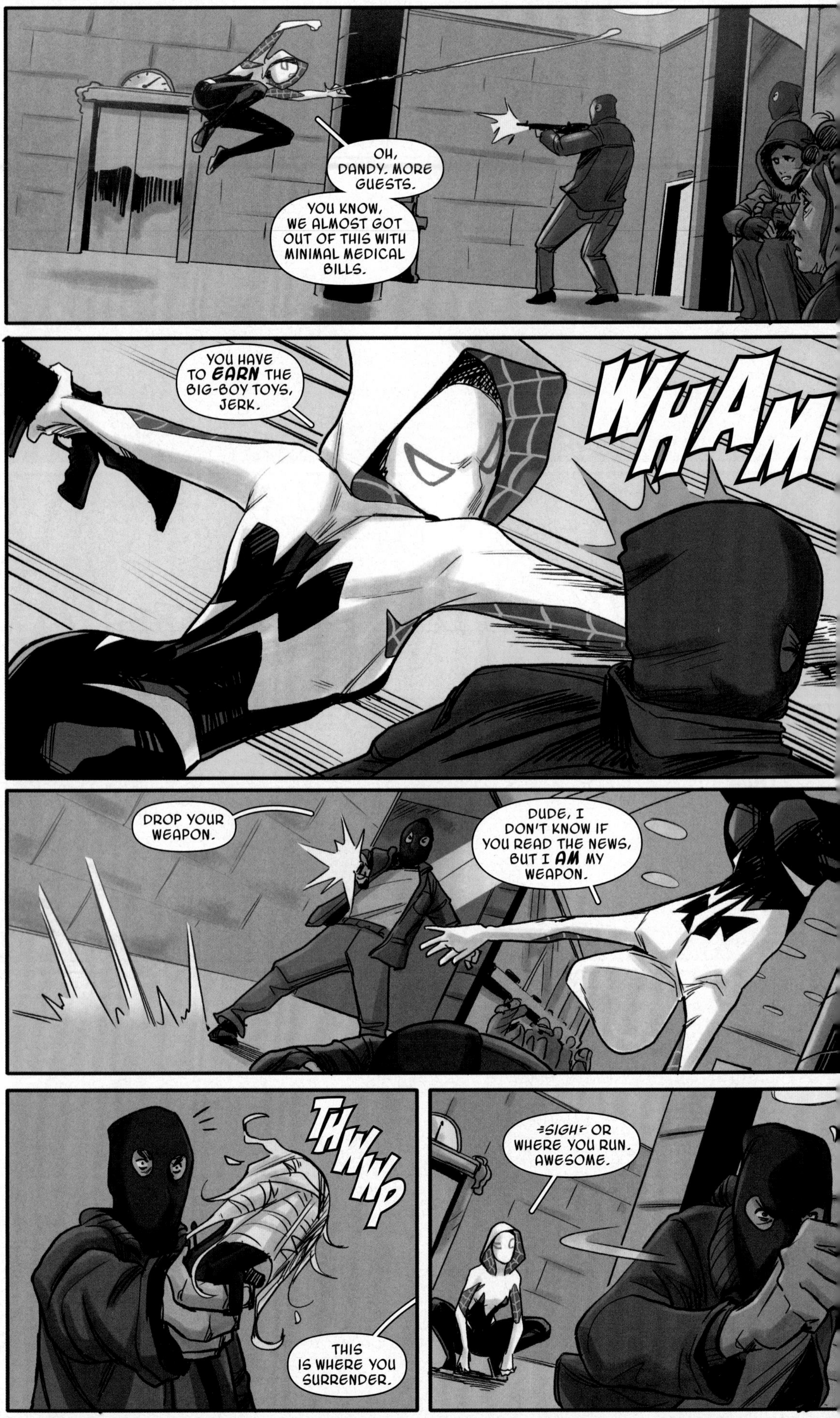
OH, DANDY. MORE GUESTS.
YOU KNOW, WE ALMOST GOT OUT OF THIS WITH MINIMAL MEDICAL BILLS.
YOU HAVE TO **EARN** THE BIG-BOY TOYS, JERK.
WHAM
DROP YOUR WEAPON.
DUDE, I DON'T KNOW IF YOU READ THE NEWS, BUT I **AM** MY WEAPON.
THWWP
THIS IS WHERE YOU SURRENDER.
=SIGH= OR WHERE YOU RUN. AWESOME.

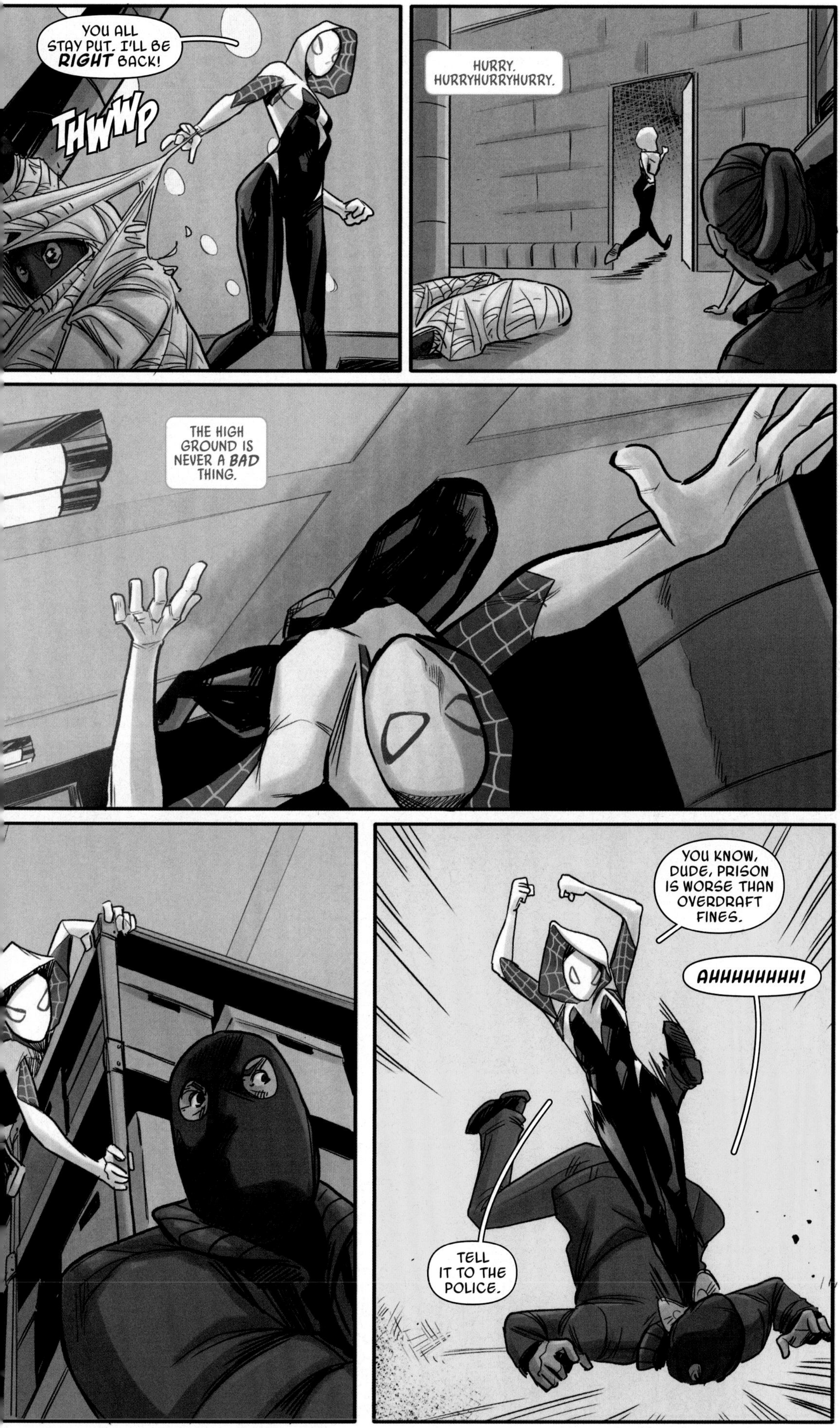
YOU ALL STAY PUT. I'LL BE **RIGHT** BACK!
THWWP
HURRY. HURRYHURRYHURRY.
THE HIGH GROUND IS NEVER A *BAD* THING.
YOU KNOW, DUDE, PRISON IS WORSE THAN OVERDRAFT FINES.
AHHHHHHHH!
TELL IT TO THE POLICE.

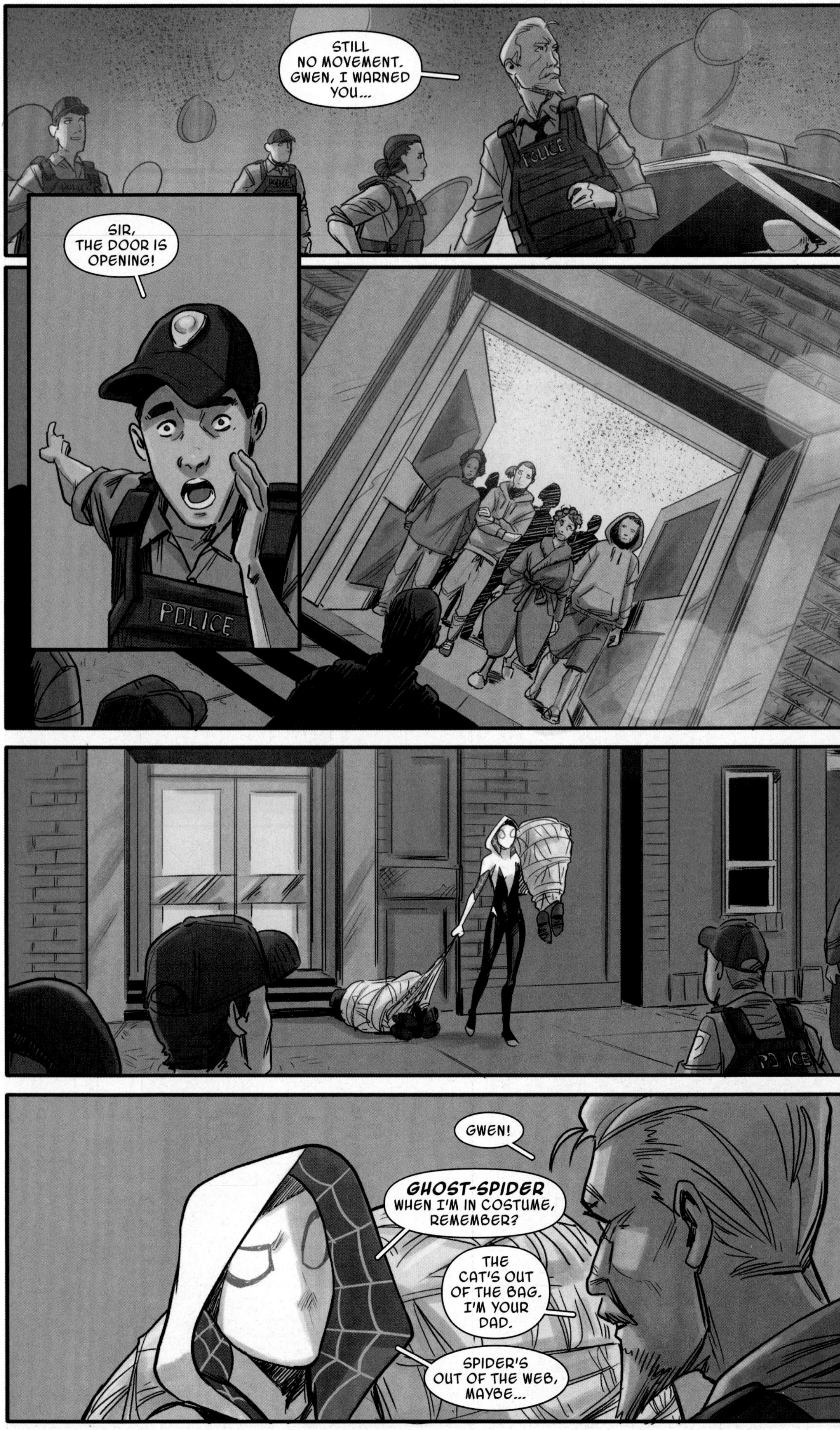
STILL NO MOVEMENT. GWEN, I WARNED YOU...
POLICE
SIR, THE DOOR IS OPENING!
POLICE
POLICE
GWEN!
GHOST-SPIDER WHEN I'M IN COSTUME, REMEMBER?
THE CAT'S OUT OF THE BAG. I'M YOUR DAD.
SPIDER'S OUT OF THE WEB, MAYBE...

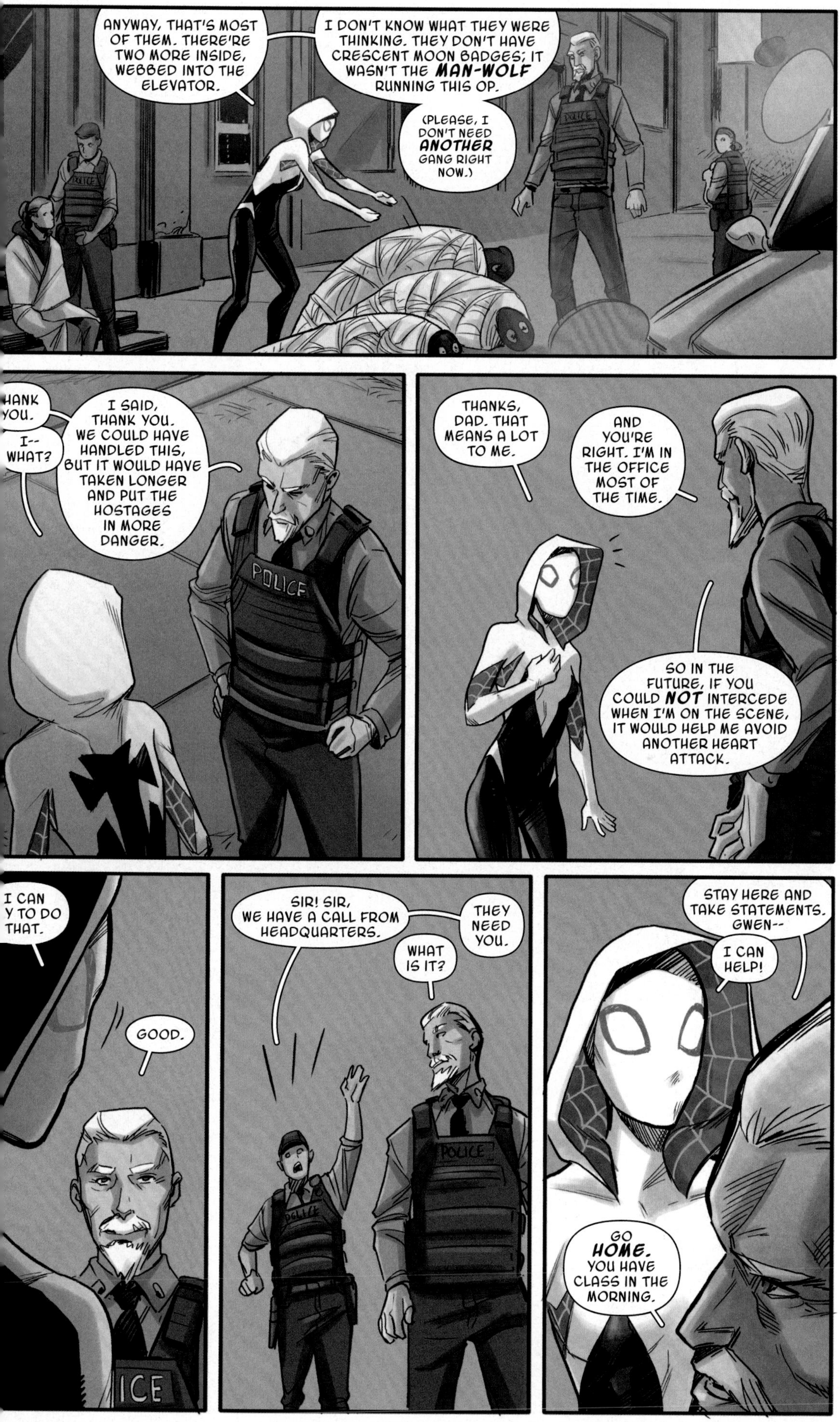
ANYWAY, THAT'S MOST OF THEM. THERE'RE TWO MORE INSIDE, WEBBED INTO THE ELEVATOR.
I DON'T KNOW WHAT THEY WERE THINKING. THEY DON'T HAVE CRESCENT MOON BADGES; IT WASN'T THE MAN-WOLF RUNNING THIS OP.
(PLEASE, I DON'T NEED ANOTHER GANG RIGHT NOW.)
POLICE
HANK YOU.
I-- WHAT?
I SAID, THANK YOU. WE COULD HAVE HANDLED THIS, BUT IT WOULD HAVE TAKEN LONGER AND PUT THE HOSTAGES IN MORE DANGER.
POLICE
THANKS, DAD. THAT MEANS A LOT TO ME.
AND YOU'RE RIGHT. I'M IN THE OFFICE MOST OF THE TIME.
SO IN THE FUTURE, IF YOU COULD NOT INTERCEDE WHEN I'M ON THE SCENE, IT WOULD HELP ME AVOID ANOTHER HEART ATTACK.
I CAN Y TO DO THAT.
GOOD.
ICE
SIR! SIR, WE HAVE A CALL FROM HEADQUARTERS.
THEY NEED YOU.
WHAT IS IT?
POLICE
STAY HERE AND TAKE STATEMENTS. GWEN--
I CAN HELP!
GO HOME. YOU HAVE CLASS IN THE MORNING.

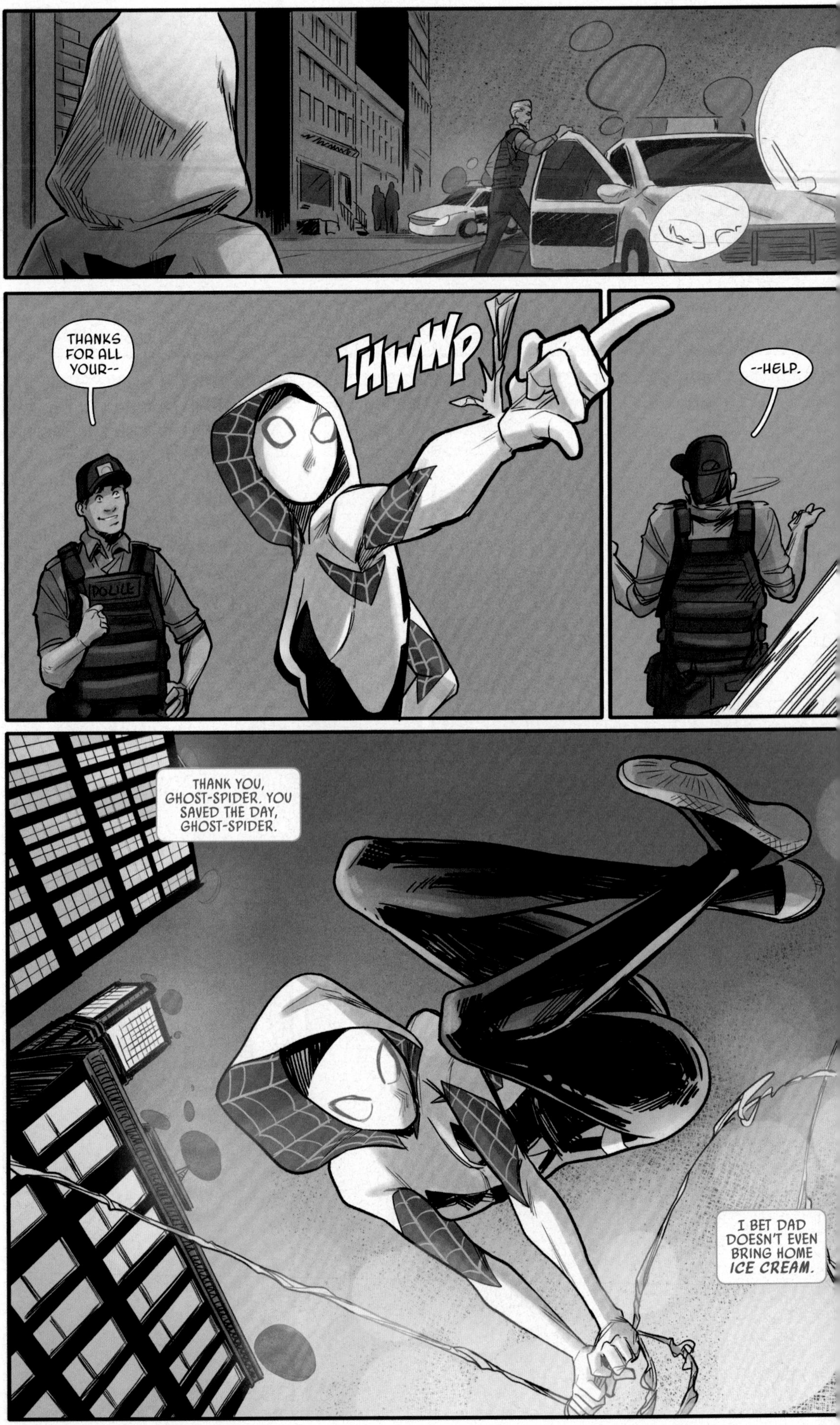
THANKS FOR ALL YOUR--
THWWP
--HELP.
THANK YOU, GHOST-SPIDER. YOU SAVED THE DAY, GHOST-SPIDER.
I BET DAD DOESN'T EVEN BRING HOME ICE CREAM.

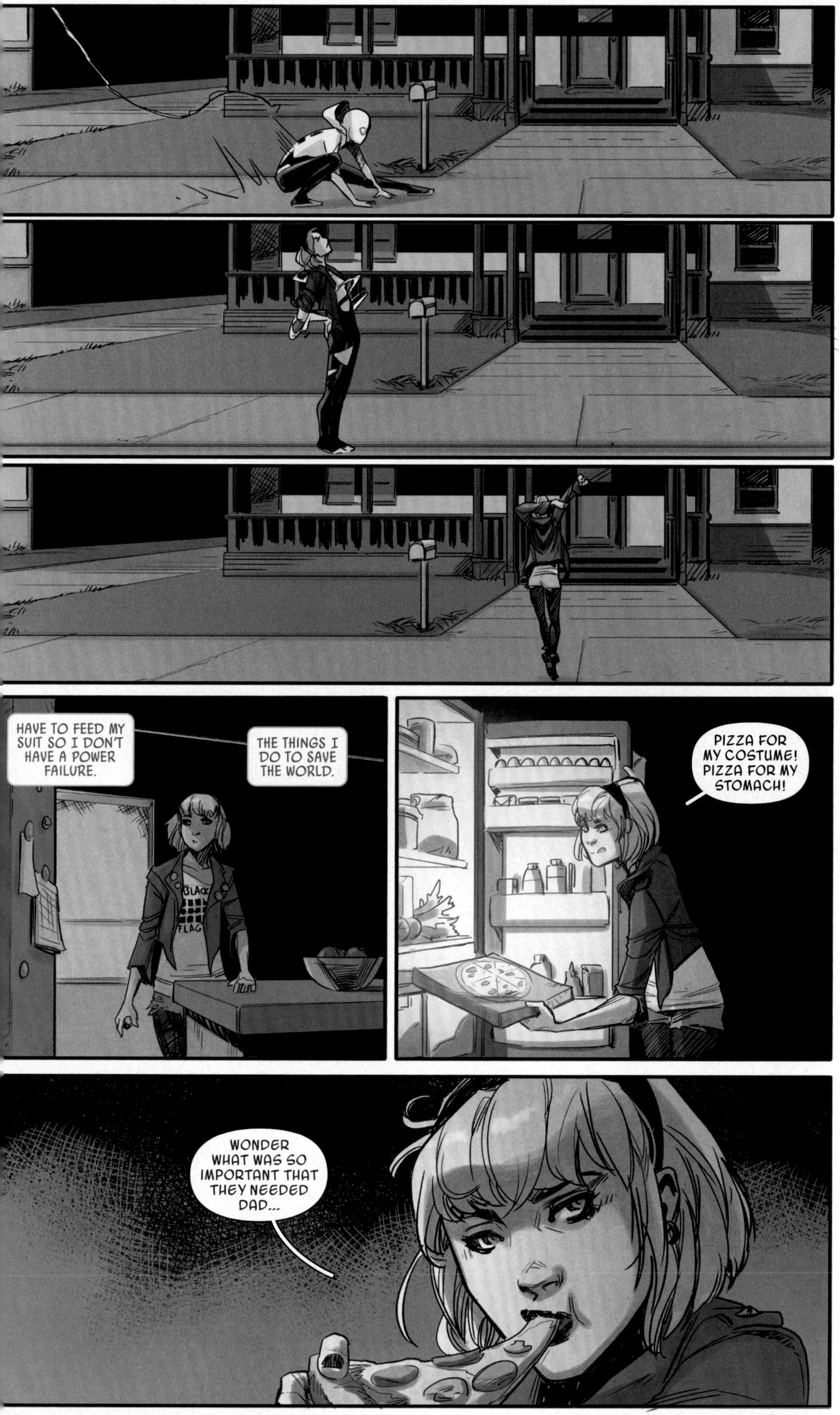
HAVE TO FEED MY SUIT SO I DON'T HAVE A POWER FAILURE.
THE THINGS I DO TO SAVE THE WORLD.
PIZZA FOR MY COSTUME! PIZZA FOR MY STOMACH!
WONDER WHAT WAS SO IMPORTANT THAT THEY NEEDED DAD...

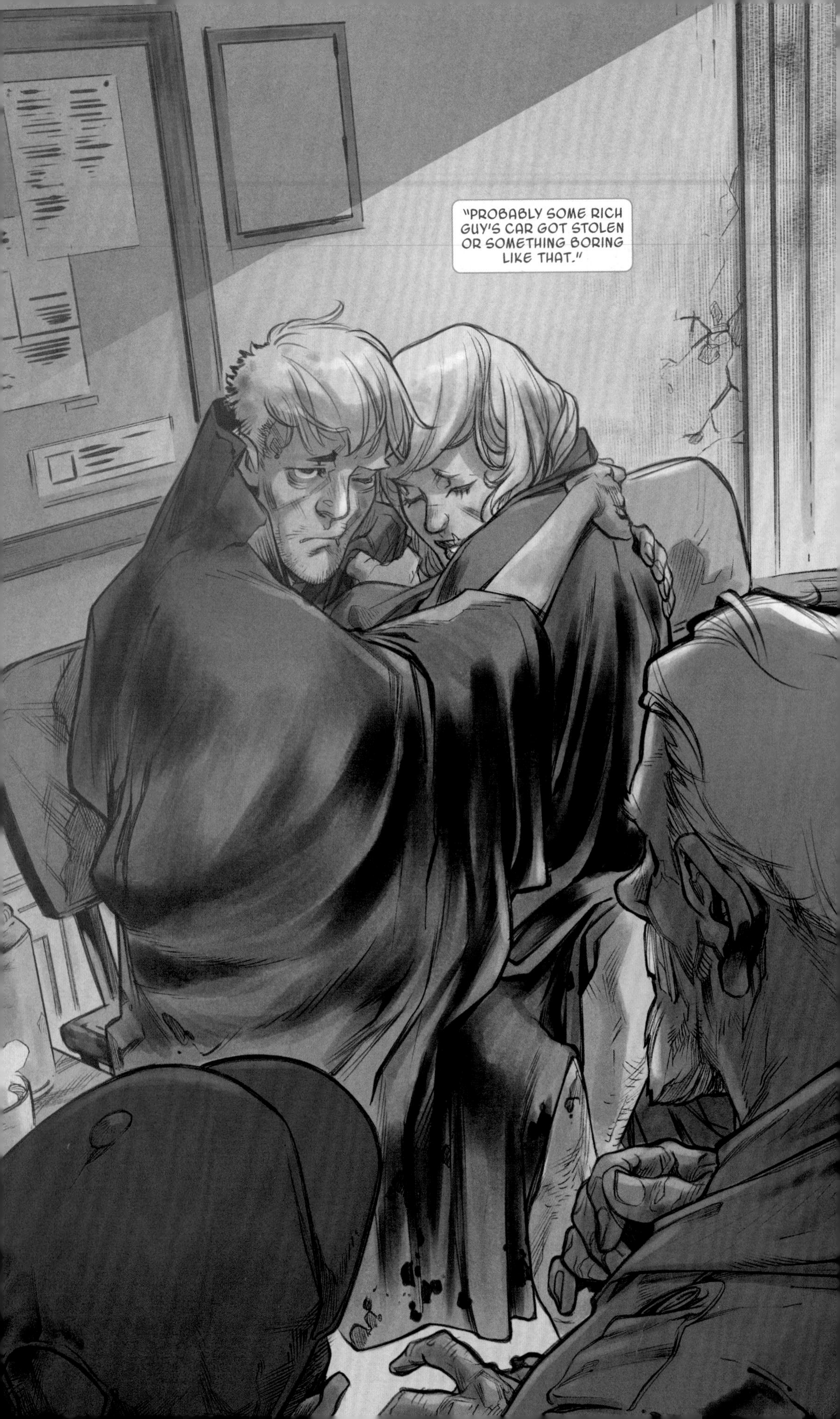
"PROBABLY SOME RICH GUY'S CAR GOT STOLEN OR SOMETHING BORING LIKE THAT."

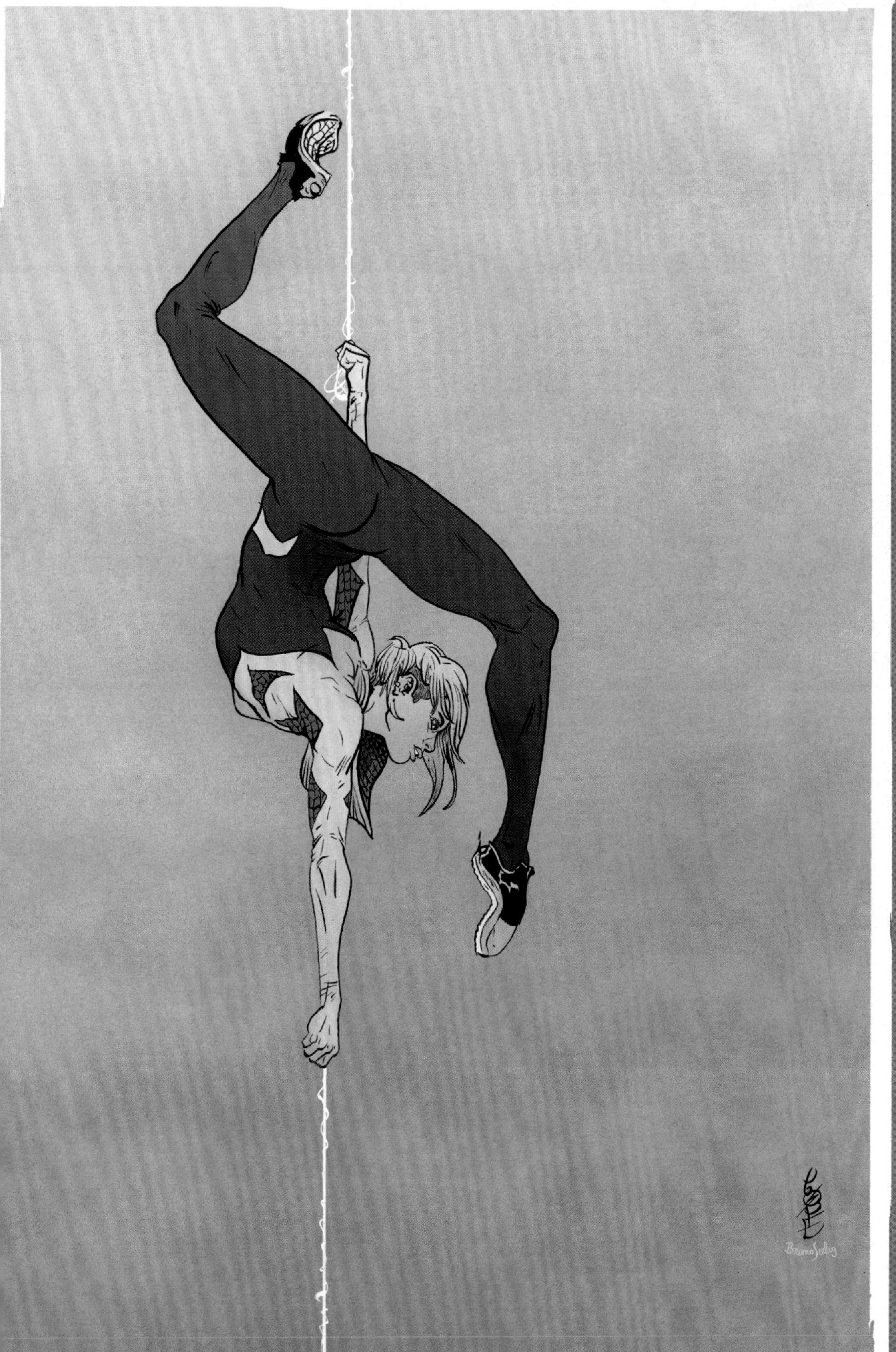

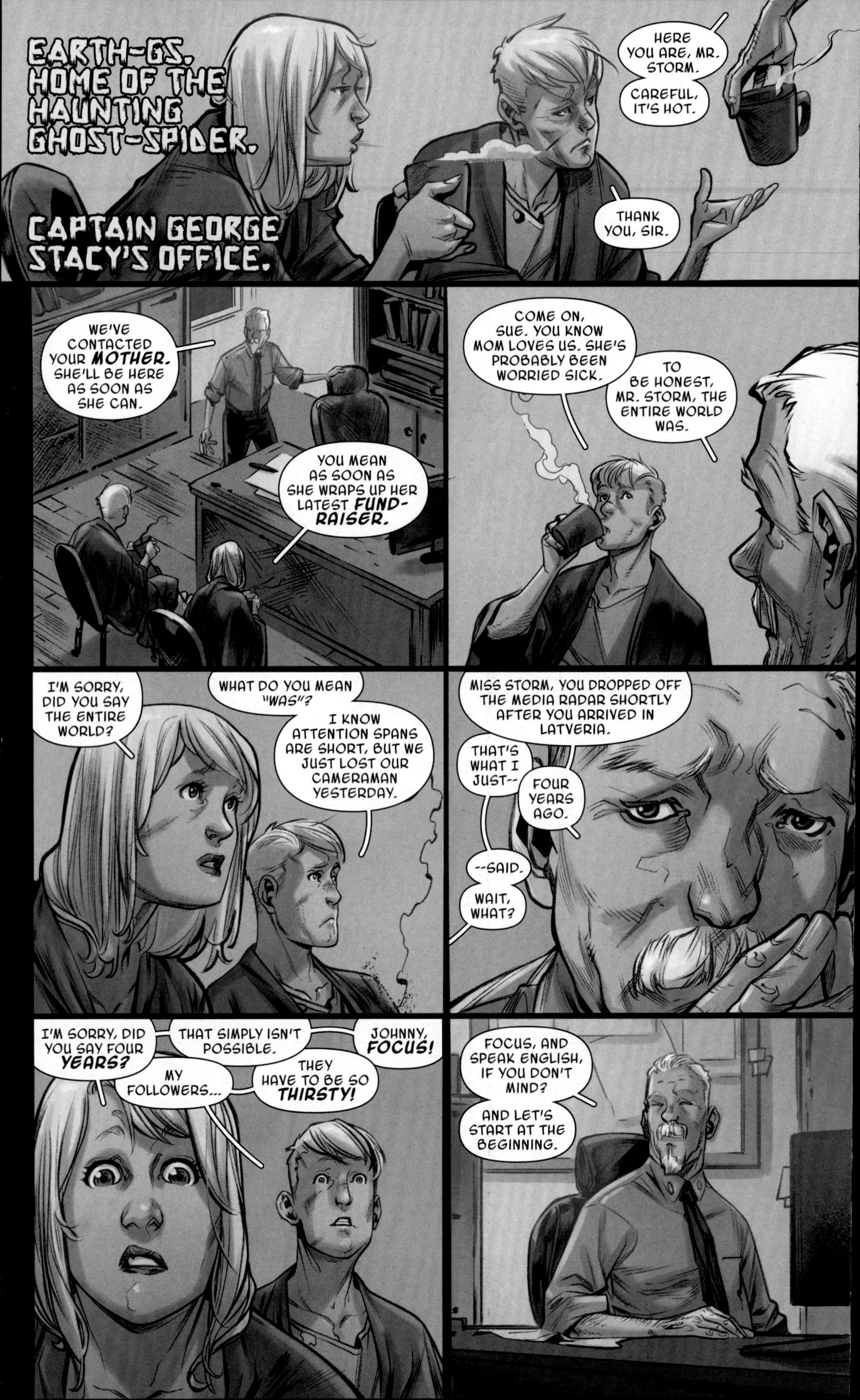
EARTH-65. HOME OF THE HAUNTING GHOST-SPIDER.
CAPTAIN GEORGE STACY'S OFFICE.
HERE YOU ARE, MR. STORM.
CAREFUL, IT'S HOT.
THANK YOU, SIR.
WE'VE CONTACTED YOUR MOTHER. SHE'LL BE HERE AS SOON AS SHE CAN.
YOU MEAN AS SOON AS SHE WRAPS UP HER LATEST FUND-RAISER.
COME ON, SUE. YOU KNOW MOM LOVES US. SHE'S PROBABLY BEEN WORRIED SICK.
TO BE HONEST, MR. STORM, THE ENTIRE WORLD WAS.
I'M SORRY, DID YOU SAY THE ENTIRE WORLD?
WHAT DO YOU MEAN "WAS"?
I KNOW ATTENTION SPANS ARE SHORT, BUT WE JUST LOST OUR CAMERAMAN YESTERDAY.
MISS STORM, YOU DROPPED OFF THE MEDIA RADAR SHORTLY AFTER YOU ARRIVED IN LATVERIA.
THAT'S WHAT I JUST--
FOUR YEARS AGO.
--SAID.
WAIT, WHAT?
I'M SORRY, DID YOU SAY FOUR YEARS?
THAT SIMPLY ISN'T POSSIBLE.
JOHNNY, FOCUS!
MY FOLLOWERS...
THEY HAVE TO BE SO THIRSTY!
FOCUS, AND SPEAK ENGLISH, IF YOU DON'T MIND?
AND LET'S START AT THE BEGINNING.

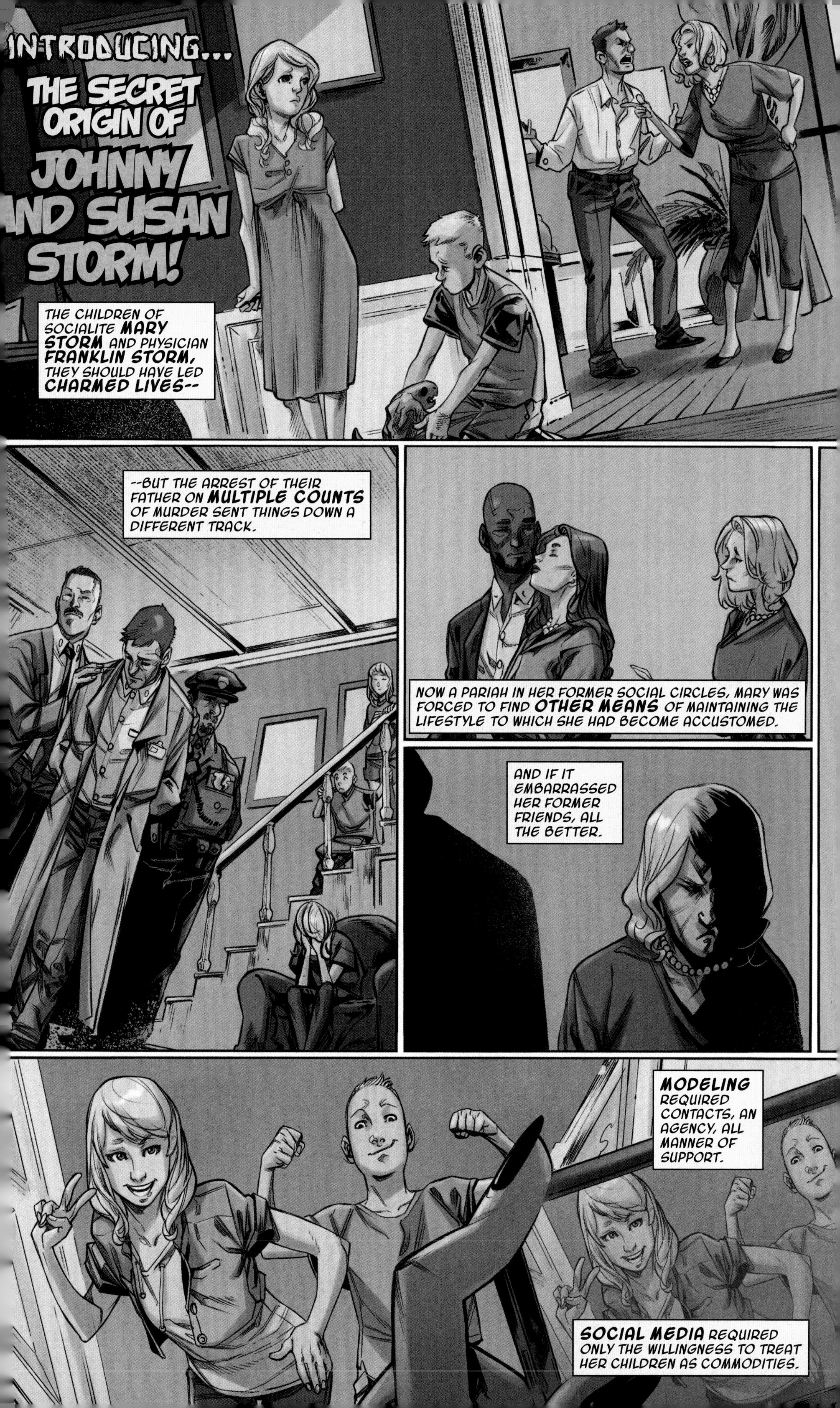
INTRODUCING...
THE SECRET ORIGIN OF JOHNNY AND SUSAN STORM!
THE CHILDREN OF SOCIALITE MARY STORM AND PHYSICIAN FRANKLIN STORM, THEY SHOULD HAVE LED CHARMED LIVES--
--BUT THE ARREST OF THEIR FATHER ON MULTIPLE COUNTS OF MURDER SENT THINGS DOWN A DIFFERENT TRACK.
NOW A PARIAH IN HER FORMER SOCIAL CIRCLES, MARY WAS FORCED TO FIND OTHER MEANS OF MAINTAINING THE LIFESTYLE TO WHICH SHE HAD BECOME ACCUSTOMED.
AND IF IT EMBARRASSED HER FORMER FRIENDS, ALL THE BETTER.
MODELING REQUIRED CONTACTS, AN AGENCY, ALL MANNER OF SUPPORT.
SOCIAL MEDIA REQUIRED ONLY THE WILLINGNESS TO TREAT HER CHILDREN AS COMMODITIES.

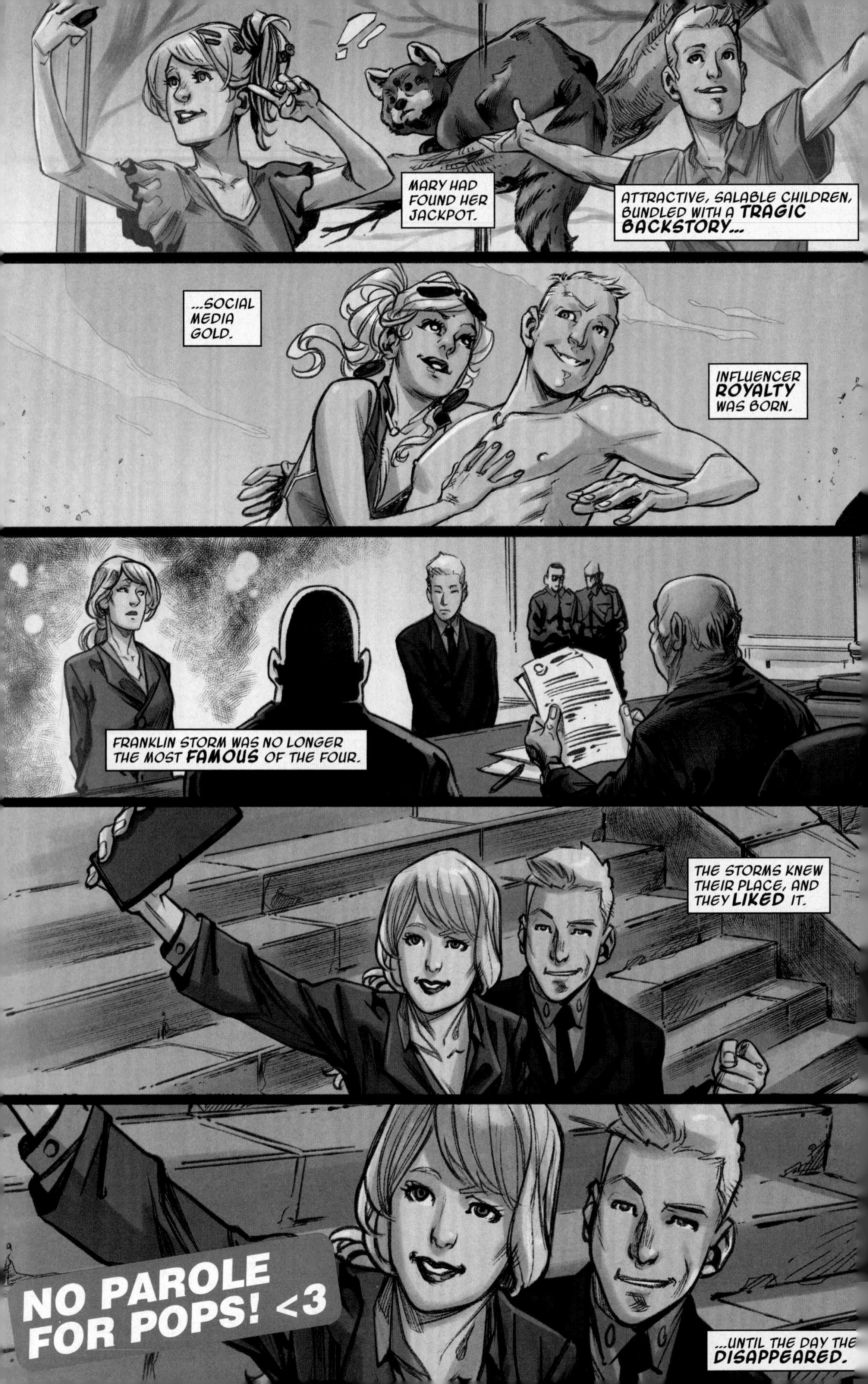
!!
MARY HAD FOUND HER JACKPOT.
ATTRACTIVE, SALABLE CHILDREN, BUNDLED WITH A TRAGIC BACKSTORY...
...SOCIAL MEDIA GOLD.
INFLUENCER ROYALTY WAS BORN.
FRANKLIN STORM WAS NO LONGER THE MOST FAMOUS OF THE FOUR.
THE STORMS KNEW THEIR PLACE, AND THEY LIKED IT.
NO PAROLE FOR POPS! <3
...UNTIL THE DAY THE DISAPPEARED.

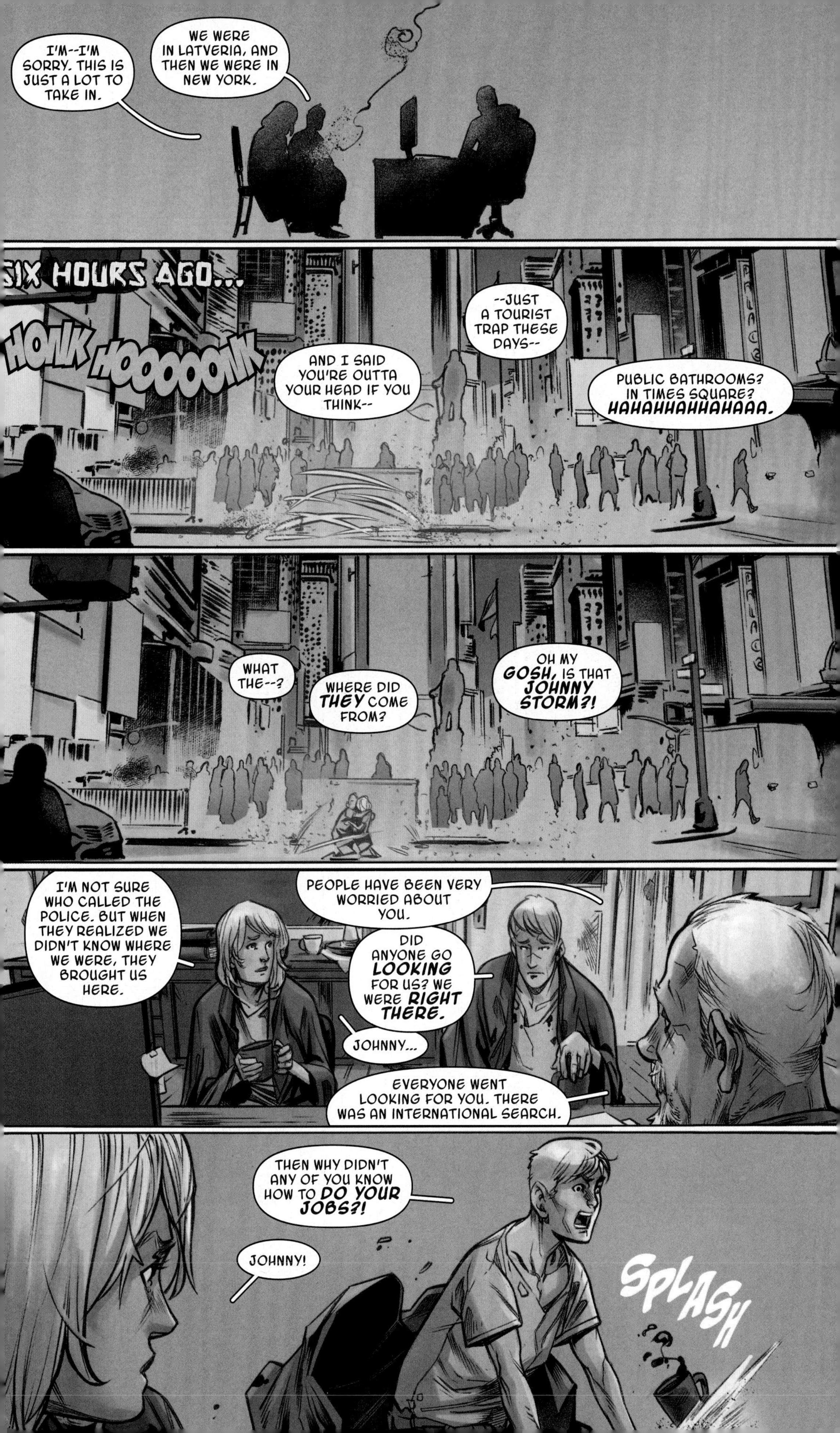
I'M--I'M SORRY. THIS IS JUST A LOT TO TAKE IN.
WE WERE IN LATVERIA, AND THEN WE WERE IN NEW YORK.
SIX HOURS AGO...
HONK HOOOOOONK
AND I SAID YOU'RE OUTTA YOUR HEAD IF YOU THINK--
--JUST A TOURIST TRAP THESE DAYS--
PUBLIC BATHROOMS? IN TIMES SQUARE? HAHAHHAHHAHAAA.
WHAT THE--?
WHERE DID THEY COME FROM?
OH MY GOSH, IS THAT JOHNNY STORM?!
I'M NOT SURE WHO CALLED THE POLICE. BUT WHEN THEY REALIZED WE DIDN'T KNOW WHERE WE WERE, THEY BROUGHT US HERE.
PEOPLE HAVE BEEN VERY WORRIED ABOUT YOU.
DID ANYONE GO LOOKING FOR US? WE WERE RIGHT THERE.
JOHNNY...
EVERYONE WENT LOOKING FOR YOU. THERE WAS AN INTERNATIONAL SEARCH.
THEN WHY DIDN'T ANY OF YOU KNOW HOW TO DO YOUR JOBS?!
JOHNNY!
SPLASH

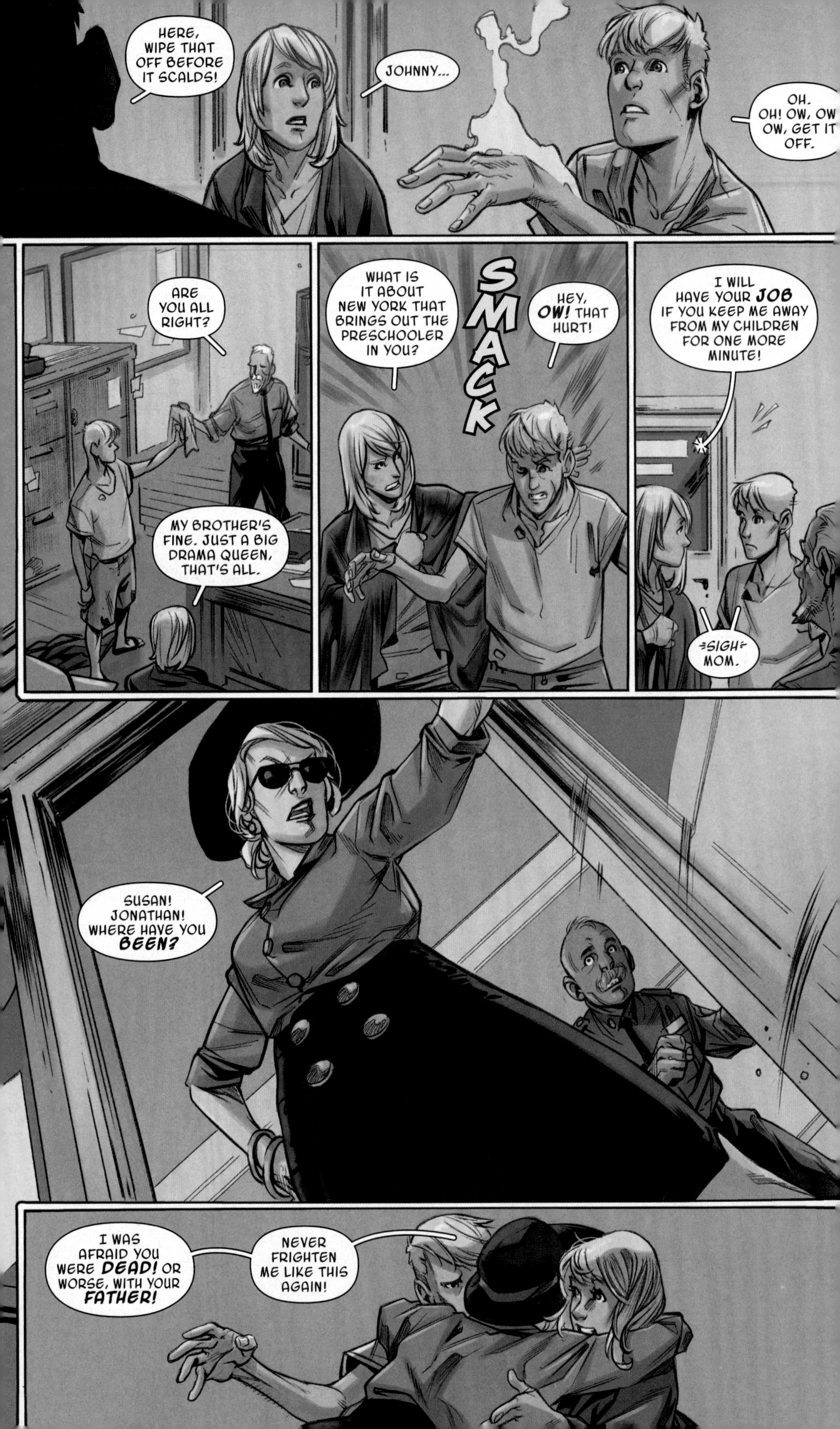
HERE, WIPE THAT OFF BEFORE IT SCALDS!
JOHNNY...
OH. OH! OW, OW OW, GET IT OFF.
ARE YOU ALL RIGHT?
MY BROTHER'S FINE. JUST A BIG DRAMA QUEEN, THAT'S ALL.
SMACK
WHAT IS IT ABOUT NEW YORK THAT BRINGS OUT THE PRESCHOOLER IN YOU?
HEY, OW! THAT HURT!
I WILL HAVE YOUR JOB IF YOU KEEP ME AWAY FROM MY CHILDREN FOR ONE MORE MINUTE!
SIGH MOM.
SUSAN! JONATHAN! WHERE HAVE YOU BEEN?
I WAS AFRAID YOU WERE DEAD! OR WORSE, WITH YOUR FATHER!
NEVER FRIGHTEN ME LIKE THIS AGAIN!

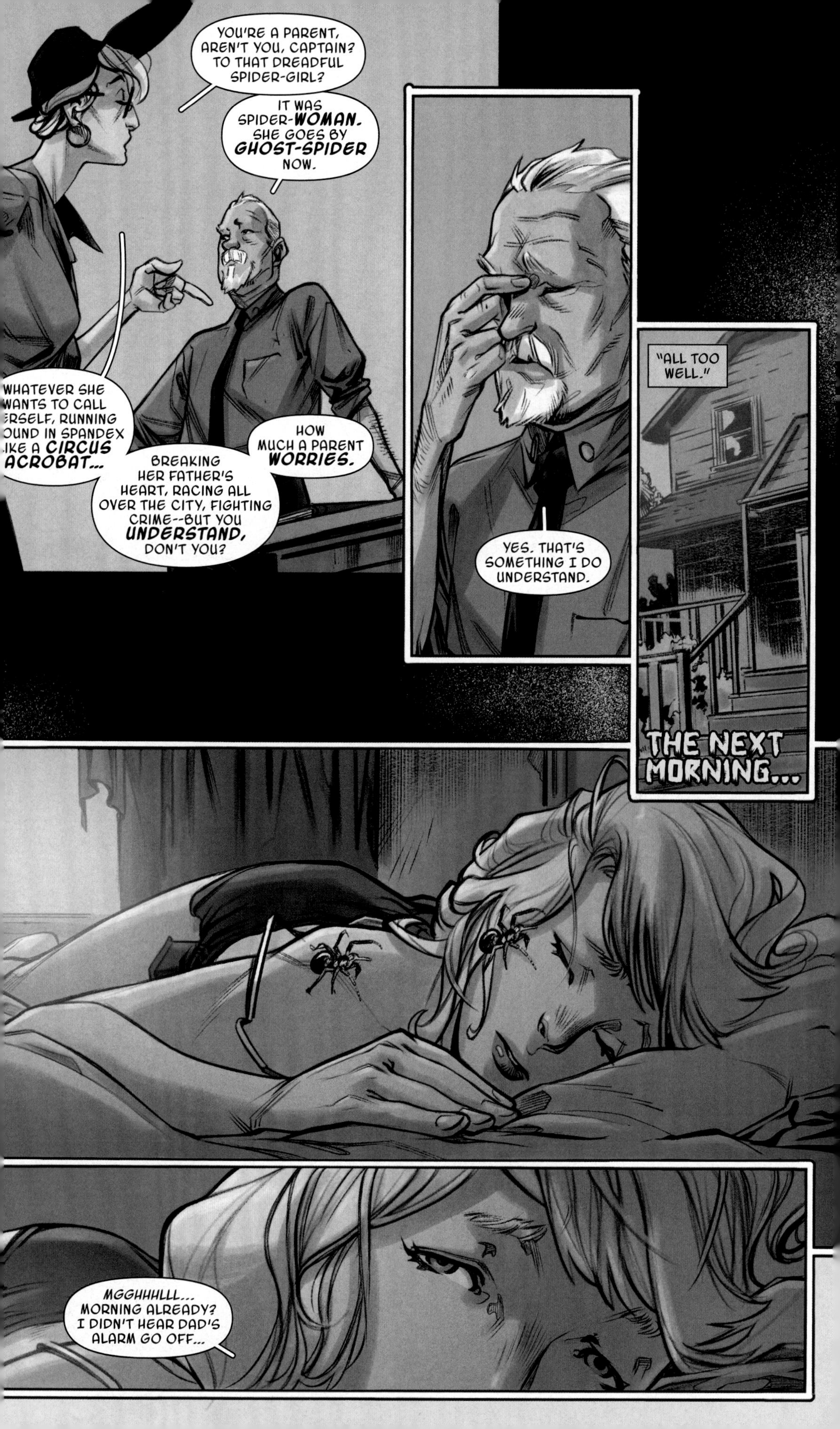
YOU'RE A PARENT, AREN'T YOU, CAPTAIN? TO THAT DREADFUL SPIDER-GIRL?
IT WAS SPIDER-WOMAN. SHE GOES BY GHOST-SPIDER NOW.
WHATEVER SHE WANTS TO CALL ERSELF, RUNNING OUND IN SPANDEX IKE A CIRCUS ACROBAT...
BREAKING HER FATHER'S HEART, RACING ALL OVER THE CITY, FIGHTING CRIME--BUT YOU UNDERSTAND, DON'T YOU?
HOW MUCH A PARENT WORRIES.
YES. THAT'S SOMETHING I DO UNDERSTAND.
"ALL TOO WELL."
THE NEXT MORNING...
MGGHHHLLL... MORNING ALREADY? I DIDN'T HEAR DAD'S ALARM GO OFF...

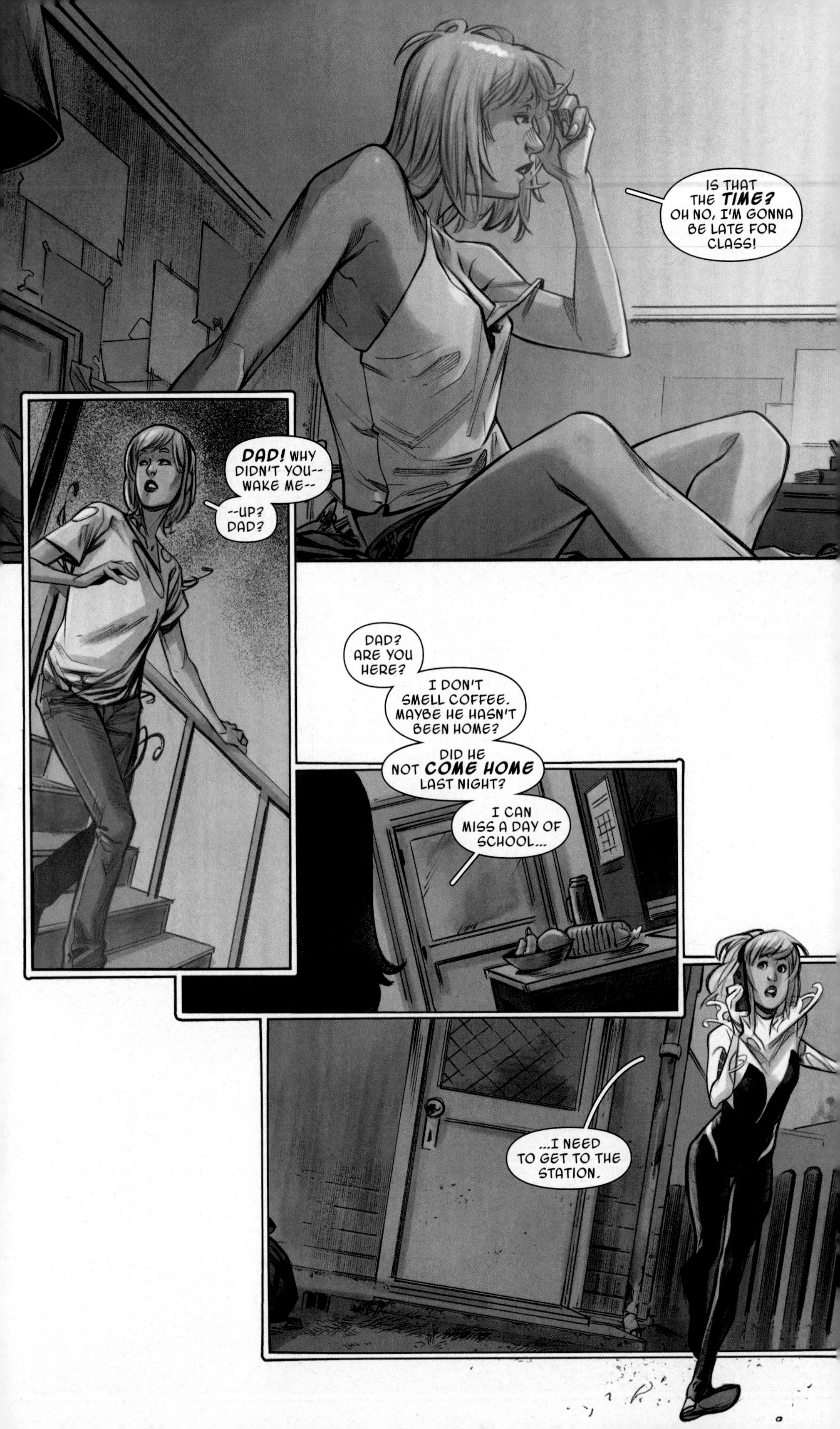
IS THAT THE TIME? OH NO, I'M GONNA BE LATE FOR CLASS!
DAD! WHY DIDN'T YOU-- WAKE ME--
--UP? DAD?
DAD? ARE YOU HERE?
I DON'T SMELL COFFEE. MAYBE HE HASN'T BEEN HOME?
DID HE NOT COME HOME LAST NIGHT?
I CAN MISS A DAY OF SCHOOL...
...I NEED TO GET TO THE STATION.

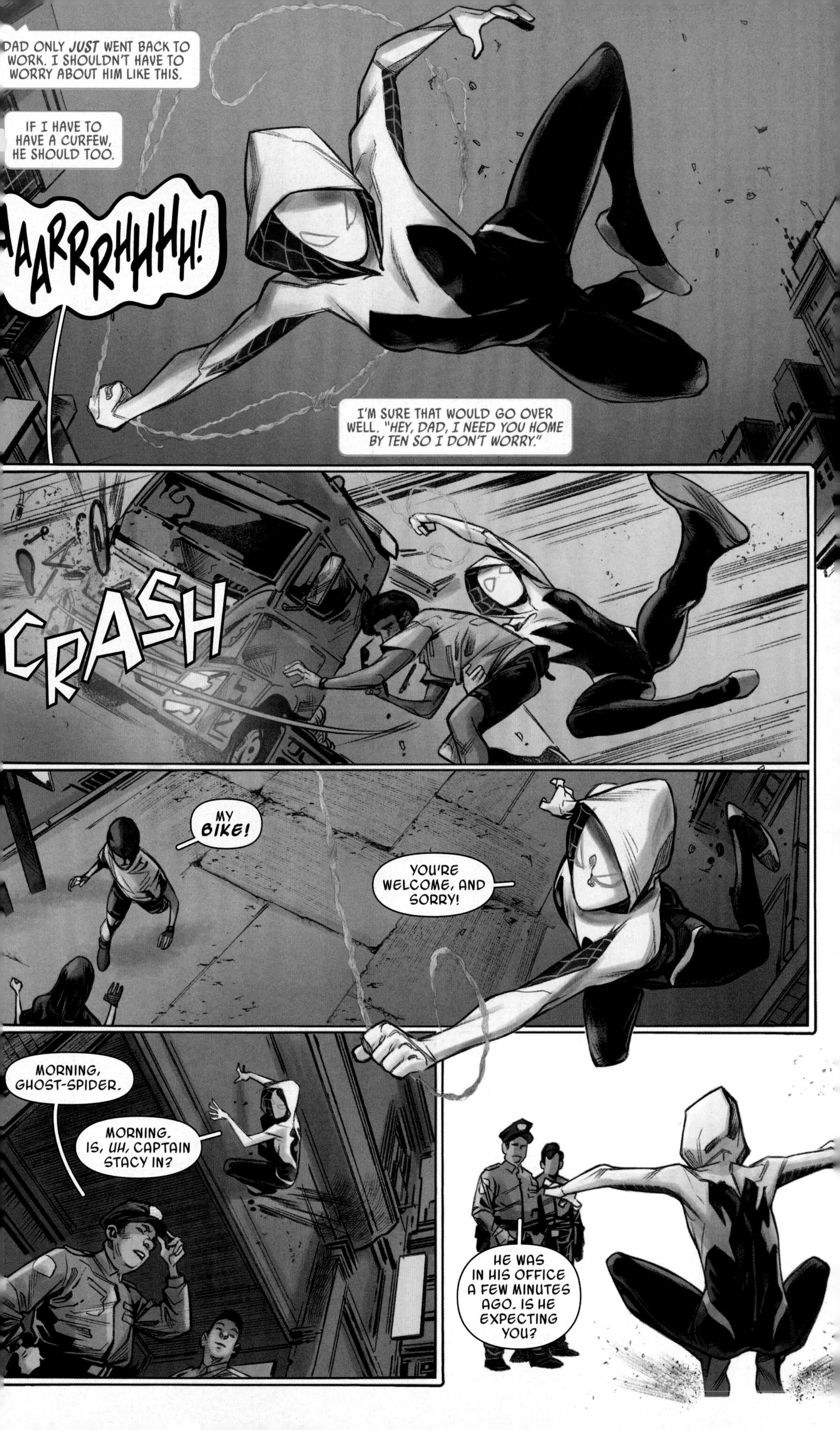
DAD ONLY JUST WENT BACK TO WORK. I SHOULDN'T HAVE TO WORRY ABOUT HIM LIKE THIS.
IF I HAVE TO HAVE A CURFEW, HE SHOULD TOO.
AARRRHHHH!
I'M SURE THAT WOULD GO OVER WELL. "HEY, DAD, I NEED YOU HOME BY TEN SO I DON'T WORRY."
CRASH
MY BIKE!
YOU'RE WELCOME, AND SORRY!
MORNING, GHOST-SPIDER.
MORNING. IS, UH, CAPTAIN STACY IN?
HE WAS IN HIS OFFICE A FEW MINUTES AGO. IS HE EXPECTING YOU?

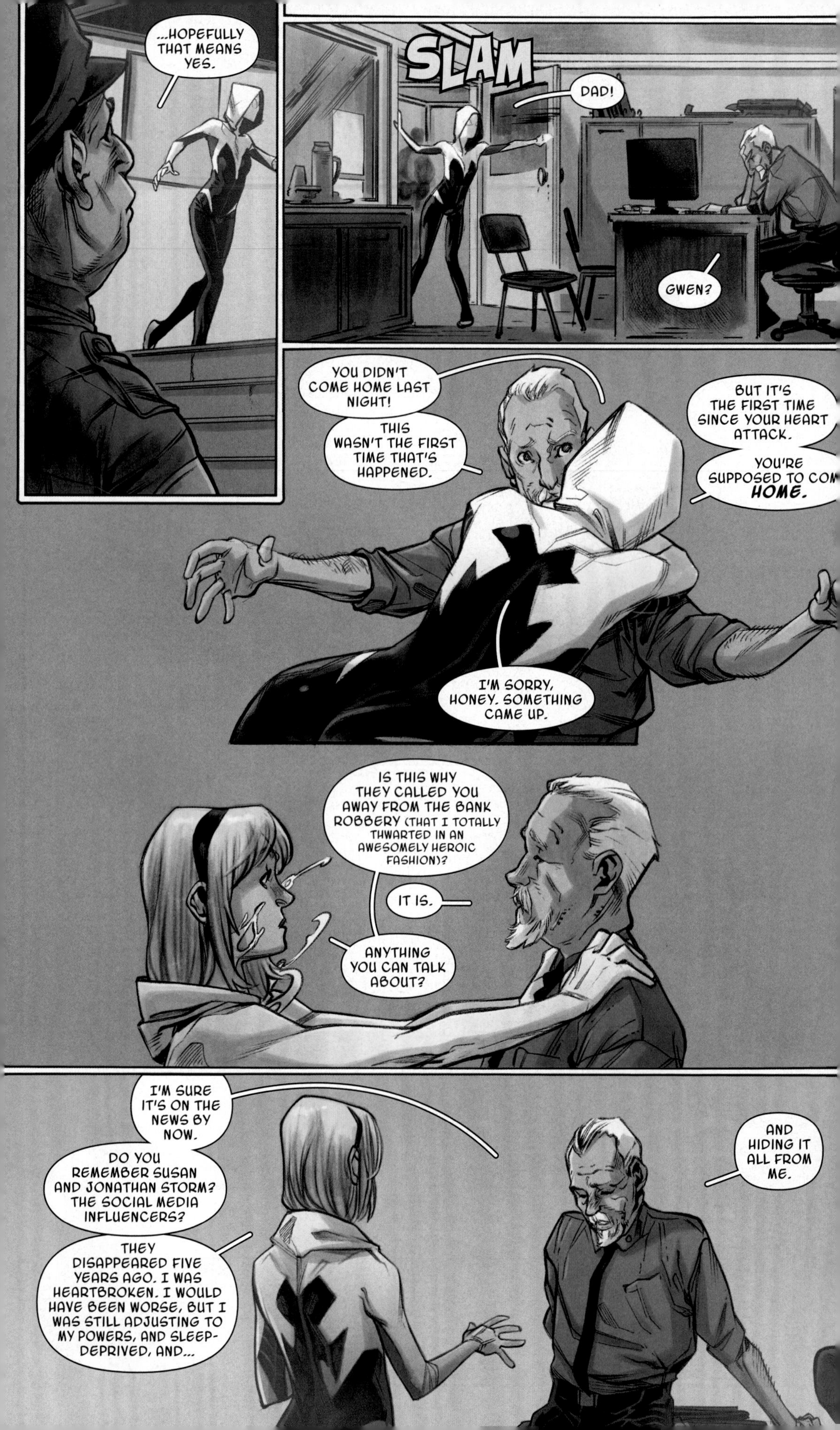

...HOPEFULLY THAT MEANS YES.
SLAM
DAD!
GWEN?
YOU DIDN'T COME HOME LAST NIGHT!
THIS WASN'T THE FIRST TIME THAT'S HAPPENED.
BUT IT'S THE FIRST TIME SINCE YOUR HEART ATTACK.
YOU'RE SUPPOSED TO COM HOME.
I'M SORRY, HONEY. SOMETHING CAME UP.
IS THIS WHY THEY CALLED YOU AWAY FROM THE BANK ROBBERY (THAT I TOTALLY THWARTED IN AN AWESOMELY HEROIC FASHION)?
IT IS.
ANYTHING YOU CAN TALK ABOUT?
I'M SURE IT'S ON THE NEWS BY NOW.
DO YOU REMEMBER SUSAN AND JONATHAN STORM? THE SOCIAL MEDIA INFLUENCERS?
THEY DISAPPEARED FIVE YEARS AGO. I WAS HEARTBROKEN. I WOULD HAVE BEEN WORSE, BUT I WAS STILL ADJUSTING TO MY POWERS, AND SLEEP-DEPRIVED, AND...
AND HIDING IT ALL FROM ME.

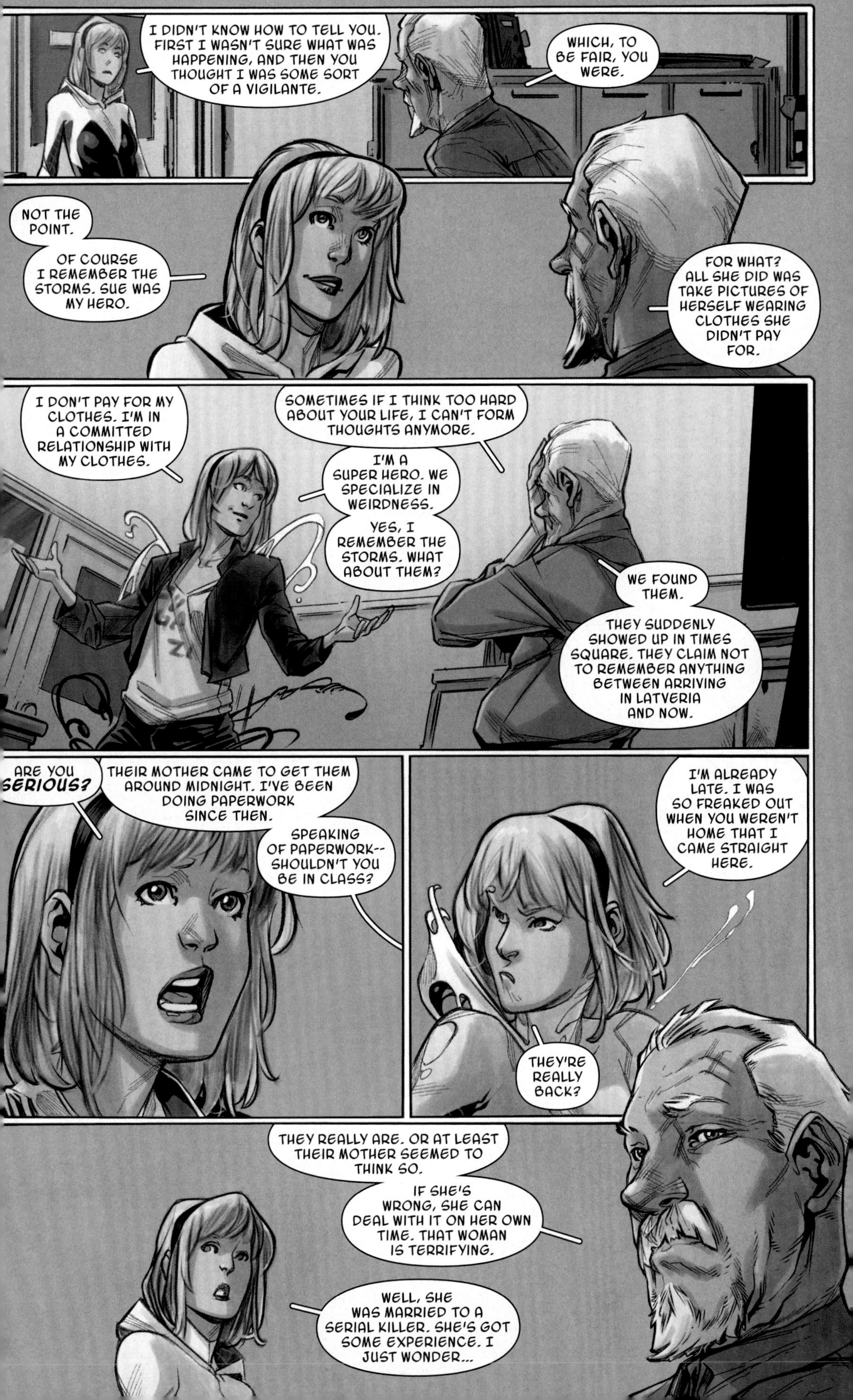
I DIDN'T KNOW HOW TO TELL YOU. FIRST I WASN'T SURE WHAT WAS HAPPENING, AND THEN YOU THOUGHT I WAS SOME SORT OF A VIGILANTE.
WHICH, TO BE FAIR, YOU WERE.
NOT THE POINT.
OF COURSE I REMEMBER THE STORMS. SUE WAS MY HERO.
FOR WHAT? ALL SHE DID WAS TAKE PICTURES OF HERSELF WEARING CLOTHES SHE DIDN'T PAY FOR.
I DON'T PAY FOR MY CLOTHES. I'M IN A COMMITTED RELATIONSHIP WITH MY CLOTHES.
SOMETIMES IF I THINK TOO HARD ABOUT YOUR LIFE, I CAN'T FORM THOUGHTS ANYMORE.
I'M A SUPER HERO. WE SPECIALIZE IN WEIRDNESS.
YES, I REMEMBER THE STORMS. WHAT ABOUT THEM?
WE FOUND THEM.
THEY SUDDENLY SHOWED UP IN TIMES SQUARE. THEY CLAIM NOT TO REMEMBER ANYTHING BETWEEN ARRIVING IN LATVERIA AND NOW.
ARE YOU *SERIOUS?*
THEIR MOTHER CAME TO GET THEM AROUND MIDNIGHT. I'VE BEEN DOING PAPERWORK SINCE THEN.
SPEAKING OF PAPERWORK-- SHOULDN'T YOU BE IN CLASS?
I'M ALREADY LATE. I WAS SO FREAKED OUT WHEN YOU WEREN'T HOME THAT I CAME STRAIGHT HERE.
THEY'RE REALLY BACK?
THEY REALLY ARE. OR AT LEAST THEIR MOTHER SEEMED TO THINK SO.
IF SHE'S WRONG, SHE CAN DEAL WITH IT ON HER OWN TIME. THAT WOMAN IS TERRIFYING.
WELL, SHE WAS MARRIED TO A SERIAL KILLER. SHE'S GOT SOME EXPERIENCE. I JUST WONDER...

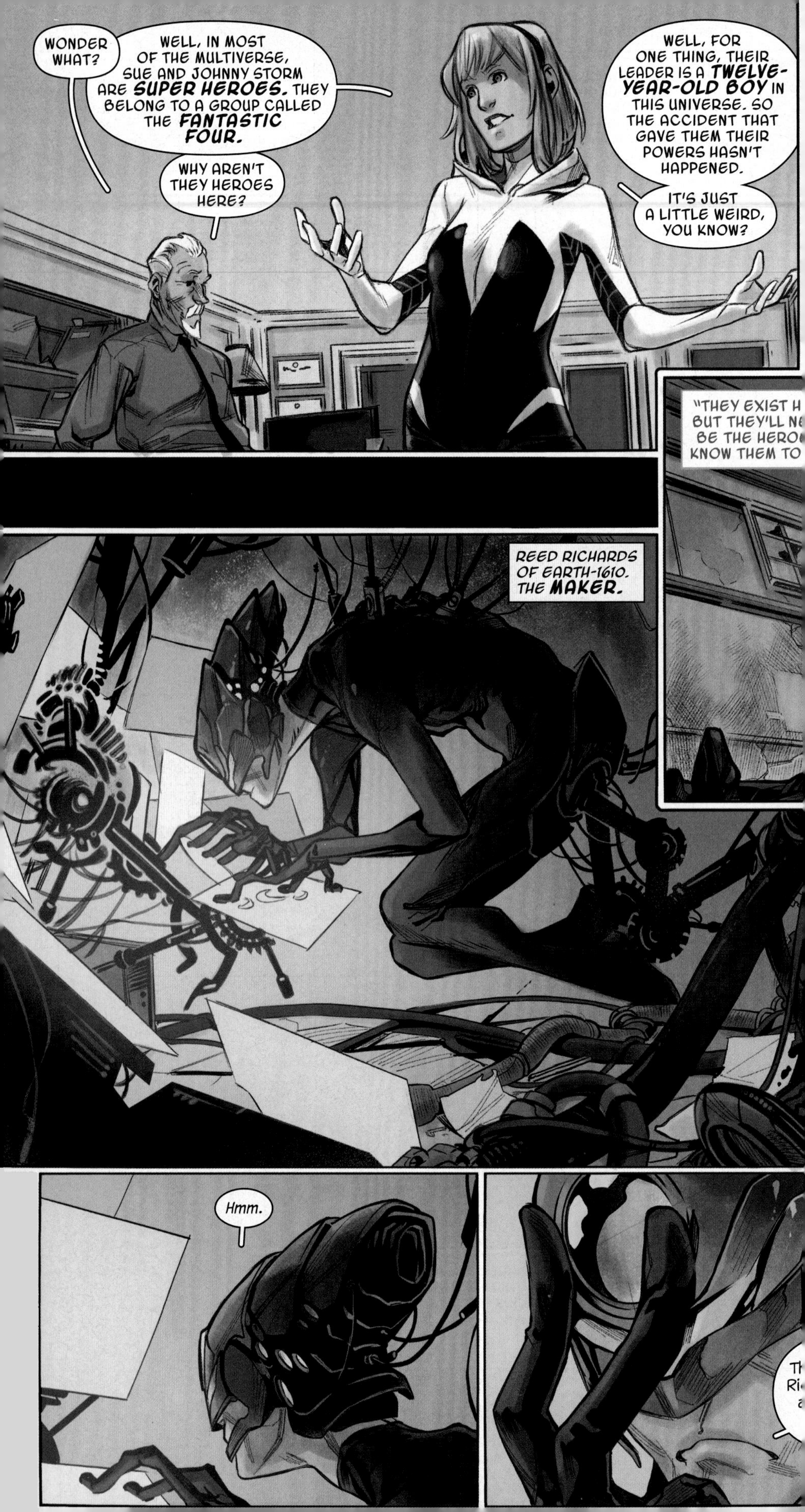
WONDER WHAT?
WELL, IN MOST OF THE MULTIVERSE, SUE AND JOHNNY STORM ARE SUPER HEROES. THEY BELONG TO A GROUP CALLED THE FANTASTIC FOUR.
WHY AREN'T THEY HEROES HERE?
WELL, FOR ONE THING, THEIR LEADER IS A TWELVE-YEAR-OLD BOY IN THIS UNIVERSE. SO THE ACCIDENT THAT GAVE THEM THEIR POWERS HASN'T HAPPENED.
IT'S JUST A LITTLE WEIRD, YOU KNOW?
"THEY EXIST H
BUT THEY'LL NE
BE THE HERO
KNOW THEM TO
REED RICHARDS OF EARTH-1610. THE MAKER.
Hmm.

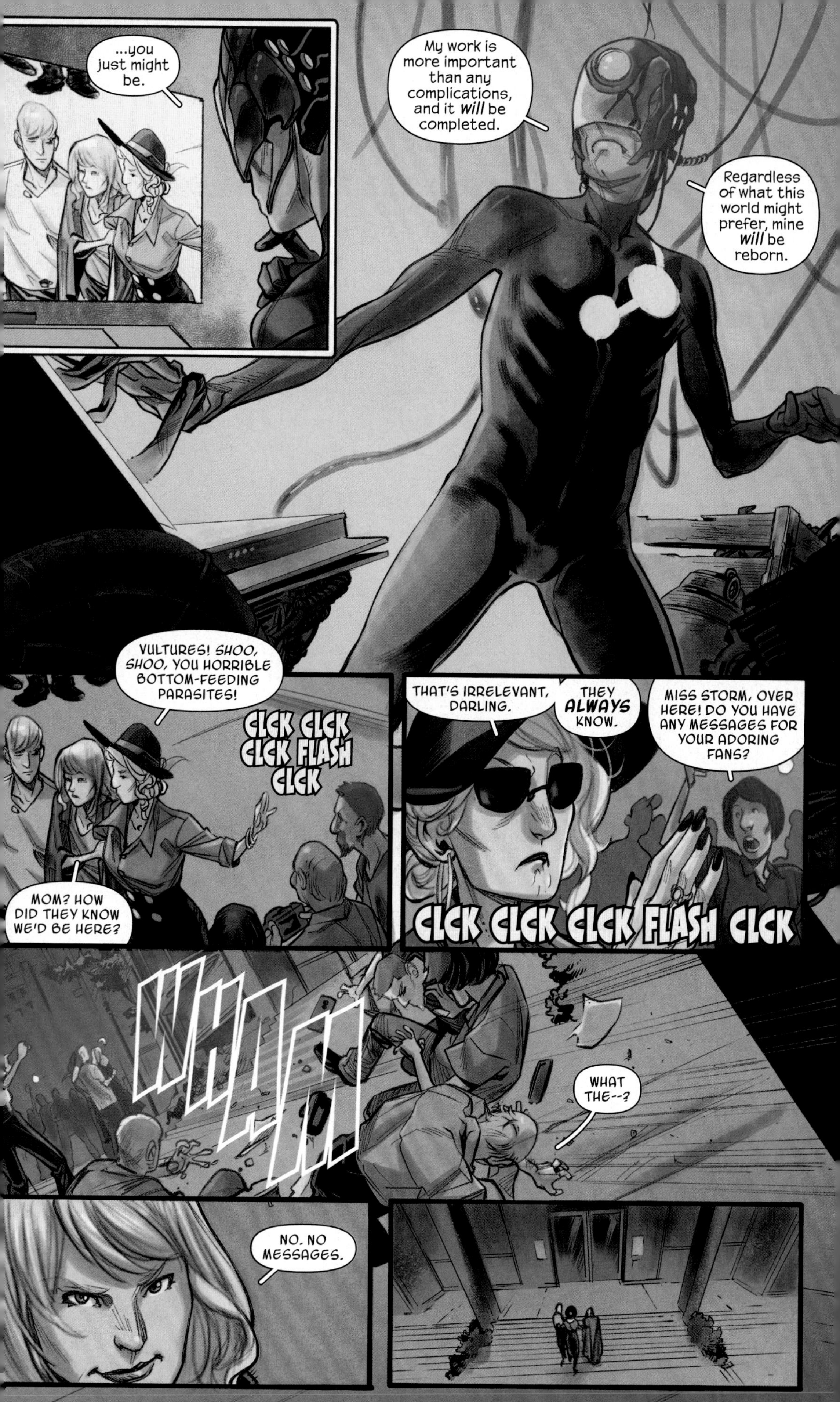
...you just might be.
My work is more important than any complications, and it WILL be completed.
Regardless of what this world might prefer, mine WILL be reborn.
VULTURES! SHOO, SHOO, YOU HORRIBLE BOTTOM-FEEDING PARASITES!
CLCK CLCK CLCK FLASH CLCK
MOM? HOW DID THEY KNOW WE'D BE HERE?
THAT'S IRRELEVANT, DARLING.
THEY ALWAYS KNOW.
MISS STORM, OVER HERE! DO YOU HAVE ANY MESSAGES FOR YOUR ADORING FANS?
CLCK CLCK CLCK FLASH CLCK
WHAM
WHAT THE--?
NO. NO MESSAGES.

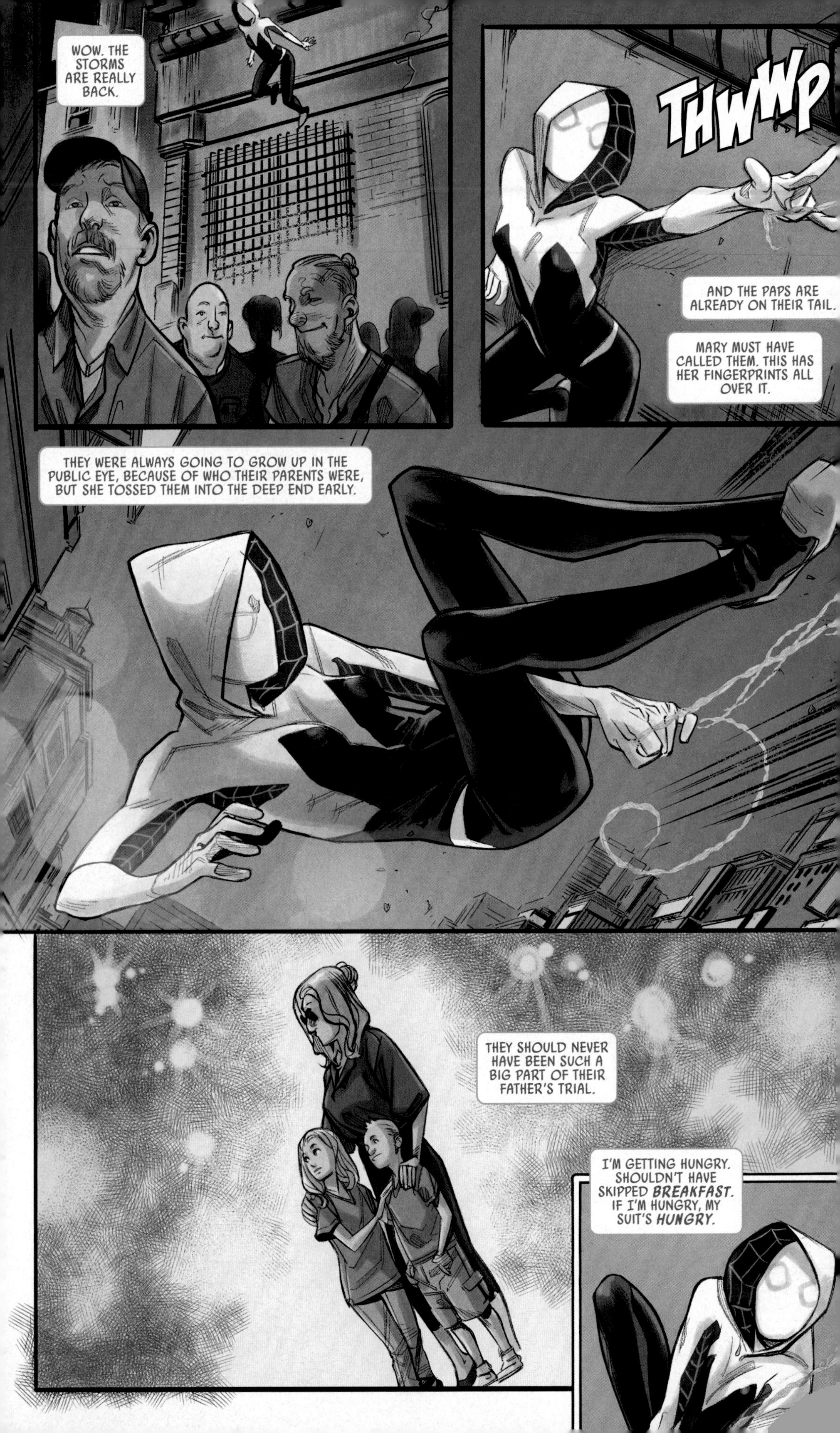
WOW. THE STORMS ARE REALLY BACK.
THWWP
AND THE PAPS ARE ALREADY ON THEIR TAIL.
MARY MUST HAVE CALLED THEM. THIS HAS HER FINGERPRINTS ALL OVER IT.
THEY WERE ALWAYS GOING TO GROW UP IN THE PUBLIC EYE, BECAUSE OF WHO THEIR PARENTS WERE, BUT SHE TOSSED THEM INTO THE DEEP END EARLY.
THEY SHOULD NEVER HAVE BEEN SUCH A BIG PART OF THEIR FATHER'S TRIAL.
I'M GETTING HUNGRY. SHOULDN'T HAVE SKIPPED BREAKFAST. IF I'M HUNGRY, MY SUIT'S HUNGRY.

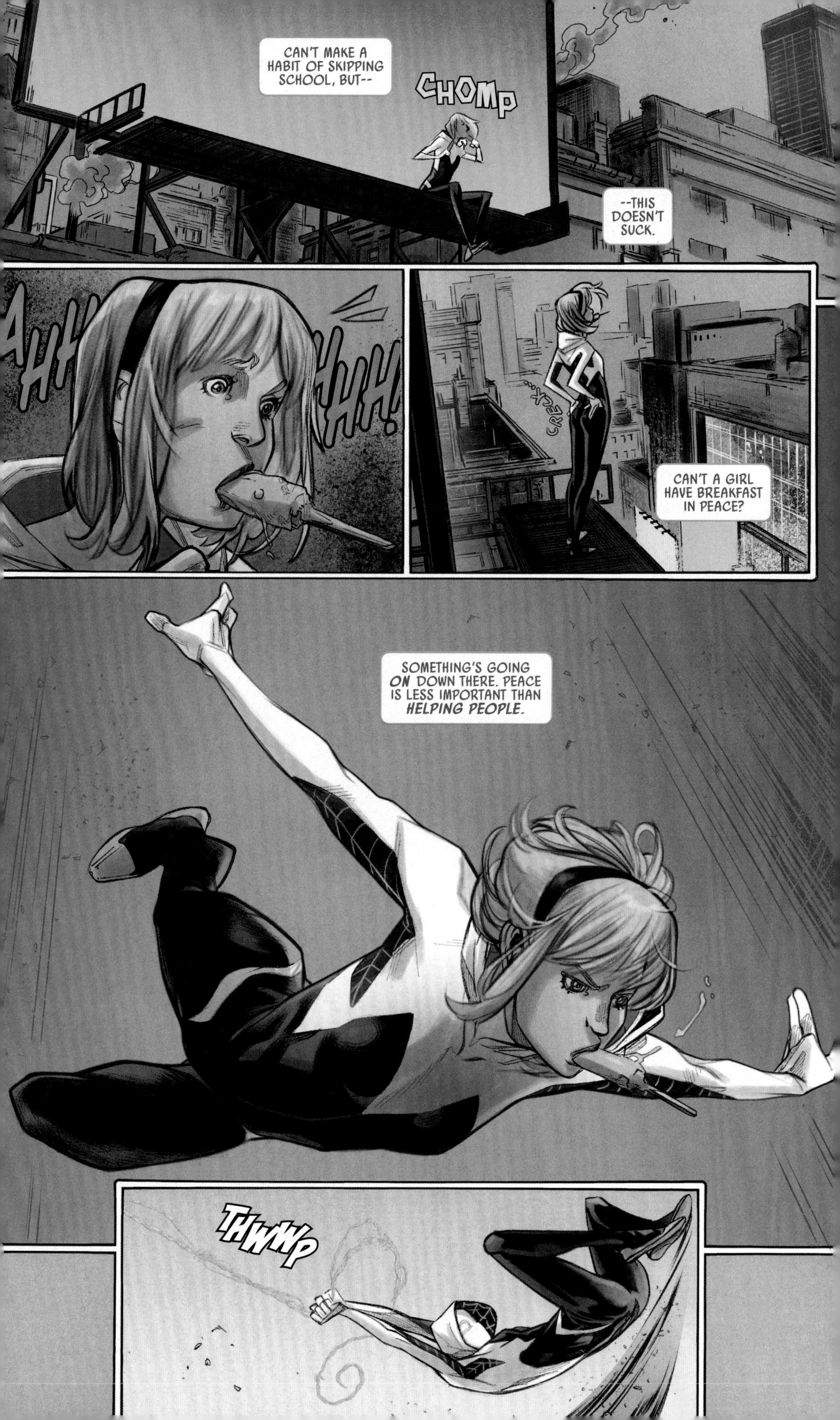
CAN'T MAKE A HABIT OF SKIPPING SCHOOL, BUT--
CHOMP
--THIS DOESN'T SUCK.
CREEK...
CAN'T A GIRL HAVE BREAKFAST IN PEACE?
SOMETHING'S GOING ON DOWN THERE. PEACE IS LESS IMPORTANT THAN HELPING PEOPLE.
THWWP

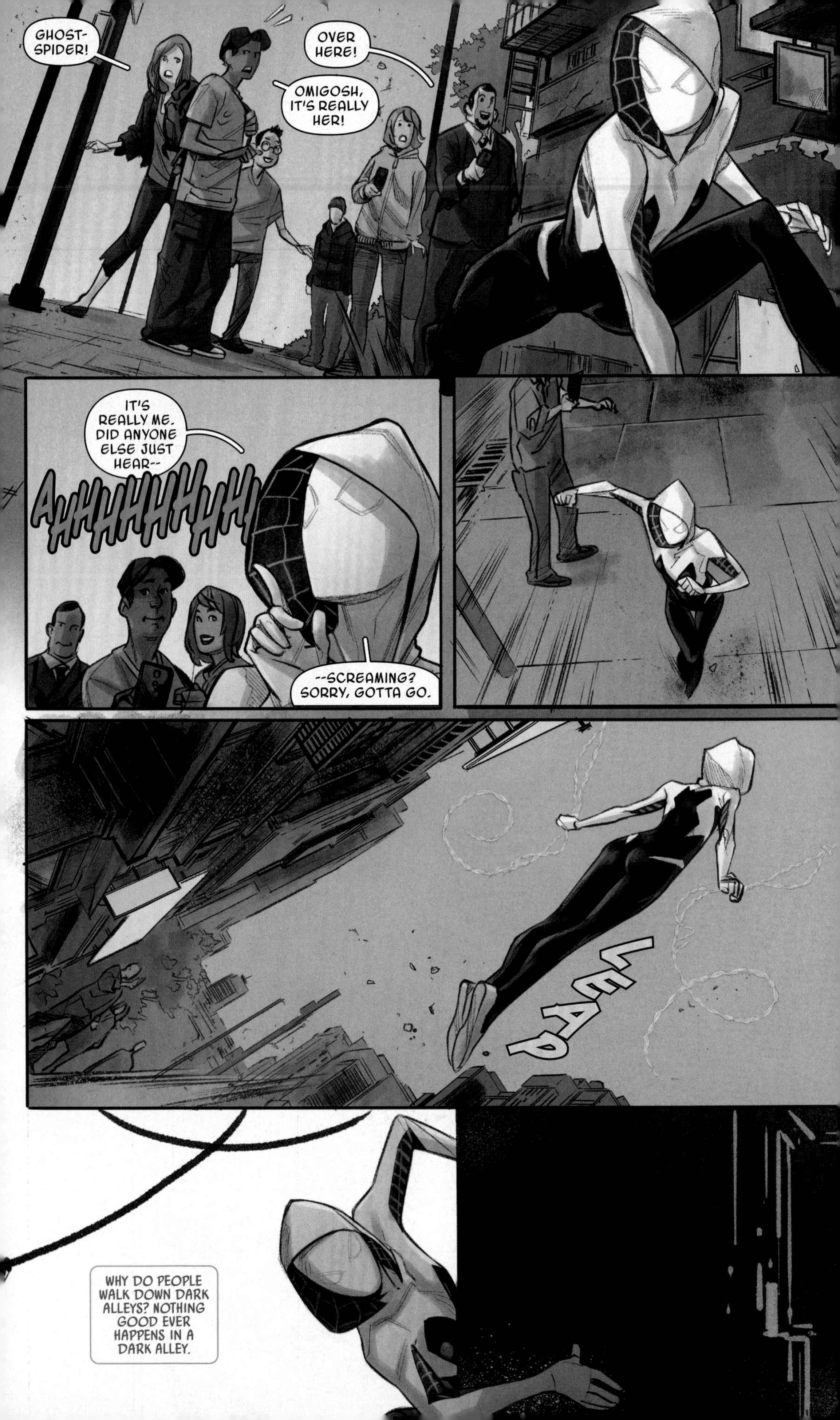
GHOST-SPIDER!
OVER HERE!
OMIGOSH, IT'S REALLY HER!
IT'S REALLY ME. DID ANYONE ELSE JUST HEAR--
AHHHHHHHH!
--SCREAMING? SORRY, GOTTA GO.
LEAP
WHY DO PEOPLE WALK DOWN DARK ALLEYS? NOTHING GOOD EVER HAPPENS IN A DARK ALLEY.

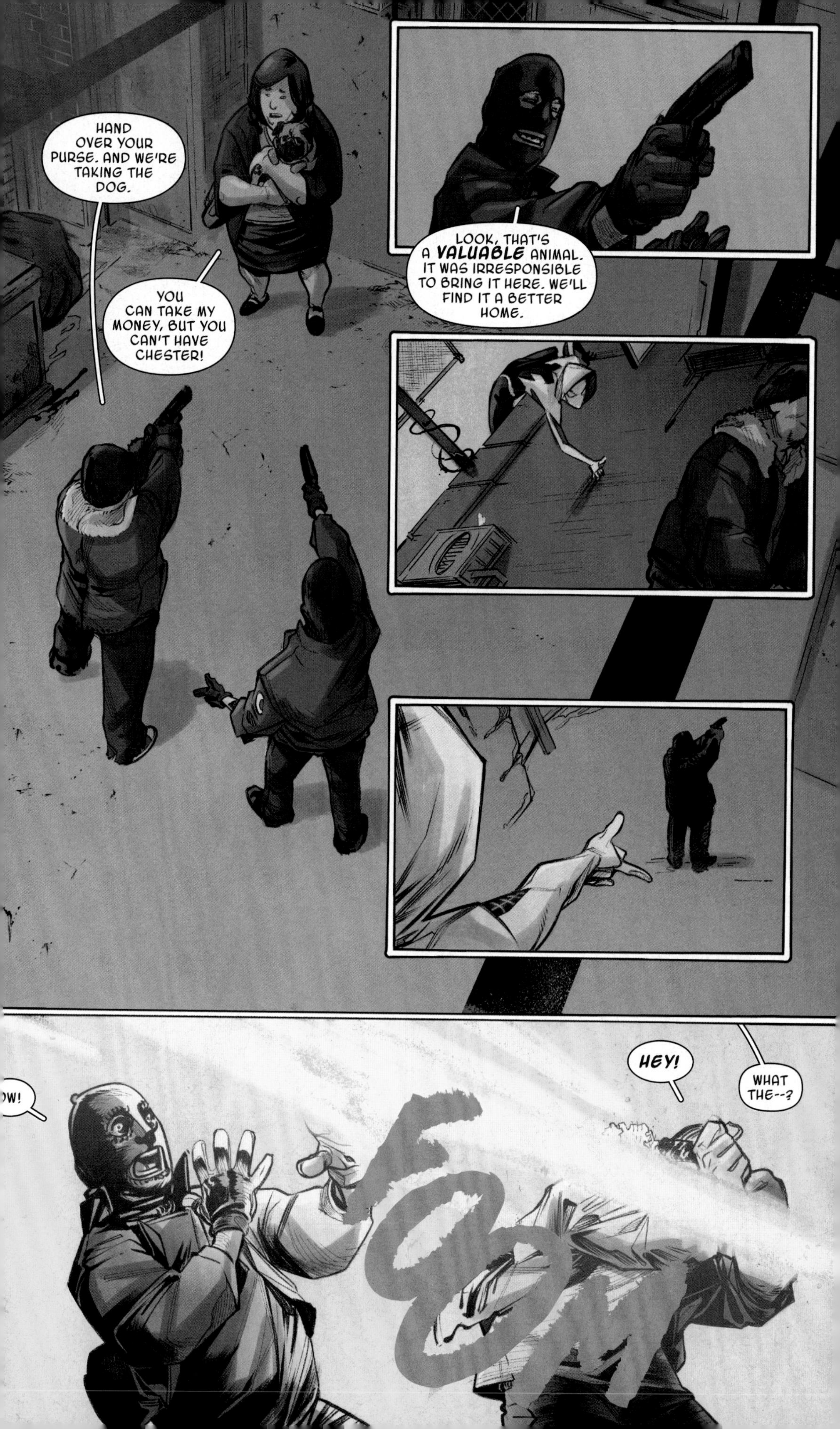
HAND OVER YOUR PURSE. AND WE'RE TAKING THE DOG.
YOU CAN TAKE MY MONEY, BUT YOU CAN'T HAVE CHESTER!
LOOK, THAT'S A VALUABLE ANIMAL. IT WAS IRRESPONSIBLE TO BRING IT HERE. WE'LL FIND IT A BETTER HOME.
OW!
HEY!
WHAT THE--?

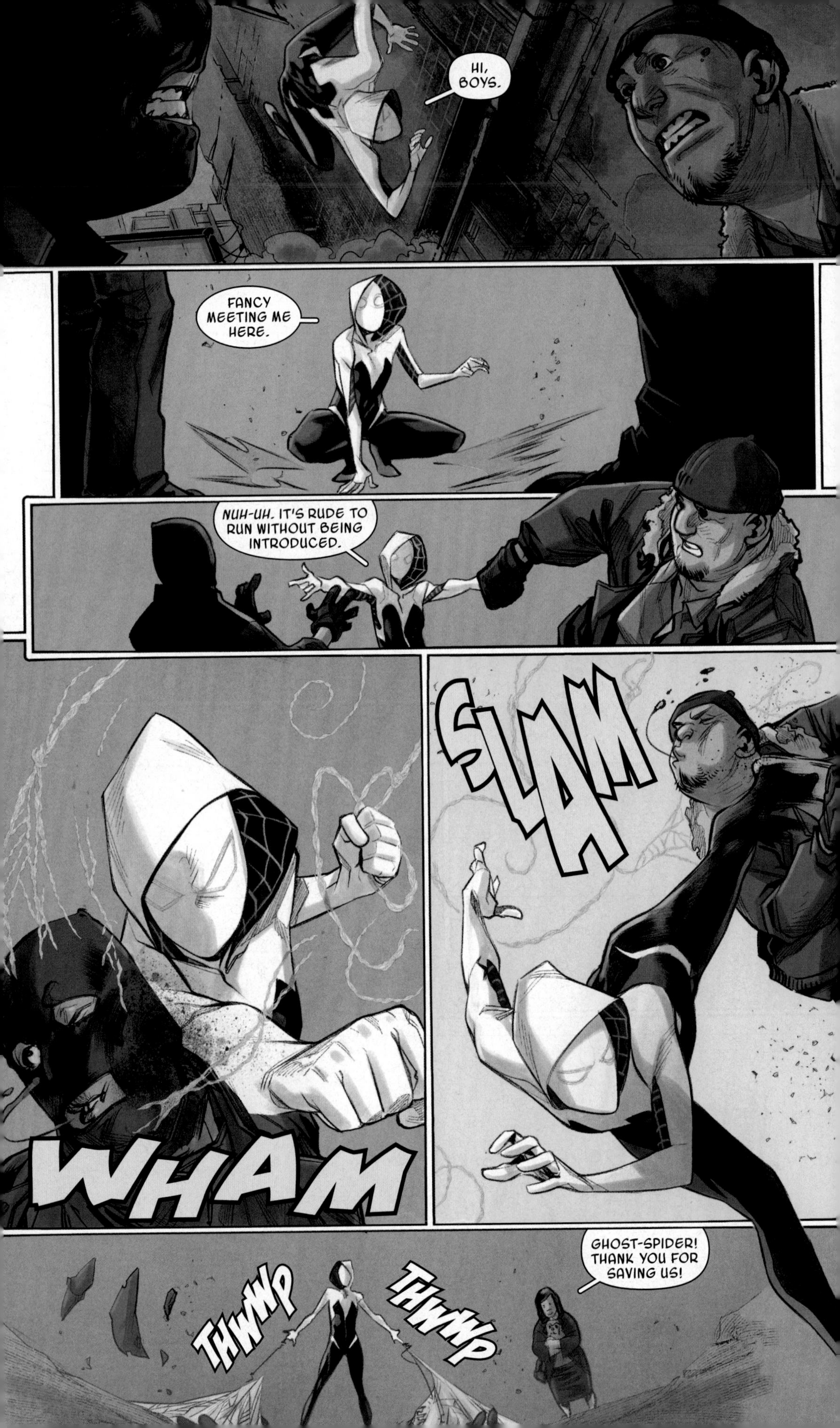
HI, BOYS.
FANCY MEETING ME HERE.
NUH-UH. IT'S RUDE TO RUN WITHOUT BEING INTRODUCED.
WHAM
SLAM
GHOST-SPIDER! THANK YOU FOR SAVING US!
THWWP
THWWP

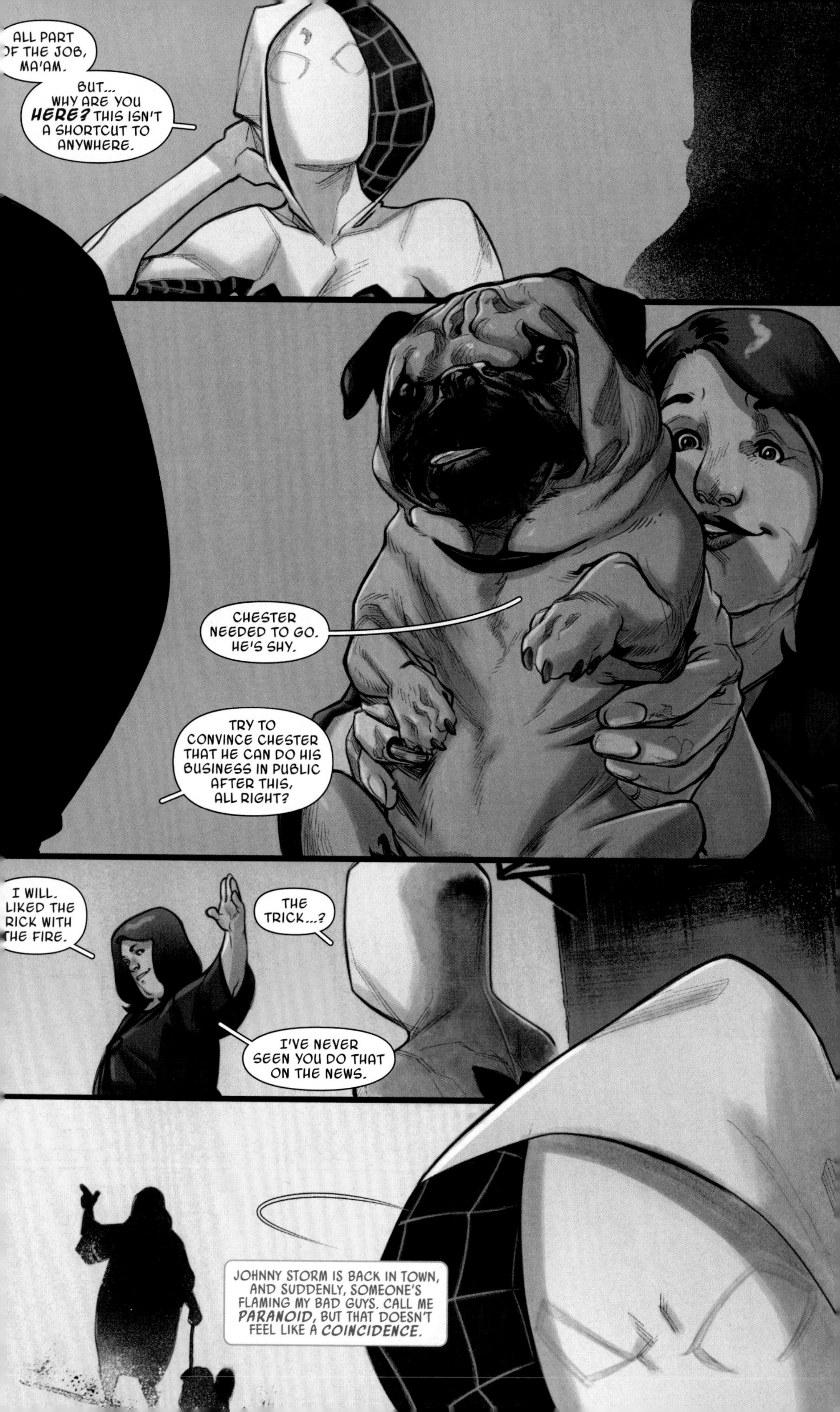
ALL PART OF THE JOB, MA'AM.
BUT... WHY ARE YOU HERE? THIS ISN'T A SHORTCUT TO ANYWHERE.
CHESTER NEEDED TO GO. HE'S SHY.
TRY TO CONVINCE CHESTER THAT HE CAN DO HIS BUSINESS IN PUBLIC AFTER THIS, ALL RIGHT?
I WILL. LIKED THE RICK WITH THE FIRE.
THE TRICK...?
I'VE NEVER SEEN YOU DO THAT ON THE NEWS.
JOHNNY STORM IS BACK IN TOWN, AND SUDDENLY, SOMEONE'S FLAMING MY BAD GUYS. CALL ME PARANOID, BUT THAT DOESN'T FEEL LIKE A COINCIDENCE.

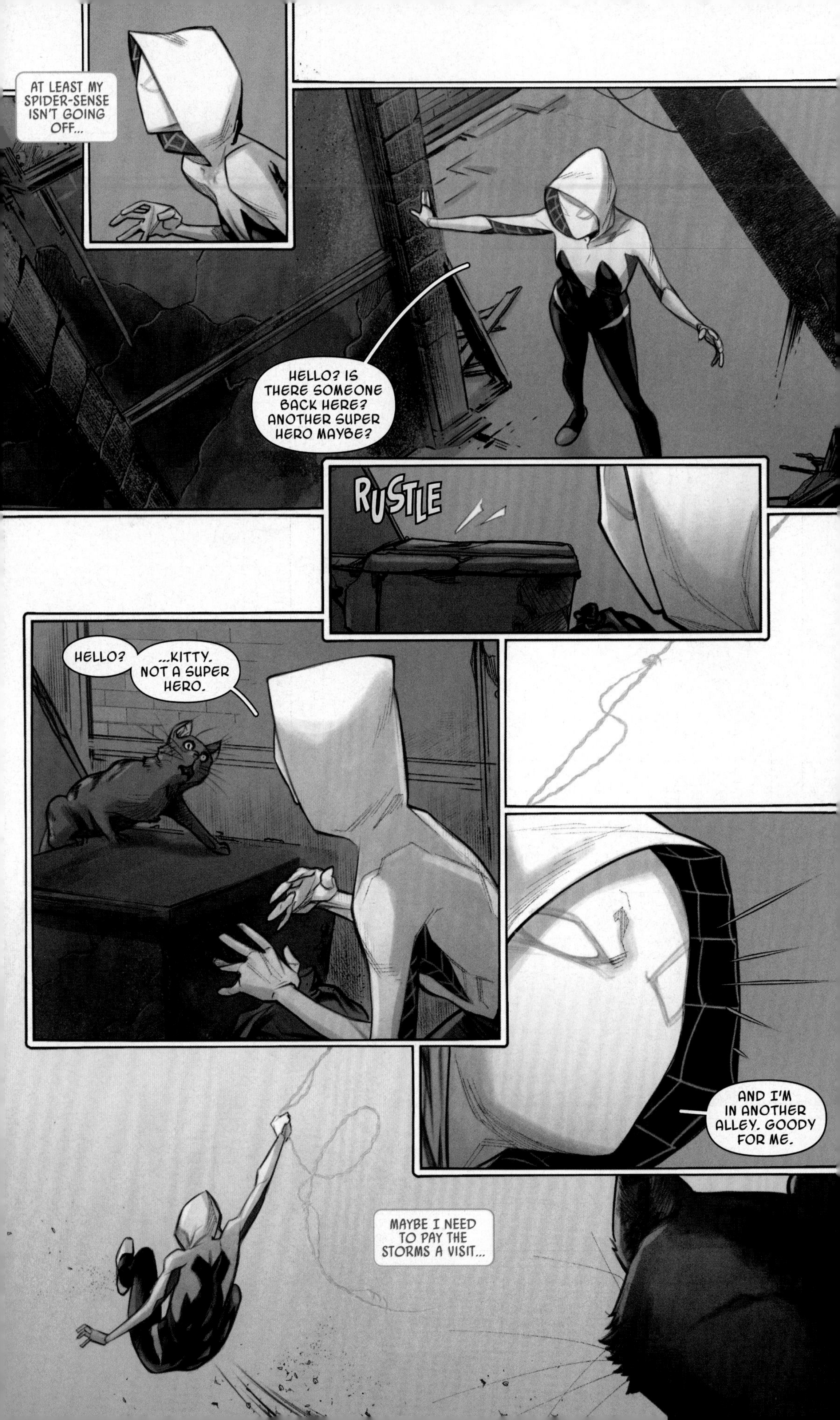
AT LEAST MY SPIDER-SENSE ISN'T GOING OFF...
HELLO? IS THERE SOMEONE BACK HERE? ANOTHER SUPER HERO MAYBE?
RUSTLE
HELLO?
...KITTY. NOT A SUPER HERO.
AND I'M IN ANOTHER ALLEY. GOODY FOR ME.
MAYBE I NEED TO PAY THE STORMS A VISIT...

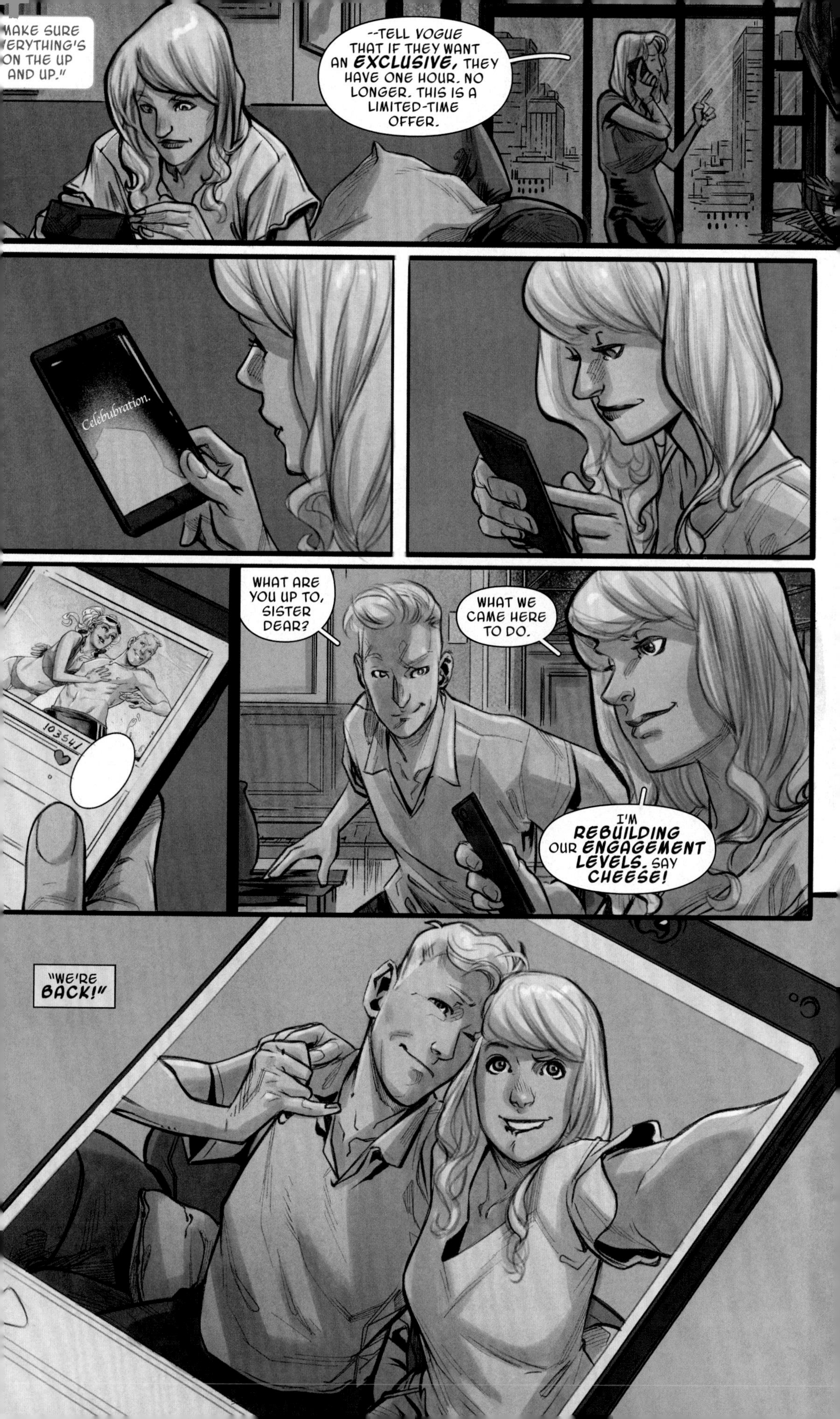
MAKE SURE
VERYTHING'S
ON THE UP
AND UP."
--TELL VOGUE THAT IF THEY WANT AN EXCLUSIVE, THEY HAVE ONE HOUR. NO LONGER. THIS IS A LIMITED-TIME OFFER.
Celebubration.
103541
WHAT ARE YOU UP TO, SISTER DEAR?
WHAT WE CAME HERE TO DO.
I'M REBUILDING OUR ENGAGEMENT LEVELS. SAY CHEESE!
"WE'RE BACK!"

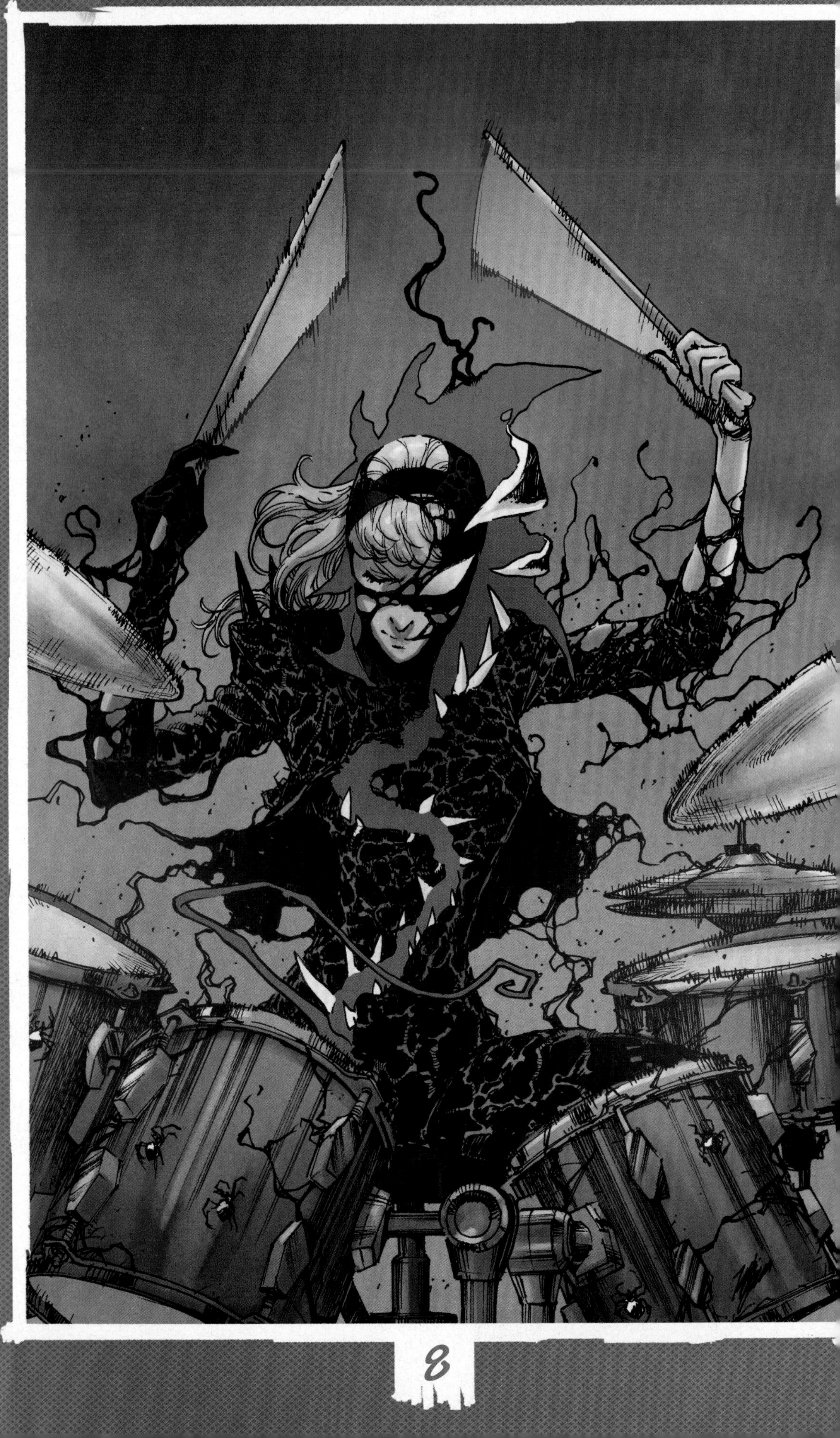
8

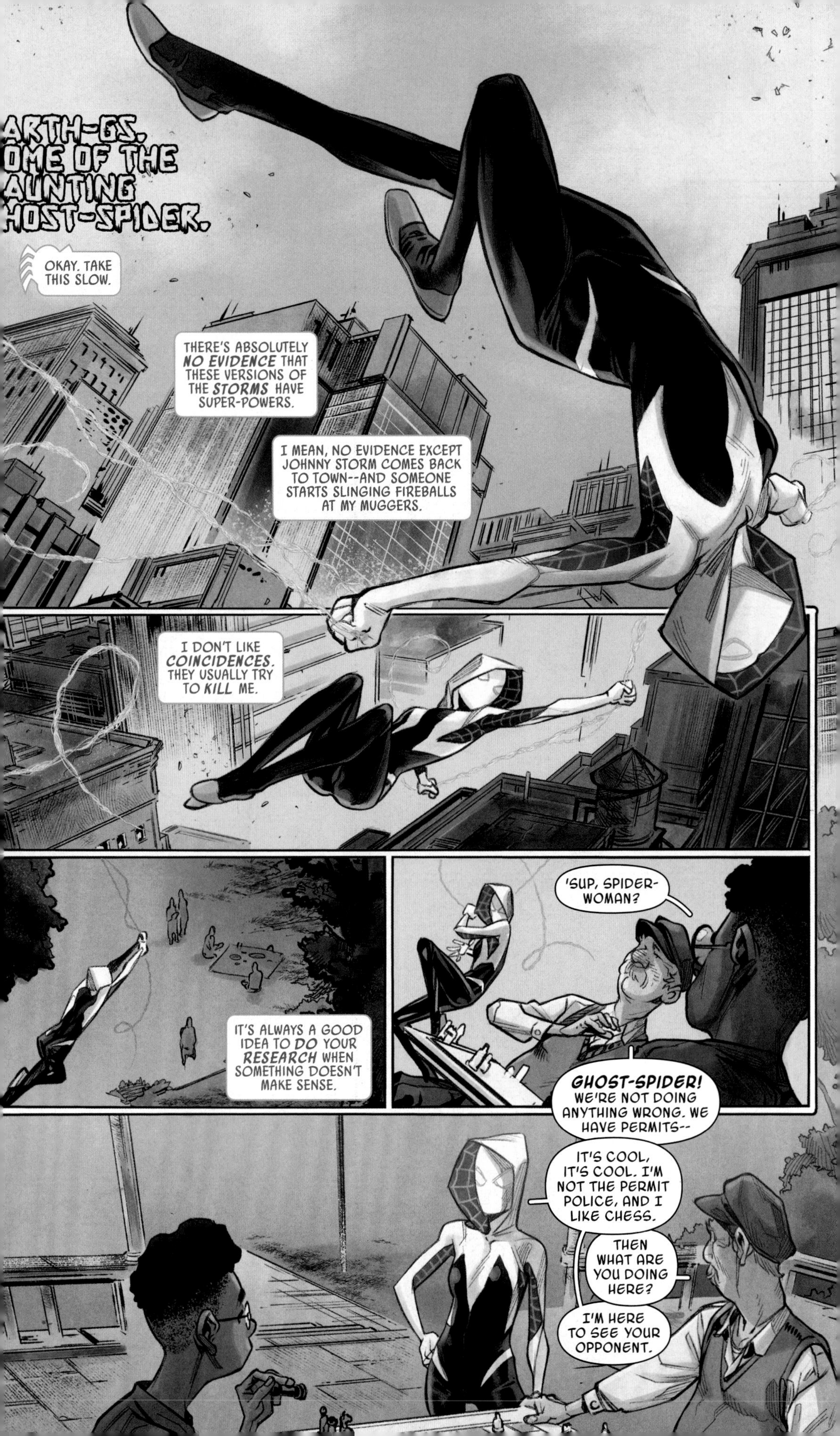
ARTH-65,
OME OF THE
AUNTING
HOST-SPIDER.
OKAY. TAKE THIS SLOW.
THERE'S ABSOLUTELY NO EVIDENCE THAT THESE VERSIONS OF THE STORMS HAVE SUPER-POWERS.
I MEAN, NO EVIDENCE EXCEPT JOHNNY STORM COMES BACK TO TOWN--AND SOMEONE STARTS SLINGING FIREBALLS AT MY MUGGERS.
I DON'T LIKE COINCIDENCES. THEY USUALLY TRY TO KILL ME.
IT'S ALWAYS A GOOD IDEA TO DO YOUR RESEARCH WHEN SOMETHING DOESN'T MAKE SENSE.
'SUP, SPIDER-WOMAN?
GHOST-SPIDER! WE'RE NOT DOING ANYTHING WRONG. WE HAVE PERMITS--
IT'S COOL, IT'S COOL. I'M NOT THE PERMIT POLICE, AND I LIKE CHESS.
THEN WHAT ARE YOU DOING HERE?
I'M HERE TO SEE YOUR OPPONENT.

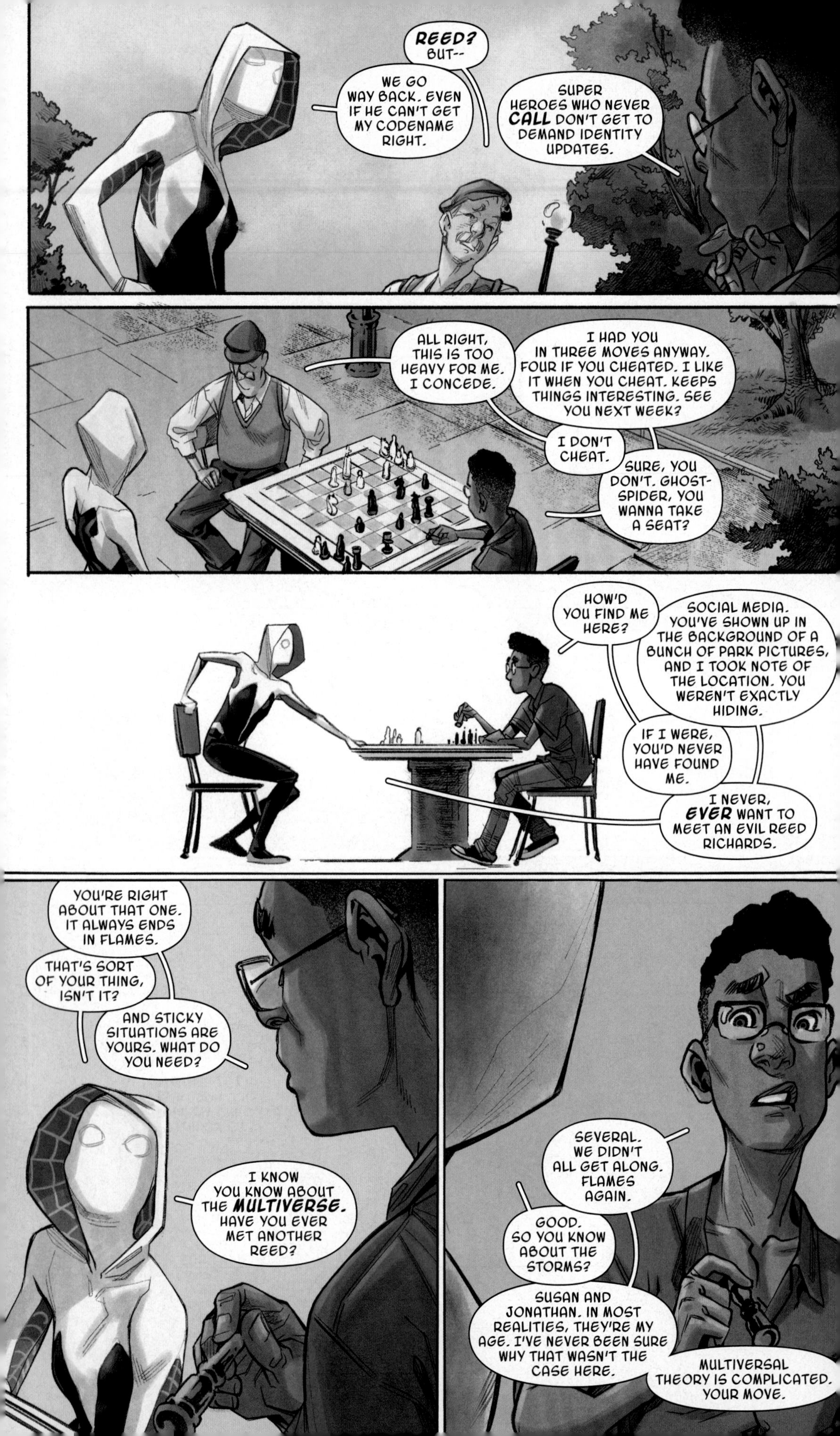
REED? BUT--
WE GO WAY BACK. EVEN IF HE CAN'T GET MY CODENAME RIGHT.
SUPER HEROES WHO NEVER CALL DON'T GET TO DEMAND IDENTITY UPDATES.
ALL RIGHT, THIS IS TOO HEAVY FOR ME. I CONCEDE.
I HAD YOU IN THREE MOVES ANYWAY. FOUR IF YOU CHEATED. I LIKE IT WHEN YOU CHEAT. KEEPS THINGS INTERESTING. SEE YOU NEXT WEEK?
I DON'T CHEAT.
SURE, YOU DON'T. GHOST-SPIDER, YOU WANNA TAKE A SEAT?
HOW'D YOU FIND ME HERE?
SOCIAL MEDIA. YOU'VE SHOWN UP IN THE BACKGROUND OF A BUNCH OF PARK PICTURES, AND I TOOK NOTE OF THE LOCATION. YOU WEREN'T EXACTLY HIDING.
IF I WERE, YOU'D NEVER HAVE FOUND ME.
I NEVER, EVER WANT TO MEET AN EVIL REED RICHARDS.
YOU'RE RIGHT ABOUT THAT ONE. IT ALWAYS ENDS IN FLAMES.
THAT'S SORT OF YOUR THING, ISN'T IT?
AND STICKY SITUATIONS ARE YOURS. WHAT DO YOU NEED?
I KNOW YOU KNOW ABOUT THE MULTIVERSE. HAVE YOU EVER MET ANOTHER REED?
SEVERAL. WE DIDN'T ALL GET ALONG. FLAMES AGAIN.
GOOD. SO YOU KNOW ABOUT THE STORMS?
SUSAN AND JONATHAN. IN MOST REALITIES, THEY'RE MY AGE. I'VE NEVER BEEN SURE WHY THAT WASN'T THE CASE HERE.
MULTIVERSAL THEORY IS COMPLICATED. YOUR MOVE.

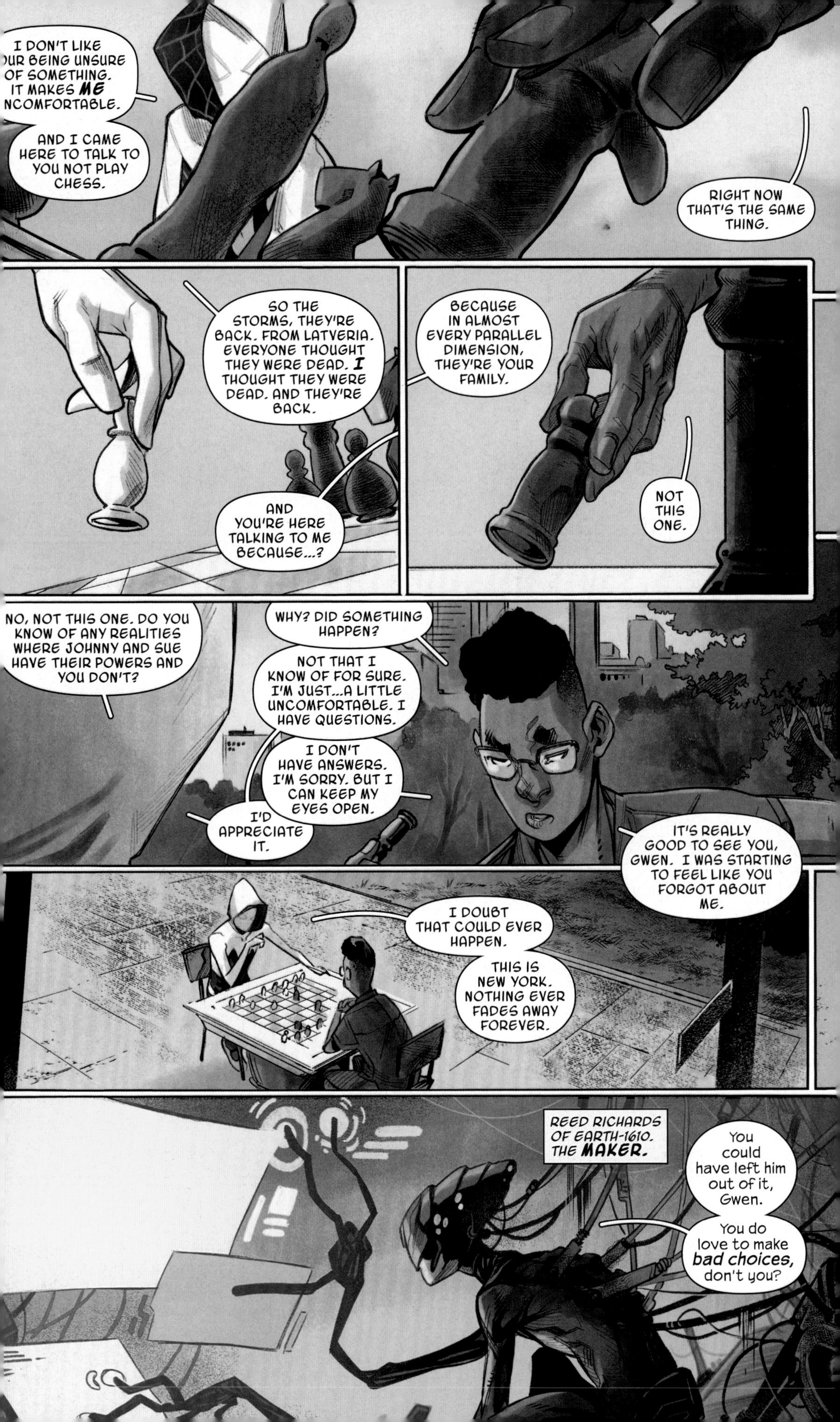

I DON'T LIKE
UR BEING UNSURE
OF SOMETHING.
IT MAKES **ME**
NCOMFORTABLE.
AND I CAME HERE TO TALK TO YOU NOT PLAY CHESS.
RIGHT NOW THAT'S THE SAME THING.
SO THE STORMS, THEY'RE BACK. FROM LATVERIA. EVERYONE THOUGHT THEY WERE DEAD. **I** THOUGHT THEY WERE DEAD. AND THEY'RE BACK.
AND YOU'RE HERE TALKING TO ME BECAUSE...?
BECAUSE IN ALMOST EVERY PARALLEL DIMENSION, THEY'RE YOUR FAMILY.
NOT THIS ONE.
NO, NOT THIS ONE. DO YOU KNOW OF ANY REALITIES WHERE JOHNNY AND SUE HAVE THEIR POWERS AND YOU DON'T?
WHY? DID SOMETHING HAPPEN?
NOT THAT I KNOW OF FOR SURE. I'M JUST...A LITTLE UNCOMFORTABLE. I HAVE QUESTIONS.
I DON'T HAVE ANSWERS. I'M SORRY. BUT I CAN KEEP MY EYES OPEN.
I'D APPRECIATE IT.
IT'S REALLY GOOD TO SEE YOU, GWEN. I WAS STARTING TO FEEL LIKE YOU FORGOT ABOUT ME.
I DOUBT THAT COULD EVER HAPPEN.
THIS IS NEW YORK. NOTHING EVER FADES AWAY FOREVER.
*REED RICHARDS OF EARTH-1610. THE **MAKER.***
You could have left him out of it, Gwen.
You do love to make ***bad choices,*** don't you?

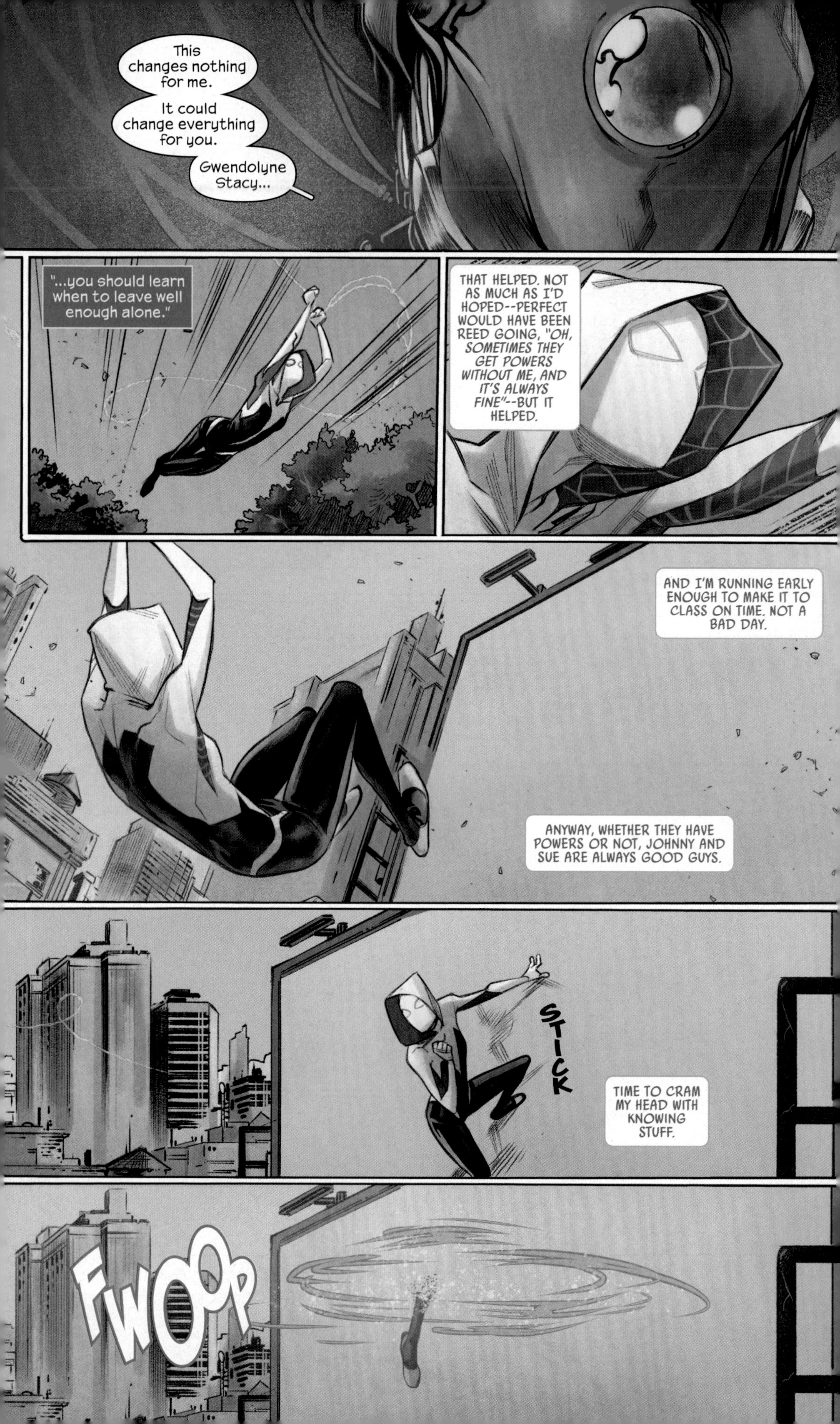
This changes nothing for me.
It could change everything for you.
Gwendolyne Stacy...
"...you should learn when to leave well enough alone."
THAT HELPED. NOT AS MUCH AS I'D HOPED--PERFECT WOULD HAVE BEEN REED GOING, "OH, SOMETIMES THEY GET POWERS WITHOUT ME, AND IT'S ALWAYS FINE"--BUT IT HELPED.
AND I'M RUNNING EARLY ENOUGH TO MAKE IT TO CLASS ON TIME. NOT A BAD DAY.
ANYWAY, WHETHER THEY HAVE POWERS OR NOT, JOHNNY AND SUE ARE ALWAYS GOOD GUYS.
STICK
TIME TO CRAM MY HEAD WITH KNOWING STUFF.
FWOOP

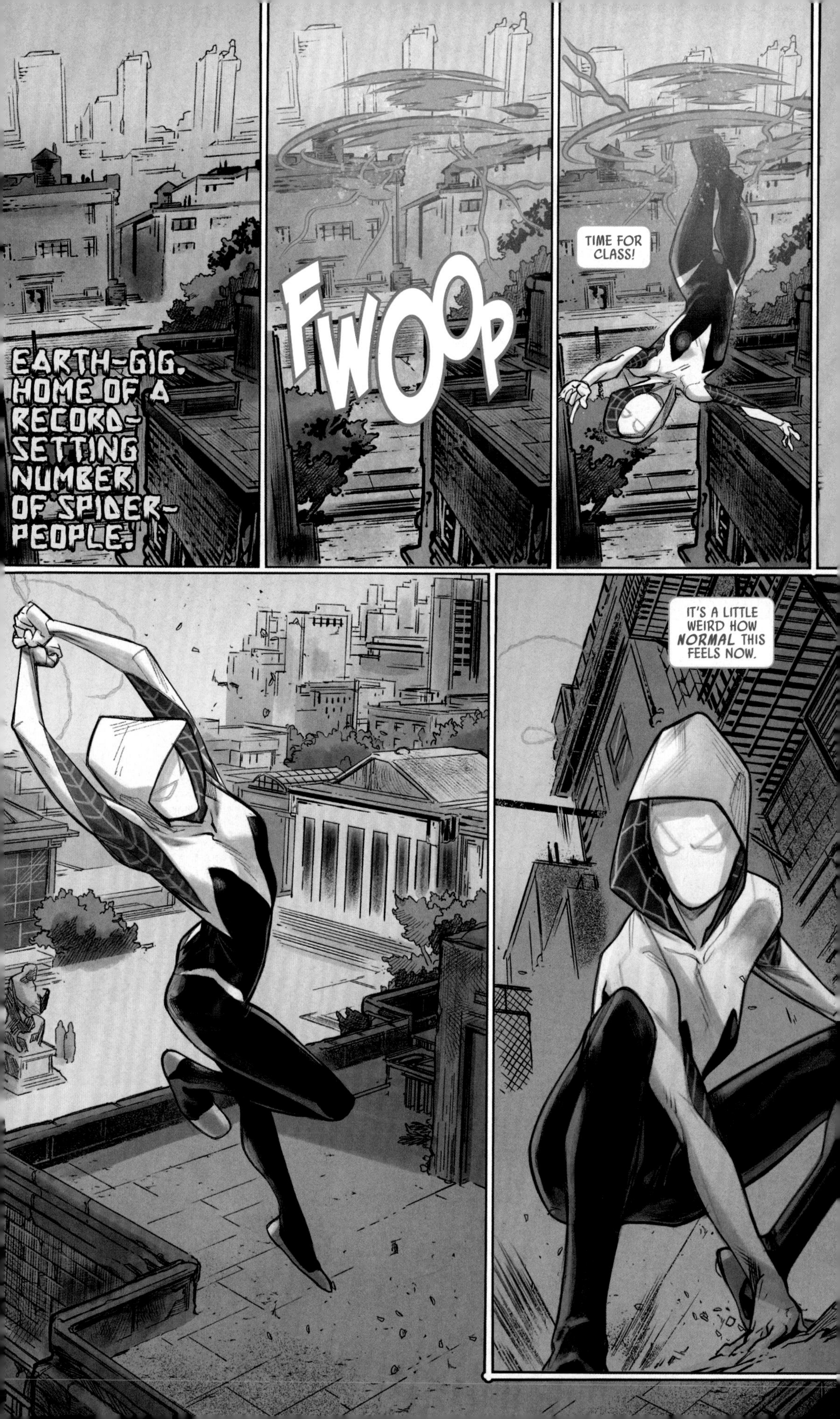
EARTH-GIG. HOME OF A RECORD-SETTING NUMBER OF SPIDER-PEOPLE.
FWOOP
TIME FOR CLASS!
IT'S A LITTLE WEIRD HOW NORMAL THIS FEELS NOW.

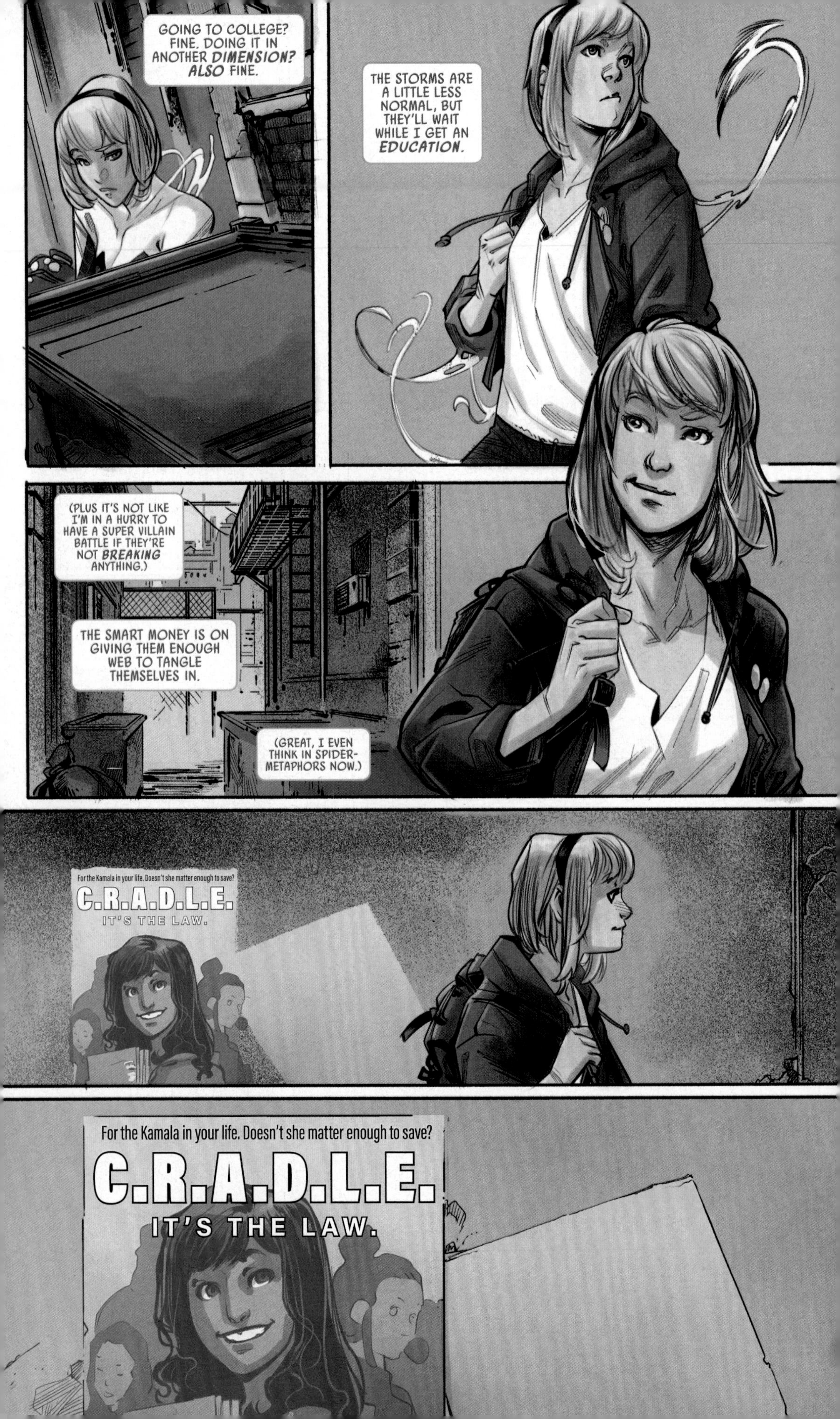

GOING TO COLLEGE? FINE. DOING IT IN ANOTHER DIMENSION? ALSO FINE.
THE STORMS ARE A LITTLE LESS NORMAL, BUT THEY'LL WAIT WHILE I GET AN EDUCATION.
(PLUS IT'S NOT LIKE I'M IN A HURRY TO HAVE A SUPER VILLAIN BATTLE IF THEY'RE NOT BREAKING ANYTHING.)
THE SMART MONEY IS ON GIVING THEM ENOUGH WEB TO TANGLE THEMSELVES IN.
(GREAT, I EVEN THINK IN SPIDER-METAPHORS NOW.)
For the Kamala in your life. Doesn't she matter enough to save?
C.R.A.D.L.E.
IT'S THE LAW.
For the Kamala in your life. Doesn't she matter enough to save?
C.R.A.D.L.E.
IT'S THE LAW.

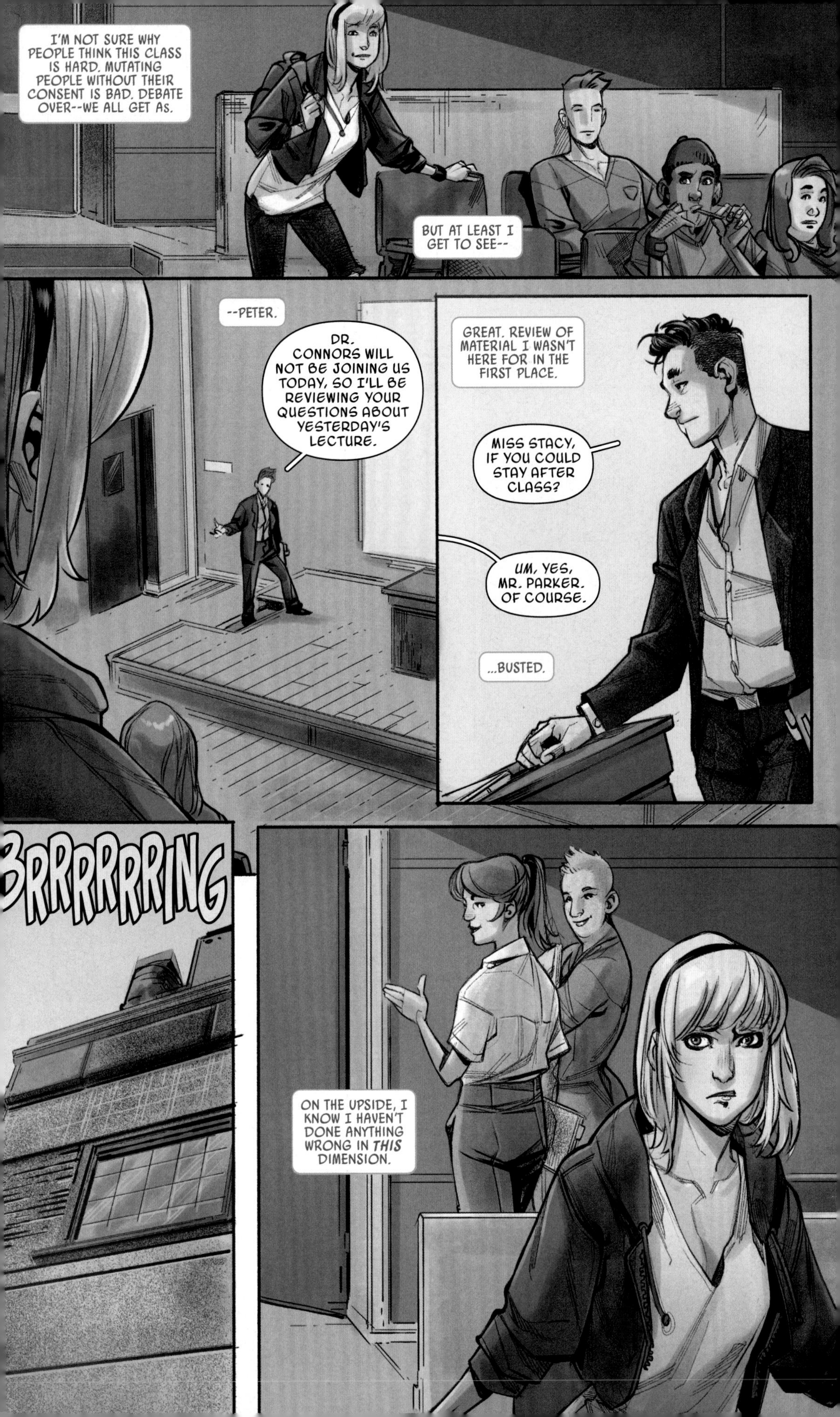

I'M NOT SURE WHY PEOPLE THINK THIS CLASS IS HARD. MUTATING PEOPLE WITHOUT THEIR CONSENT IS BAD. DEBATE OVER--WE ALL GET As.
BUT AT LEAST I GET TO SEE--
--PETER.
DR. CONNORS WILL NOT BE JOINING US TODAY, SO I'LL BE REVIEWING YOUR QUESTIONS ABOUT YESTERDAY'S LECTURE.
GREAT. REVIEW OF MATERIAL I WASN'T HERE FOR IN THE FIRST PLACE.
MISS STACY, IF YOU COULD STAY AFTER CLASS?
UM, YES, MR. PARKER. OF COURSE.
...BUSTED.
BRRRRRRING
ON THE UPSIDE, I KNOW I HAVEN'T DONE ANYTHING WRONG IN *THIS* DIMENSION.

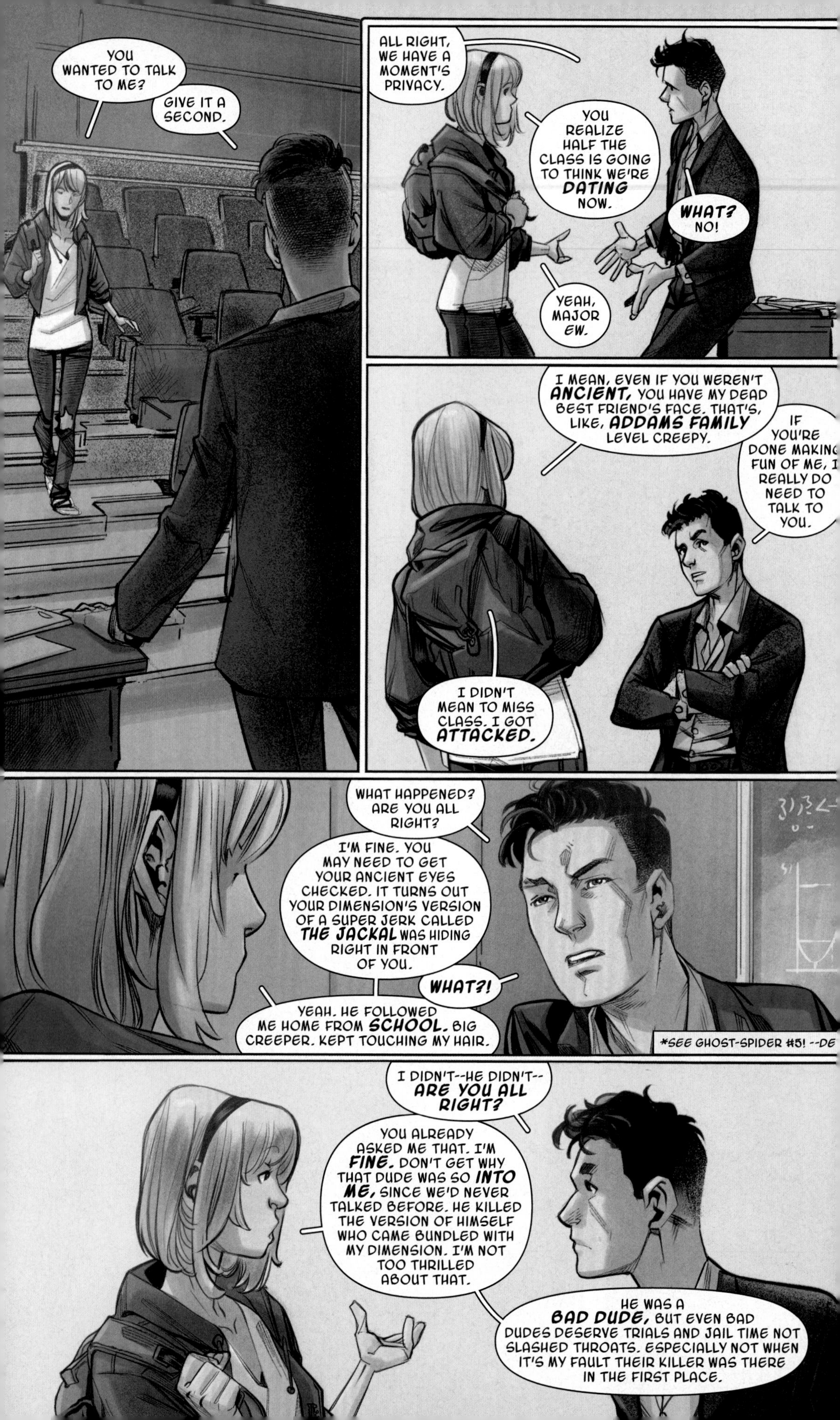

YOU WANTED TO TALK TO ME?
GIVE IT A SECOND.
ALL RIGHT, WE HAVE A MOMENT'S PRIVACY.
YOU REALIZE HALF THE CLASS IS GOING TO THINK WE'RE DATING NOW.
WHAT? NO!
YEAH, MAJOR EW.
I MEAN, EVEN IF YOU WEREN'T ANCIENT, YOU HAVE MY DEAD BEST FRIEND'S FACE. THAT'S, LIKE, ADDAMS FAMILY LEVEL CREEPY.
IF YOU'RE DONE MAKING FUN OF ME, I REALLY DO NEED TO TALK TO YOU.
I DIDN'T MEAN TO MISS CLASS. I GOT ATTACKED.
WHAT HAPPENED? ARE YOU ALL RIGHT?
I'M FINE. YOU MAY NEED TO GET YOUR ANCIENT EYES CHECKED. IT TURNS OUT YOUR DIMENSION'S VERSION OF A SUPER JERK CALLED THE JACKAL WAS HIDING RIGHT IN FRONT OF YOU.
WHAT?!
YEAH. HE FOLLOWED ME HOME FROM SCHOOL. BIG CREEPER. KEPT TOUCHING MY HAIR.
*SEE GHOST-SPIDER #5! --DE
I DIDN'T--HE DIDN'T-- ARE YOU ALL RIGHT?
YOU ALREADY ASKED ME THAT. I'M FINE. DON'T GET WHY THAT DUDE WAS SO INTO ME, SINCE WE'D NEVER TALKED BEFORE. HE KILLED THE VERSION OF HIMSELF WHO CAME BUNDLED WITH MY DIMENSION. I'M NOT TOO THRILLED ABOUT THAT.
HE WAS A BAD DUDE, BUT EVEN BAD DUDES DESERVE TRIALS AND JAIL TIME NOT SLASHED THROATS. ESPECIALLY NOT WHEN IT'S MY FAULT THEIR KILLER WAS THERE IN THE FIRST PLACE.

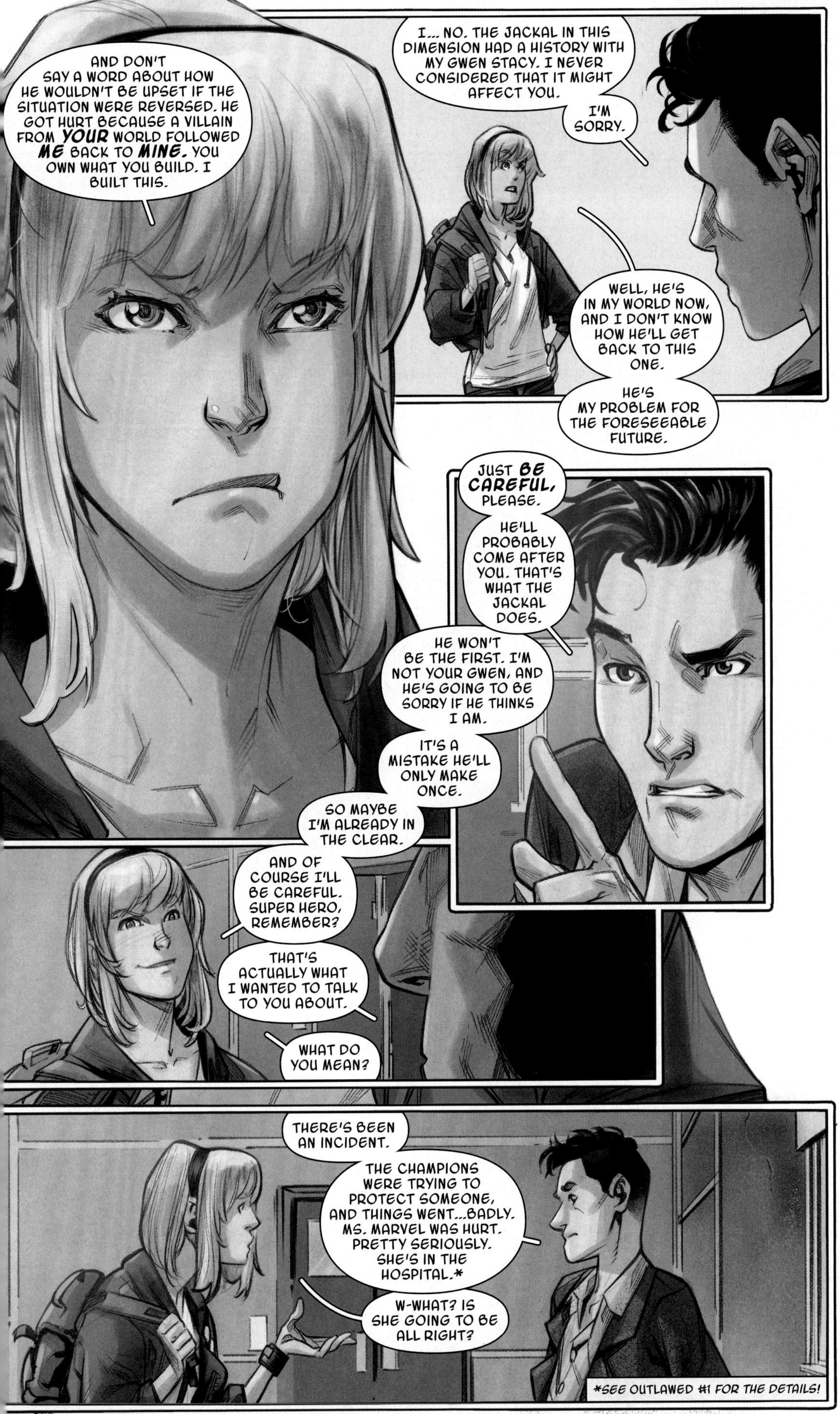
AND DON'T SAY A WORD ABOUT HOW HE WOULDN'T BE UPSET IF THE SITUATION WERE REVERSED. HE GOT HURT BECAUSE A VILLAIN FROM **YOUR** WORLD FOLLOWED **ME** BACK TO **MINE.** YOU OWN WHAT YOU BUILD. I BUILT THIS.
I... NO. THE JACKAL IN THIS DIMENSION HAD A HISTORY WITH MY GWEN STACY. I NEVER CONSIDERED THAT IT MIGHT AFFECT YOU.
I'M SORRY.
WELL, HE'S IN MY WORLD NOW, AND I DON'T KNOW HOW HE'LL GET BACK TO THIS ONE.
HE'S MY PROBLEM FOR THE FORESEEABLE FUTURE.
JUST **BE CAREFUL,** PLEASE.
HE'LL PROBABLY COME AFTER YOU. THAT'S WHAT THE JACKAL DOES.
HE WON'T BE THE FIRST. I'M NOT YOUR GWEN, AND HE'S GOING TO BE SORRY IF HE THINKS I AM.
IT'S A MISTAKE HE'LL ONLY MAKE ONCE.
SO MAYBE I'M ALREADY IN THE CLEAR.
AND OF COURSE I'LL BE CAREFUL. SUPER HERO, REMEMBER?
THAT'S ACTUALLY WHAT I WANTED TO TALK TO YOU ABOUT.
WHAT DO YOU MEAN?
THERE'S BEEN AN INCIDENT.
THE CHAMPIONS WERE TRYING TO PROTECT SOMEONE, AND THINGS WENT...BADLY. MS. MARVEL WAS HURT. PRETTY SERIOUSLY. SHE'S IN THE HOSPITAL.*
W-WHAT? IS SHE GOING TO BE ALL RIGHT?
*SEE OUTLAWED #1 FOR THE DETAILS!

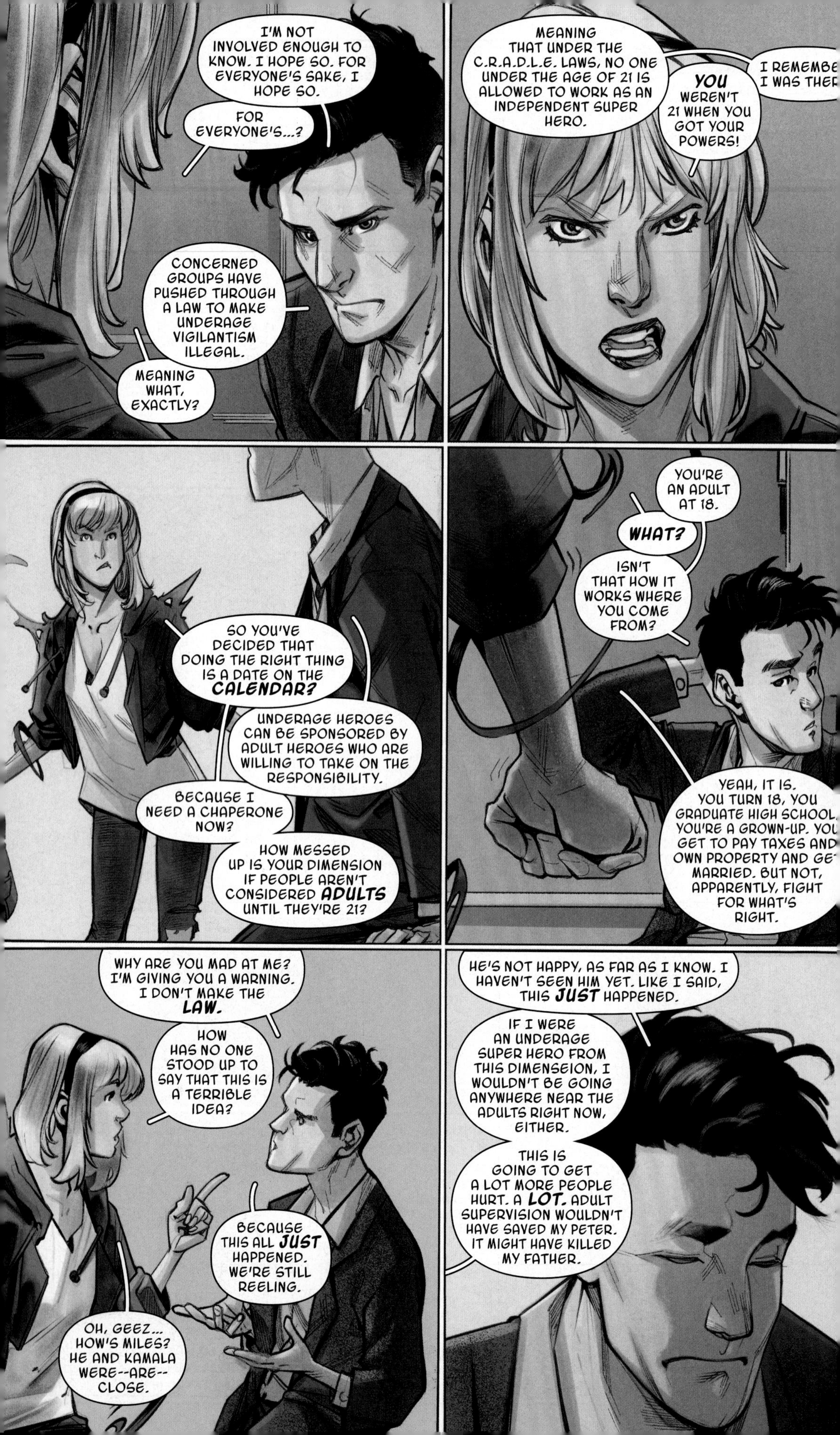

I'M NOT INVOLVED ENOUGH TO KNOW. I HOPE SO. FOR EVERYONE'S SAKE, I HOPE SO.
FOR EVERYONE'S...?
CONCERNED GROUPS HAVE PUSHED THROUGH A LAW TO MAKE UNDERAGE VIGILANTISM ILLEGAL.
MEANING WHAT, EXACTLY?
MEANING THAT UNDER THE C.R.A.D.L.E. LAWS, NO ONE UNDER THE AGE OF 21 IS ALLOWED TO WORK AS AN INDEPENDENT SUPER HERO.
YOU WEREN'T 21 WHEN YOU GOT YOUR POWERS!
SO YOU'VE DECIDED THAT DOING THE RIGHT THING IS A DATE ON THE CALENDAR?
UNDERAGE HEROES CAN BE SPONSORED BY ADULT HEROES WHO ARE WILLING TO TAKE ON THE RESPONSIBILITY.
BECAUSE I NEED A CHAPERONE NOW?
HOW MESSED UP IS YOUR DIMENSION IF PEOPLE AREN'T CONSIDERED ADULTS UNTIL THEY'RE 21?
YOU'RE AN ADULT AT 18.
WHAT?
ISN'T THAT HOW IT WORKS WHERE YOU COME FROM?
WHY ARE YOU MAD AT ME? I'M GIVING YOU A WARNING. I DON'T MAKE THE LAW.
HOW HAS NO ONE STOOD UP TO SAY THAT THIS IS A TERRIBLE IDEA?
BECAUSE THIS ALL JUST HAPPENED. WE'RE STILL REELING.
OH, GEEZ... HOW'S MILES? HE AND KAMALA WERE--ARE--CLOSE.
HE'S NOT HAPPY, AS FAR AS I KNOW. I HAVEN'T SEEN HIM YET. LIKE I SAID, THIS JUST HAPPENED.
IF I WERE AN UNDERAGE SUPER HERO FROM THIS DIMENSEION, I WOULDN'T BE GOING ANYWHERE NEAR THE ADULTS RIGHT NOW, EITHER.
THIS IS GOING TO GET A LOT MORE PEOPLE HURT. A LOT. ADULT SUPERVISION WOULDN'T HAVE SAVED MY PETER. IT MIGHT HAVE KILLED MY FATHER.

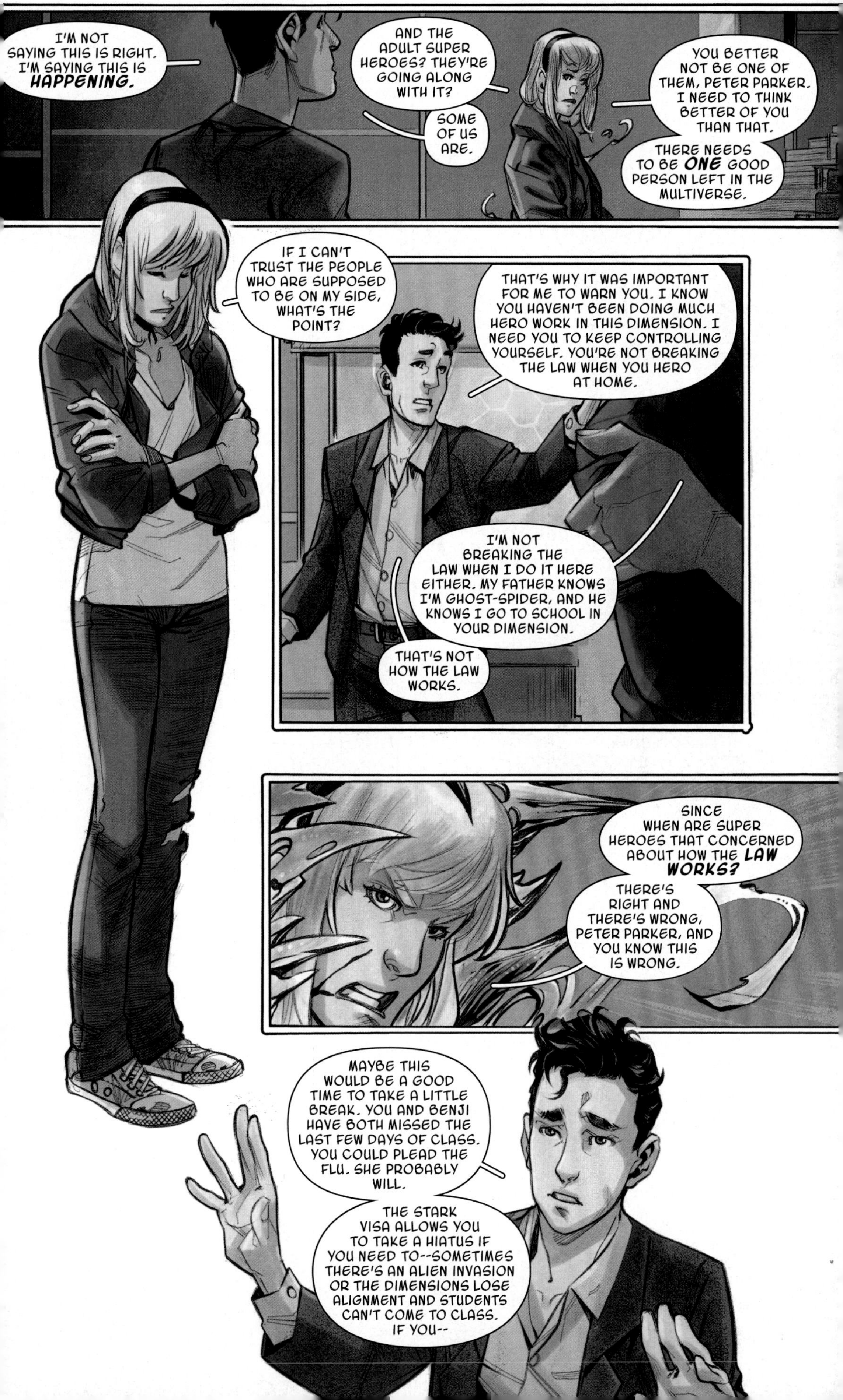

I'M NOT SAYING THIS IS RIGHT. I'M SAYING THIS IS HAPPENING.
AND THE ADULT SUPER HEROES? THEY'RE GOING ALONG WITH IT?
SOME OF US ARE.
YOU BETTER NOT BE ONE OF THEM, PETER PARKER. I NEED TO THINK BETTER OF YOU THAN THAT.
THERE NEEDS TO BE ONE GOOD PERSON LEFT IN THE MULTIVERSE.
IF I CAN'T TRUST THE PEOPLE WHO ARE SUPPOSED TO BE ON MY SIDE, WHAT'S THE POINT?
THAT'S WHY IT WAS IMPORTANT FOR ME TO WARN YOU. I KNOW YOU HAVEN'T BEEN DOING MUCH HERO WORK IN THIS DIMENSION. I NEED YOU TO KEEP CONTROLLING YOURSELF. YOU'RE NOT BREAKING THE LAW WHEN YOU HERO AT HOME.
I'M NOT BREAKING THE LAW WHEN I DO IT HERE EITHER. MY FATHER KNOWS I'M GHOST-SPIDER, AND HE KNOWS I GO TO SCHOOL IN YOUR DIMENSION.
THAT'S NOT HOW THE LAW WORKS.
SINCE WHEN ARE SUPER HEROES THAT CONCERNED ABOUT HOW THE LAW WORKS?
THERE'S RIGHT AND THERE'S WRONG, PETER PARKER, AND YOU KNOW THIS IS WRONG.
MAYBE THIS WOULD BE A GOOD TIME TO TAKE A LITTLE BREAK. YOU AND BENJI HAVE BOTH MISSED THE LAST FEW DAYS OF CLASS. YOU COULD PLEAD THE FLU. SHE PROBABLY WILL.
THE STARK VISA ALLOWS YOU TO TAKE A HIATUS IF YOU NEED TO--SOMETIMES THERE'S AN ALIEN INVASION OR THE DIMENSIONS LOSE ALIGNMENT AND STUDENTS CAN'T COME TO CLASS. IF YOU--

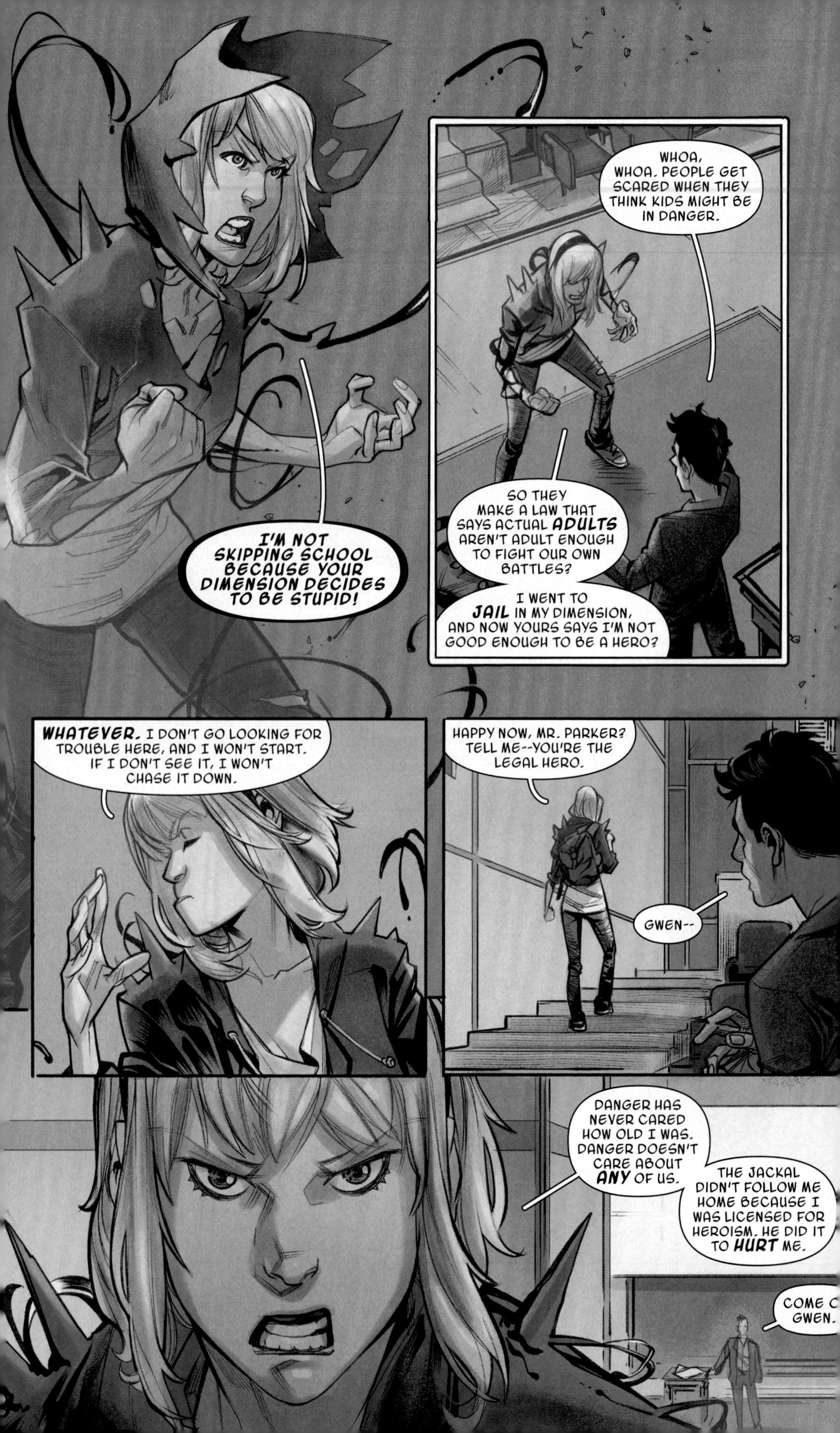
I'M NOT SKIPPING SCHOOL BECAUSE YOUR DIMENSION DECIDES TO BE STUPID!
WHOA, WHOA. PEOPLE GET SCARED WHEN THEY THINK KIDS MIGHT BE IN DANGER.
SO THEY MAKE A LAW THAT SAYS ACTUAL ADULTS AREN'T ADULT ENOUGH TO FIGHT OUR OWN BATTLES?
I WENT TO JAIL IN MY DIMENSION, AND NOW YOURS SAYS I'M NOT GOOD ENOUGH TO BE A HERO?
WHATEVER. I DON'T GO LOOKING FOR TROUBLE HERE, AND I WON'T START. IF I DON'T SEE IT, I WON'T CHASE IT DOWN.
HAPPY NOW, MR. PARKER? TELL ME--YOU'RE THE LEGAL HERO.
GWEN--
DANGER HAS NEVER CARED HOW OLD I WAS. DANGER DOESN'T CARE ABOUT ANY OF US.
THE JACKAL DIDN'T FOLLOW ME HOME BECAUSE I WAS LICENSED FOR HEROISM. HE DID IT TO HURT ME.

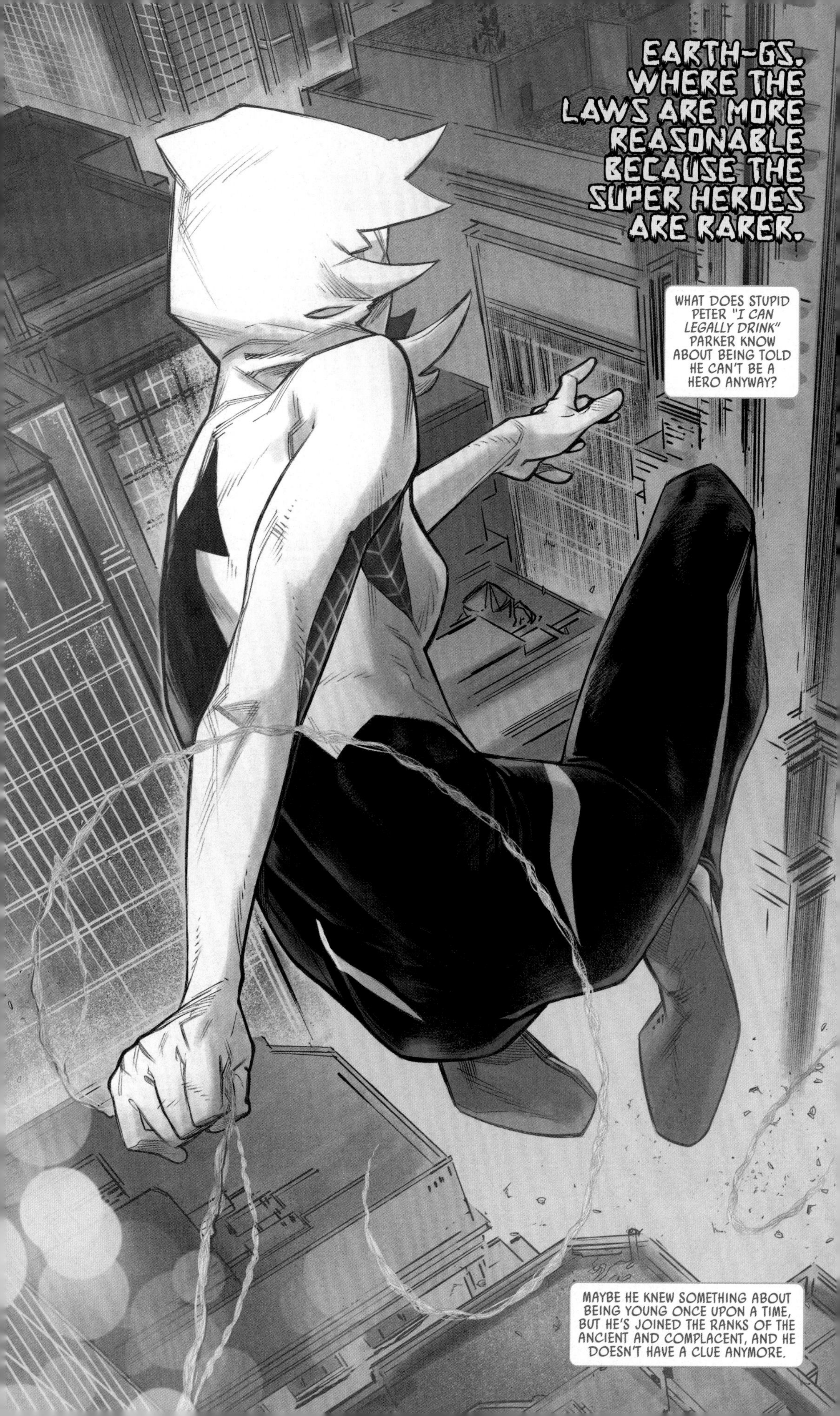
EARTH-65. WHERE THE LAWS ARE MORE REASONABLE BECAUSE THE SUPER HEROES ARE RARER.
WHAT DOES STUPID PETER "I CAN LEGALLY DRINK" PARKER KNOW ABOUT BEING TOLD HE CAN'T BE A HERO ANYWAY?
MAYBE HE KNEW SOMETHING ABOUT BEING YOUNG ONCE UPON A TIME, BUT HE'S JOINED THE RANKS OF THE ANCIENT AND COMPLACENT, AND HE DOESN'T HAVE A CLUE ANYMORE.

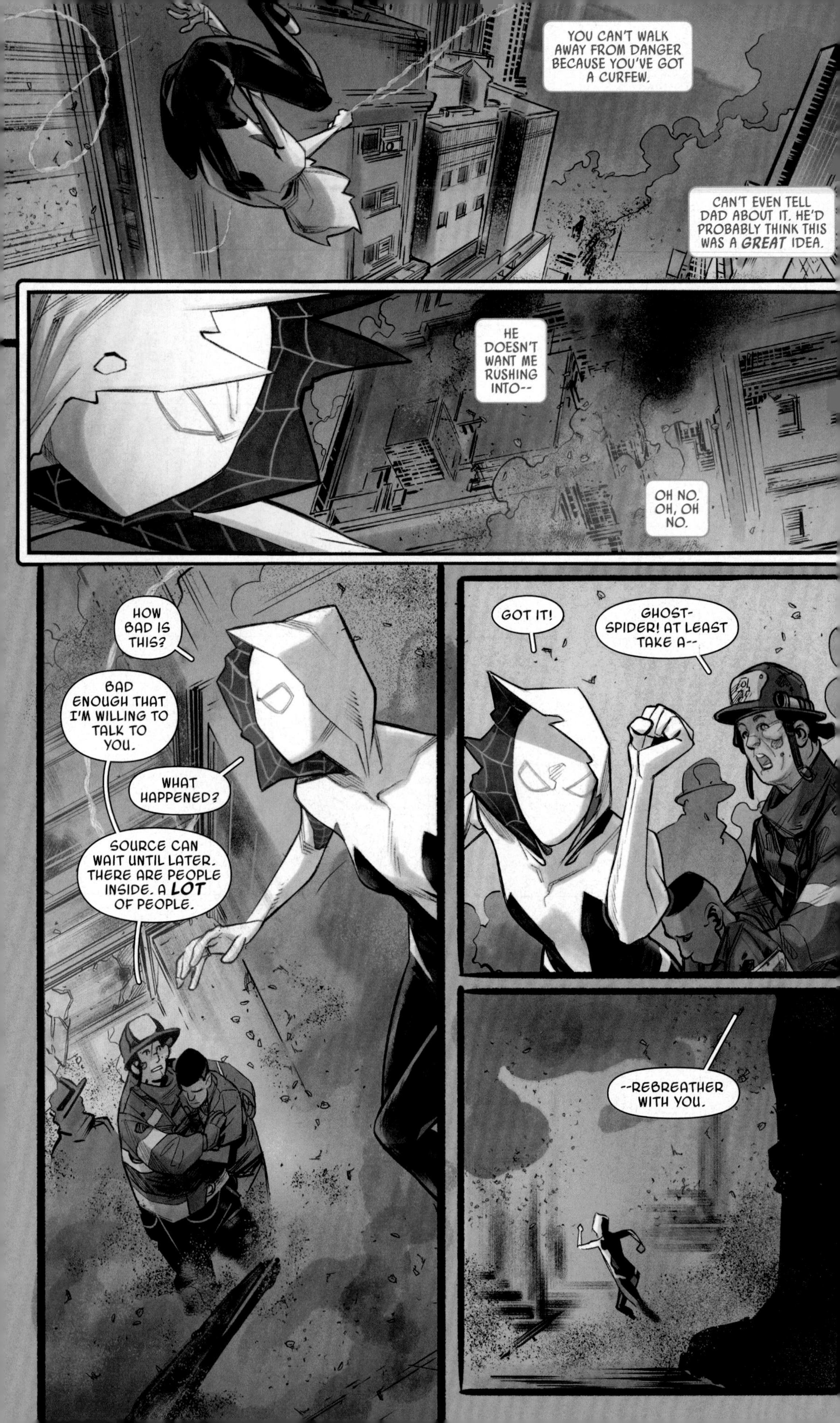
YOU CAN'T WALK AWAY FROM DANGER BECAUSE YOU'VE GOT A CURFEW.
CAN'T EVEN TELL DAD ABOUT IT. HE'D PROBABLY THINK THIS WAS A **GREAT** IDEA.
HE DOESN'T WANT ME RUSHING INTO--
OH NO. OH, OH NO.
HOW BAD IS THIS?
BAD ENOUGH THAT I'M WILLING TO TALK TO YOU.
WHAT HAPPENED?
SOURCE CAN WAIT UNTIL LATER. THERE ARE PEOPLE INSIDE. A **LOT** OF PEOPLE.
GOT IT!
GHOST-SPIDER! AT LEAST TAKE A--
--REBREATHER WITH YOU.

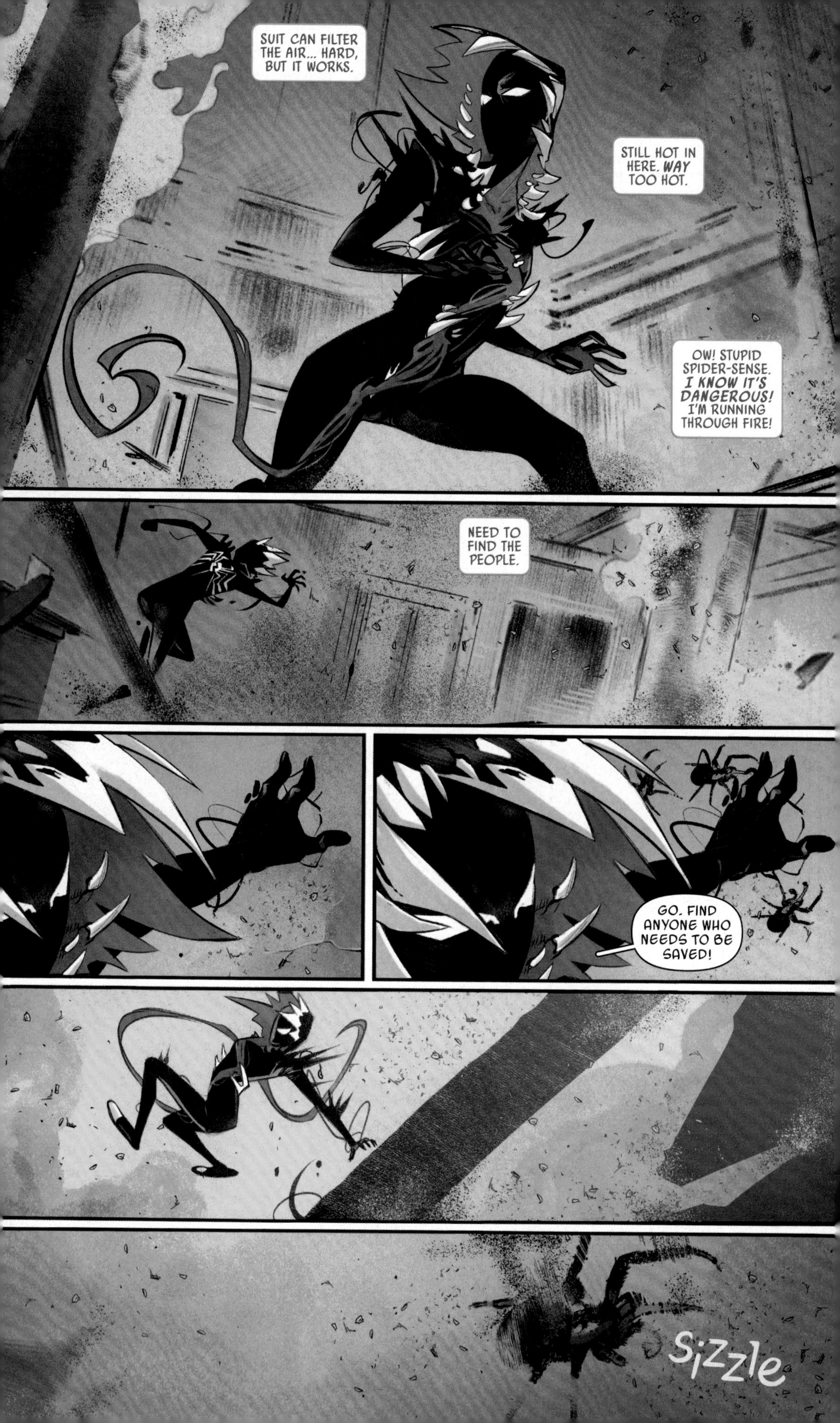
SUIT CAN FILTER THE AIR... HARD, BUT IT WORKS.
STILL HOT IN HERE. **WAY** TOO HOT.
OW! STUPID SPIDER-SENSE. ***I KNOW IT'S DANGEROUS!*** I'M RUNNING THROUGH FIRE!
NEED TO FIND THE PEOPLE.
GO. FIND ANYONE WHO NEEDS TO BE SAVED!
SIZZLE

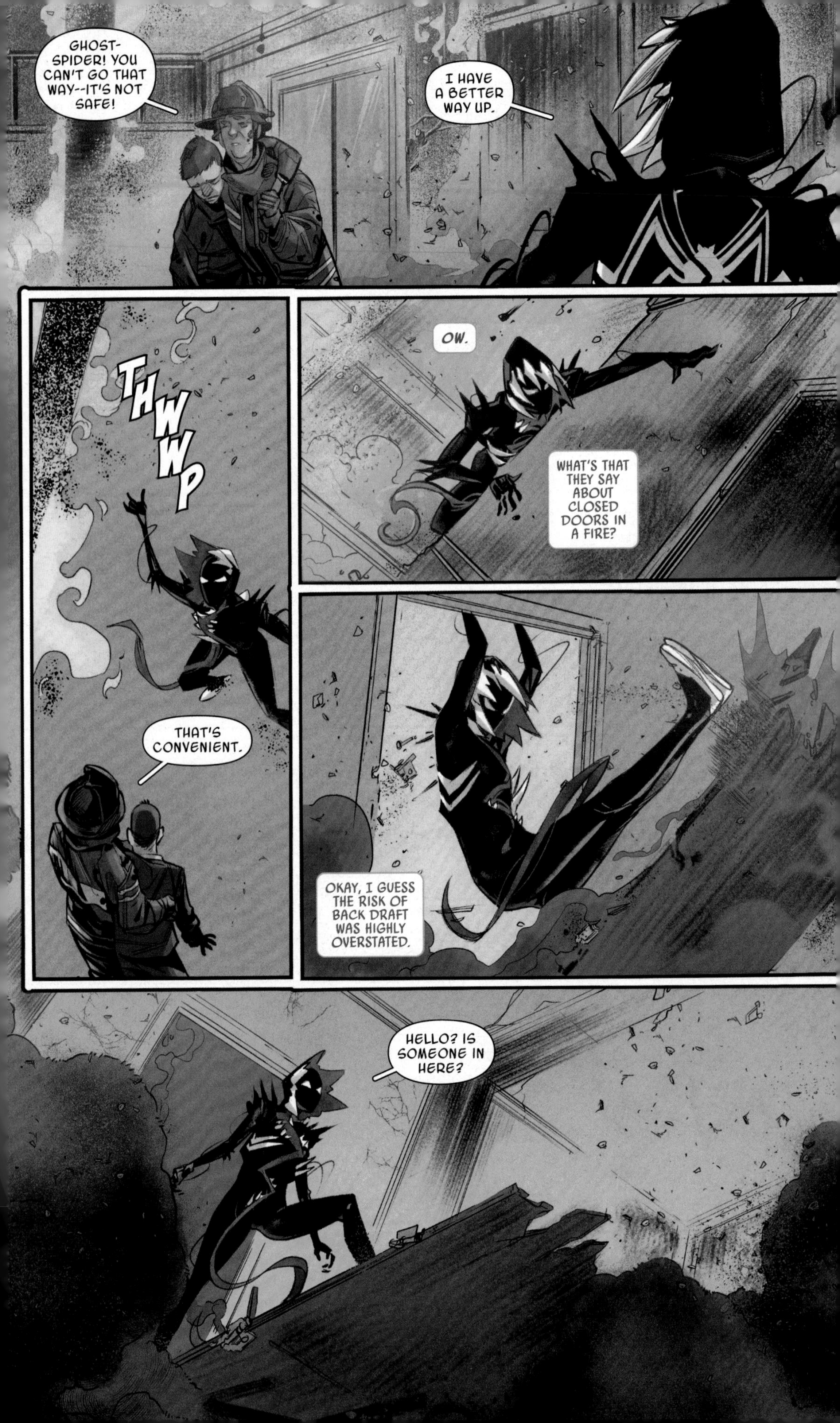
GHOST-SPIDER! YOU CAN'T GO THAT WAY--IT'S NOT SAFE!
I HAVE A BETTER WAY UP.
THWWP
THAT'S CONVENIENT.
OW.
WHAT'S THAT THEY SAY ABOUT CLOSED DOORS IN A FIRE?
OKAY, I GUESS THE RISK OF BACK DRAFT WAS HIGHLY OVERSTATED.
HELLO? IS SOMEONE IN HERE?

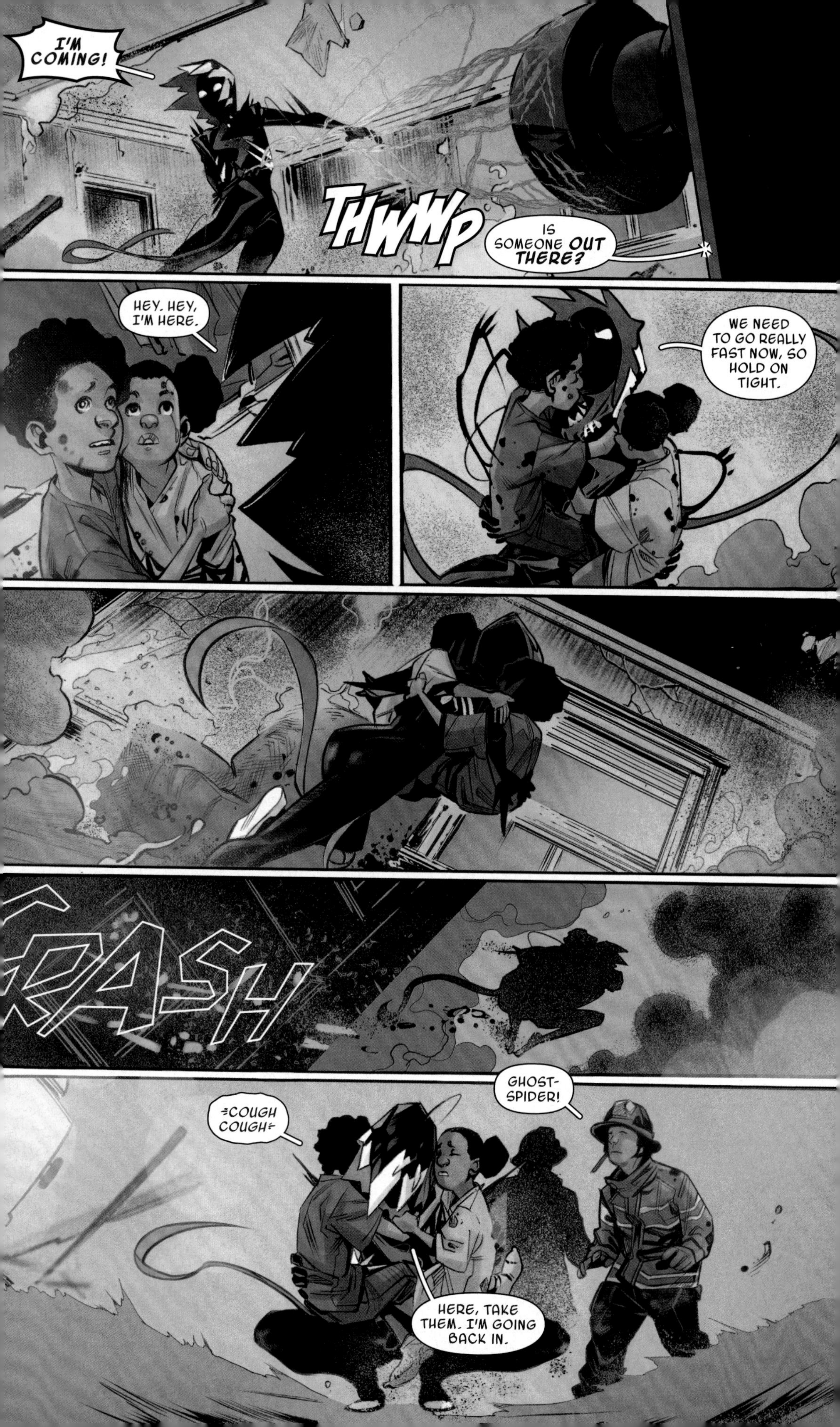
I'M COMING!
THWWP
IS SOMEONE OUT THERE?
HEY. HEY, I'M HERE.
WE NEED TO GO REALLY FAST NOW, SO HOLD ON TIGHT.
CRASH
=COUGH COUGH=
GHOST-SPIDER!
HERE, TAKE THEM. I'M GOING BACK IN.

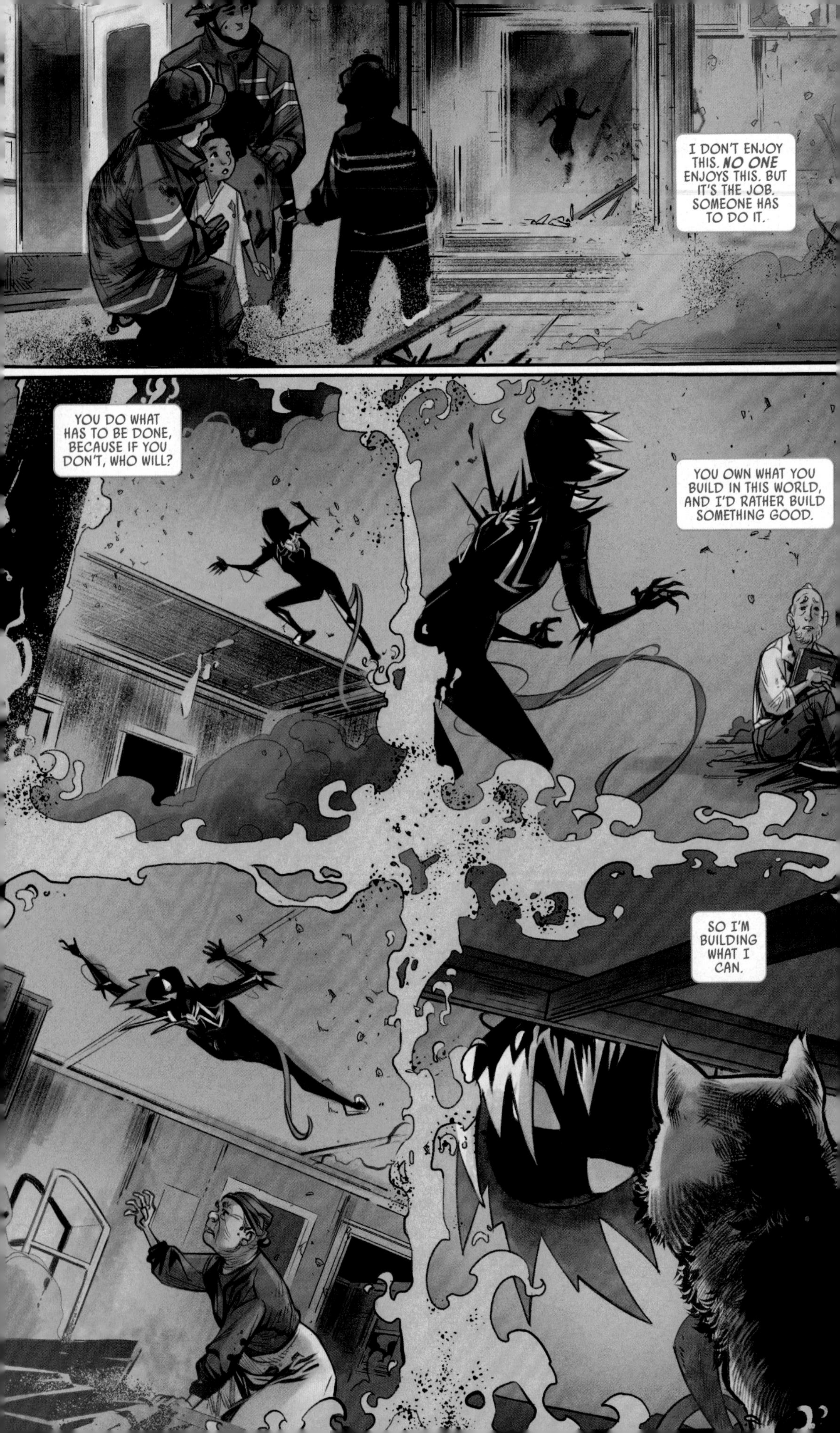
I DON'T ENJOY THIS. NO ONE ENJOYS THIS. BUT IT'S THE JOB. SOMEONE HAS TO DO IT.
YOU DO WHAT HAS TO BE DONE, BECAUSE IF YOU DON'T, WHO WILL?
YOU OWN WHAT YOU BUILD IN THIS WORLD, AND I'D RATHER BUILD SOMETHING GOOD.
SO I'M BUILDING WHAT I CAN.

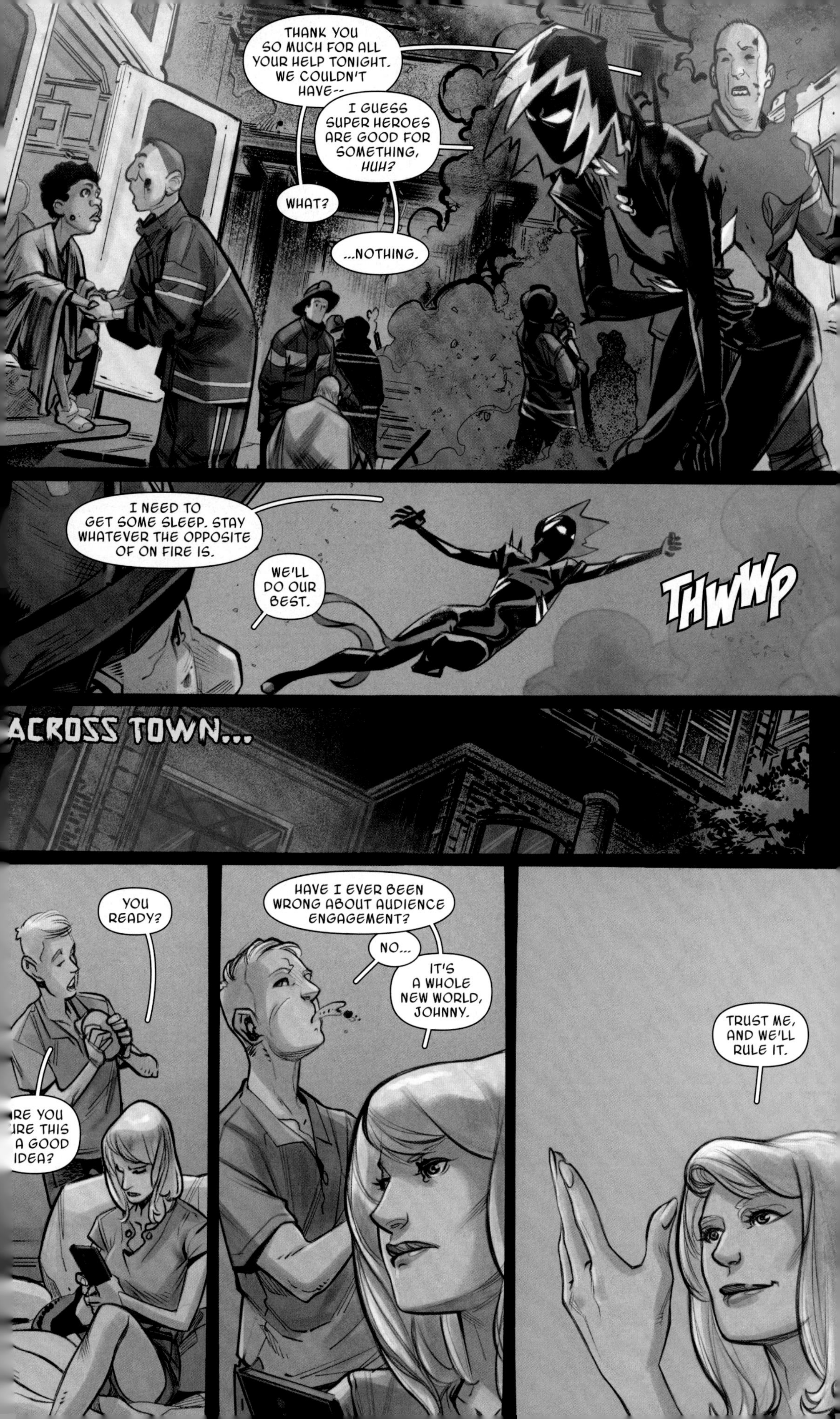
THANK YOU SO MUCH FOR ALL YOUR HELP TONIGHT. WE COULDN'T HAVE--
I GUESS SUPER HEROES ARE GOOD FOR SOMETHING, HUH?
WHAT?
...NOTHING.
I NEED TO GET SOME SLEEP. STAY WHATEVER THE OPPOSITE OF ON FIRE IS.
WE'LL DO OUR BEST.
THWWP
ACROSS TOWN...
YOU READY?
RE YOU
RE THIS
A GOOD
IDEA?
HAVE I EVER BEEN WRONG ABOUT AUDIENCE ENGAGEMENT?
NO...
IT'S A WHOLE NEW WORLD, JOHNNY.
TRUST ME, AND WE'LL RULE IT.

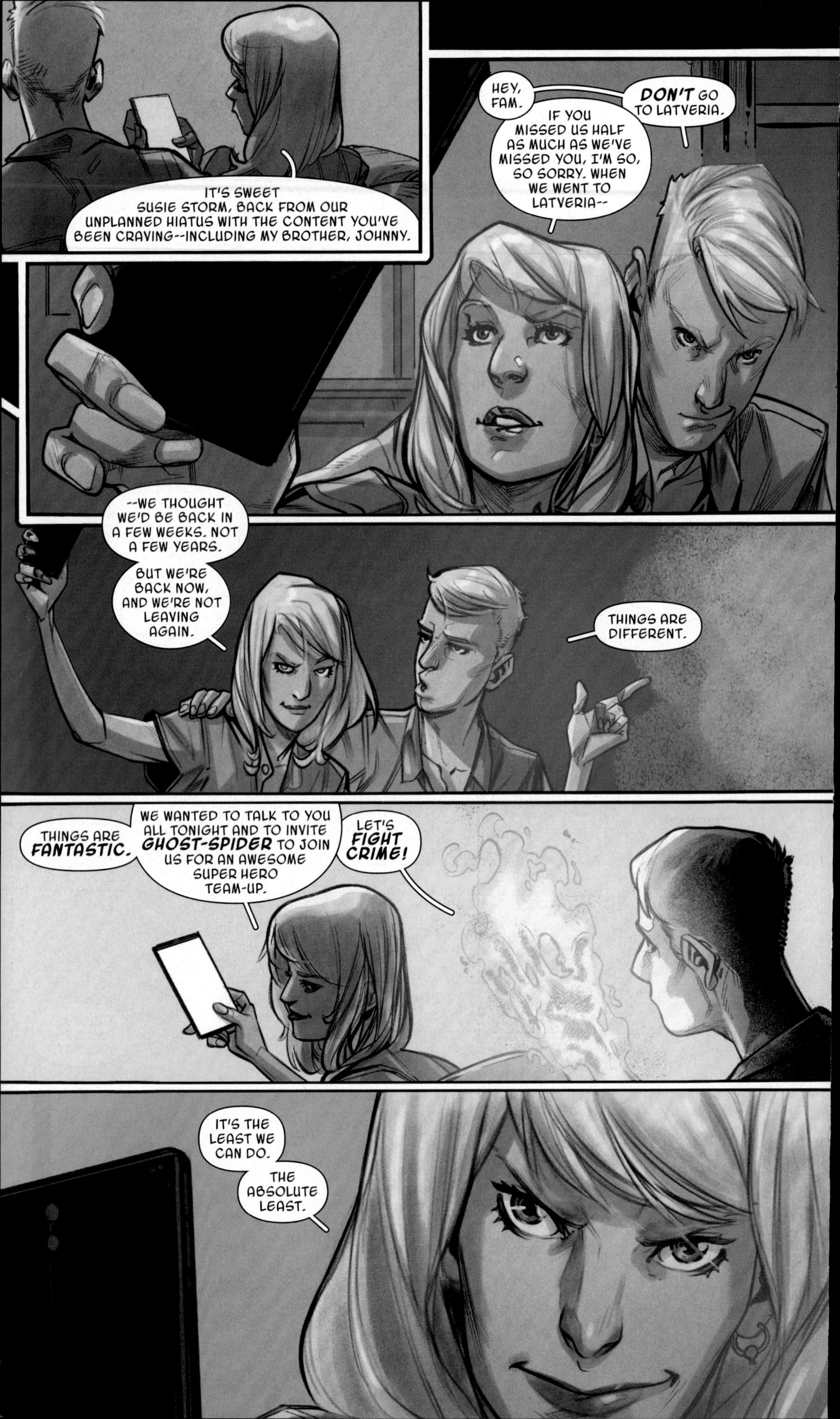
IT'S SWEET SUSIE STORM, BACK FROM OUR UNPLANNED HIATUS WITH THE CONTENT YOU'VE BEEN CRAVING--INCLUDING MY BROTHER, JOHNNY.
HEY, FAM.
DON'T GO TO LATVERIA.
IF YOU MISSED US HALF AS MUCH AS WE'VE MISSED YOU, I'M SO, SO SORRY. WHEN WE WENT TO LATVERIA--
--WE THOUGHT WE'D BE BACK IN A FEW WEEKS. NOT A FEW YEARS.
BUT WE'RE BACK NOW, AND WE'RE NOT LEAVING AGAIN.
THINGS ARE DIFFERENT.
THINGS ARE FANTASTIC.
WE WANTED TO TALK TO YOU ALL TONIGHT AND TO INVITE GHOST-SPIDER TO JOIN US FOR AN AWESOME SUPER HERO TEAM-UP.
LET'S FIGHT CRIME!
IT'S THE LEAST WE CAN DO.
THE ABSOLUTE LEAST.

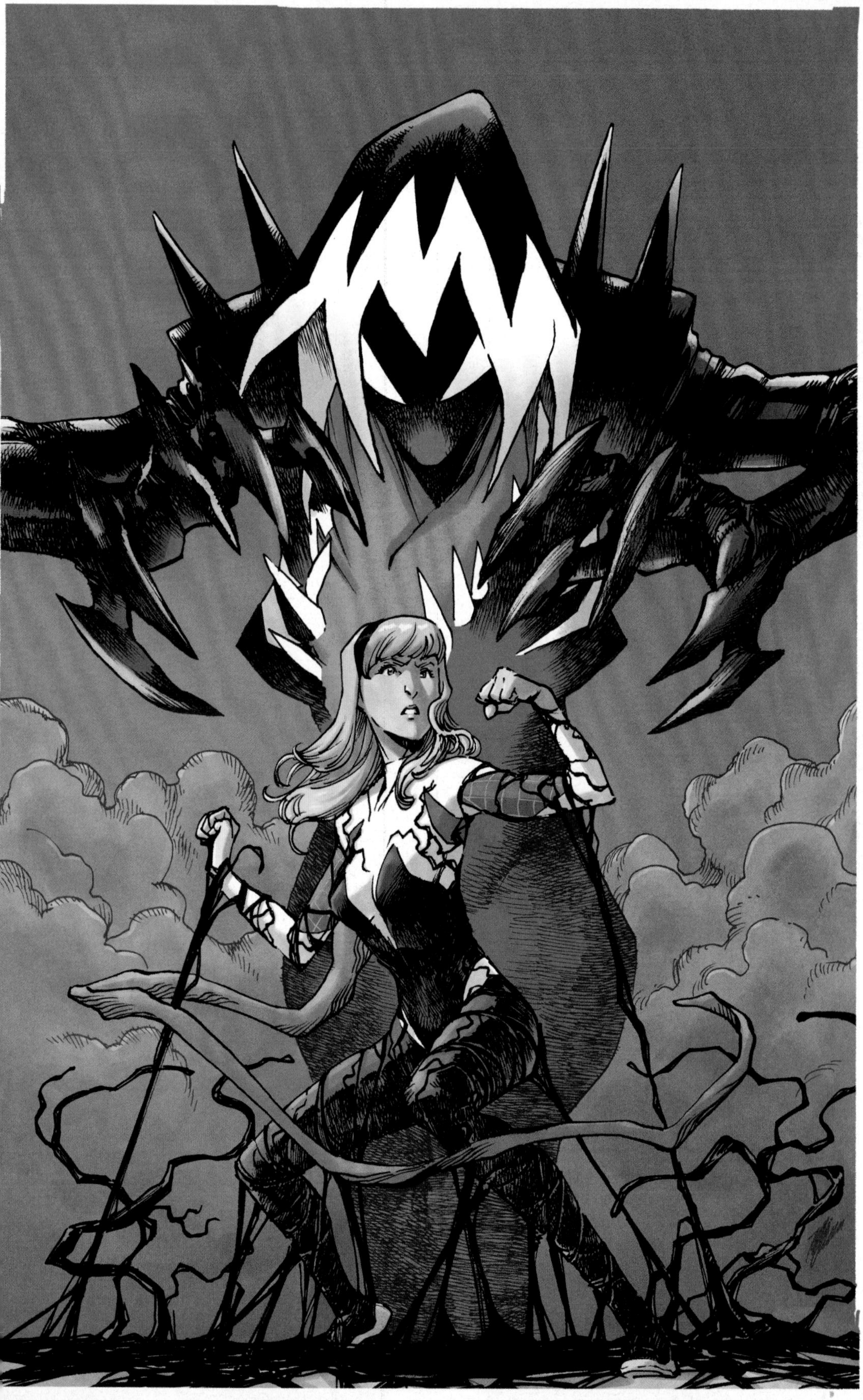

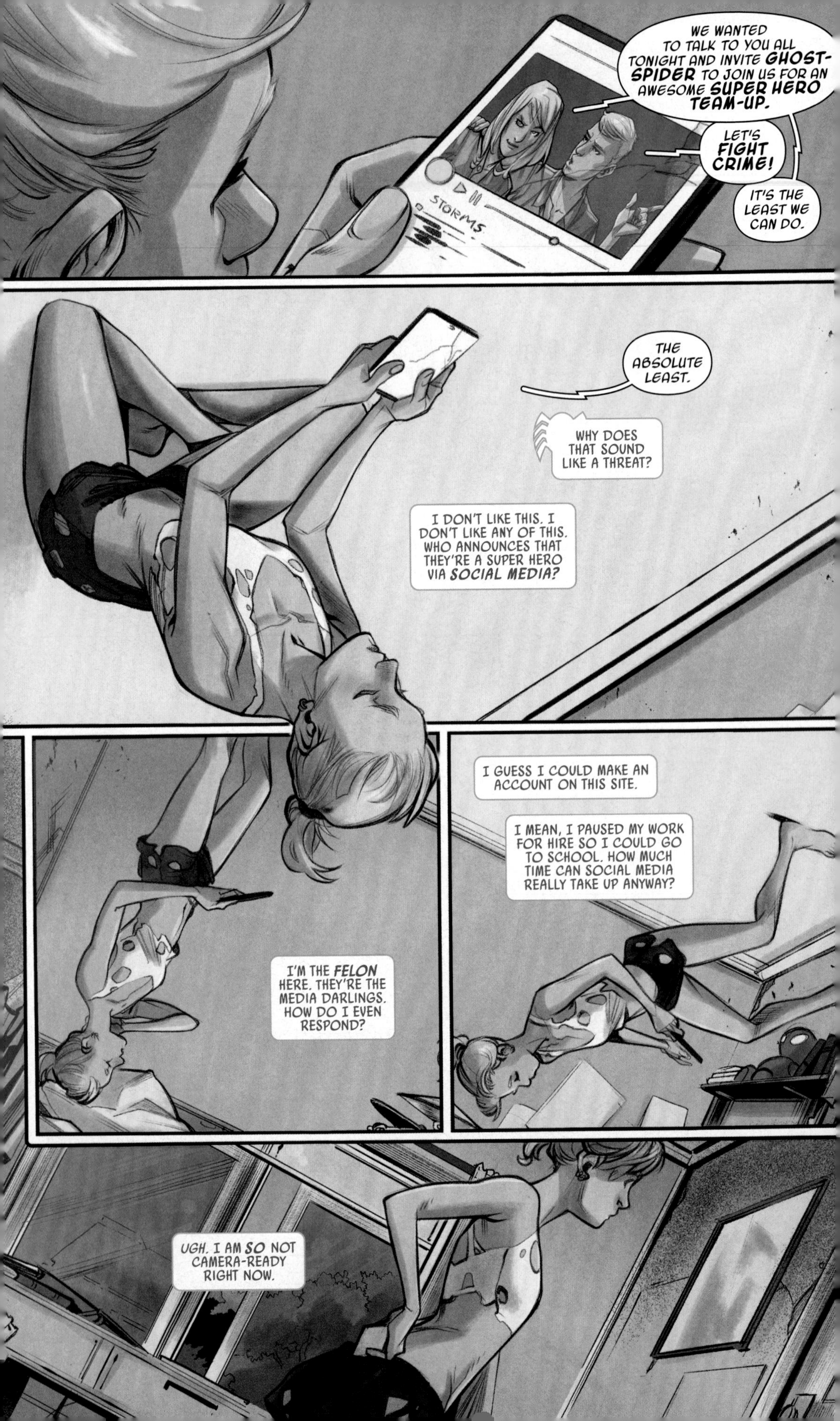
WE WANTED TO TALK TO YOU ALL TONIGHT AND INVITE GHOST-SPIDER TO JOIN US FOR AN AWESOME SUPER HERO TEAM-UP.
LET'S FIGHT CRIME!
IT'S THE LEAST WE CAN DO.
STORMS
THE ABSOLUTE LEAST.
WHY DOES THAT SOUND LIKE A THREAT?
I DON'T LIKE THIS. I DON'T LIKE ANY OF THIS. WHO ANNOUNCES THAT THEY'RE A SUPER HERO VIA SOCIAL MEDIA?
I'M THE FELON HERE. THEY'RE THE MEDIA DARLINGS. HOW DO I EVEN RESPOND?
I GUESS I COULD MAKE AN ACCOUNT ON THIS SITE.
I MEAN, I PAUSED MY WORK FOR HIRE SO I COULD GO TO SCHOOL. HOW MUCH TIME CAN SOCIAL MEDIA REALLY TAKE UP ANYWAY?
UGH. I AM SO NOT CAMERA-READY RIGHT NOW.

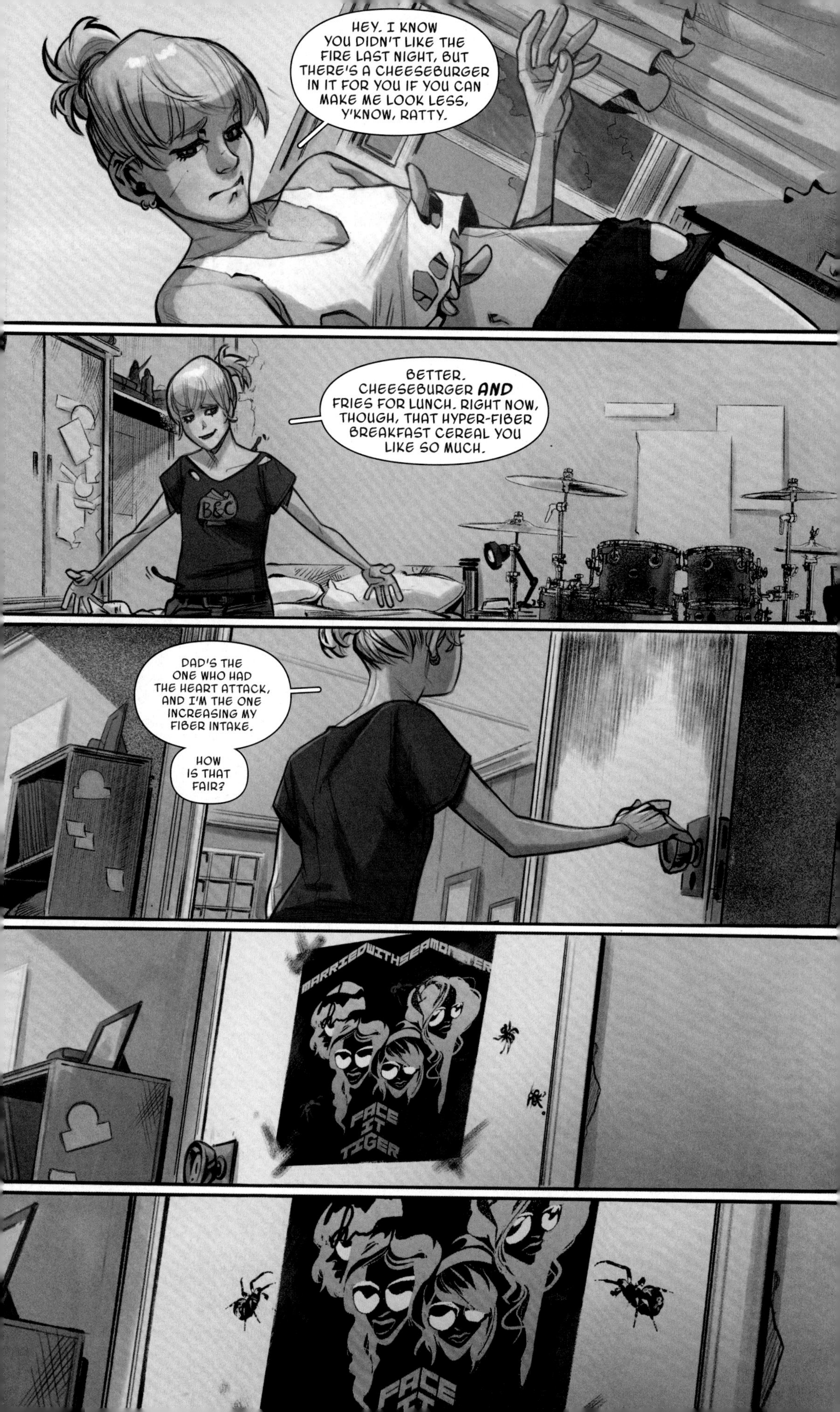
HEY. I KNOW YOU DIDN'T LIKE THE FIRE LAST NIGHT, BUT THERE'S A CHEESEBURGER IN IT FOR YOU IF YOU CAN MAKE ME LOOK LESS, Y'KNOW, RATTY.
BETTER. CHEESEBURGER **AND** FRIES FOR LUNCH. RIGHT NOW, THOUGH, THAT HYPER-FIBER BREAKFAST CEREAL YOU LIKE SO MUCH.
B&C
DAD'S THE ONE WHO HAD THE HEART ATTACK, AND I'M THE ONE INCREASING MY FIBER INTAKE.
HOW IS THAT FAIR?
MARRIEDWITHSEAMONSTER
FACE IT TIGER

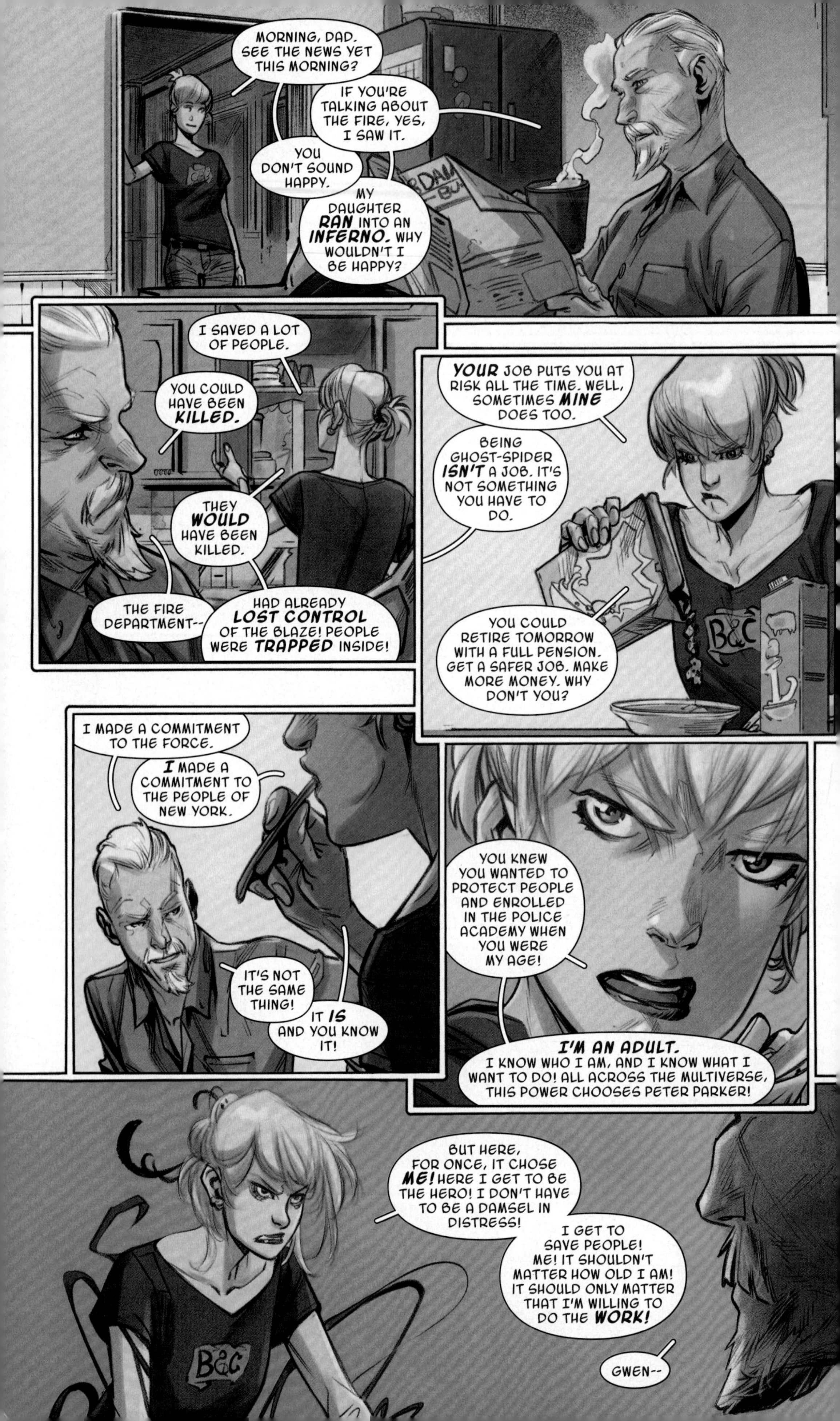

MORNING, DAD. SEE THE NEWS YET THIS MORNING?
IF YOU'RE TALKING ABOUT THE FIRE, YES, I SAW IT.
YOU DON'T SOUND HAPPY.
MY DAUGHTER RAN INTO AN INFERNO. WHY WOULDN'T I BE HAPPY?
I SAVED A LOT OF PEOPLE.
YOU COULD HAVE BEEN KILLED.
THEY WOULD HAVE BEEN KILLED.
THE FIRE DEPARTMENT--
HAD ALREADY LOST CONTROL OF THE BLAZE! PEOPLE WERE TRAPPED INSIDE!
YOUR JOB PUTS YOU AT RISK ALL THE TIME. WELL, SOMETIMES MINE DOES TOO.
BEING GHOST-SPIDER ISN'T A JOB. IT'S NOT SOMETHING YOU HAVE TO DO.
YOU COULD RETIRE TOMORROW WITH A FULL PENSION. GET A SAFER JOB. MAKE MORE MONEY. WHY DON'T YOU?
I MADE A COMMITMENT TO THE FORCE.
I MADE A COMMITMENT TO THE PEOPLE OF NEW YORK.
IT'S NOT THE SAME THING!
IT IS AND YOU KNOW IT!
YOU KNEW YOU WANTED TO PROTECT PEOPLE AND ENROLLED IN THE POLICE ACADEMY WHEN YOU WERE MY AGE!
I'M AN ADULT. I KNOW WHO I AM, AND I KNOW WHAT I WANT TO DO! ALL ACROSS THE MULTIVERSE, THIS POWER CHOOSES PETER PARKER!
BUT HERE, FOR ONCE, IT CHOSE ME! HERE I GET TO BE THE HERO! I DON'T HAVE TO BE A DAMSEL IN DISTRESS!
I GET TO SAVE PEOPLE! ME! IT SHOULDN'T MATTER HOW OLD I AM! IT SHOULD ONLY MATTER THAT I'M WILLING TO DO THE WORK!
GWEN--

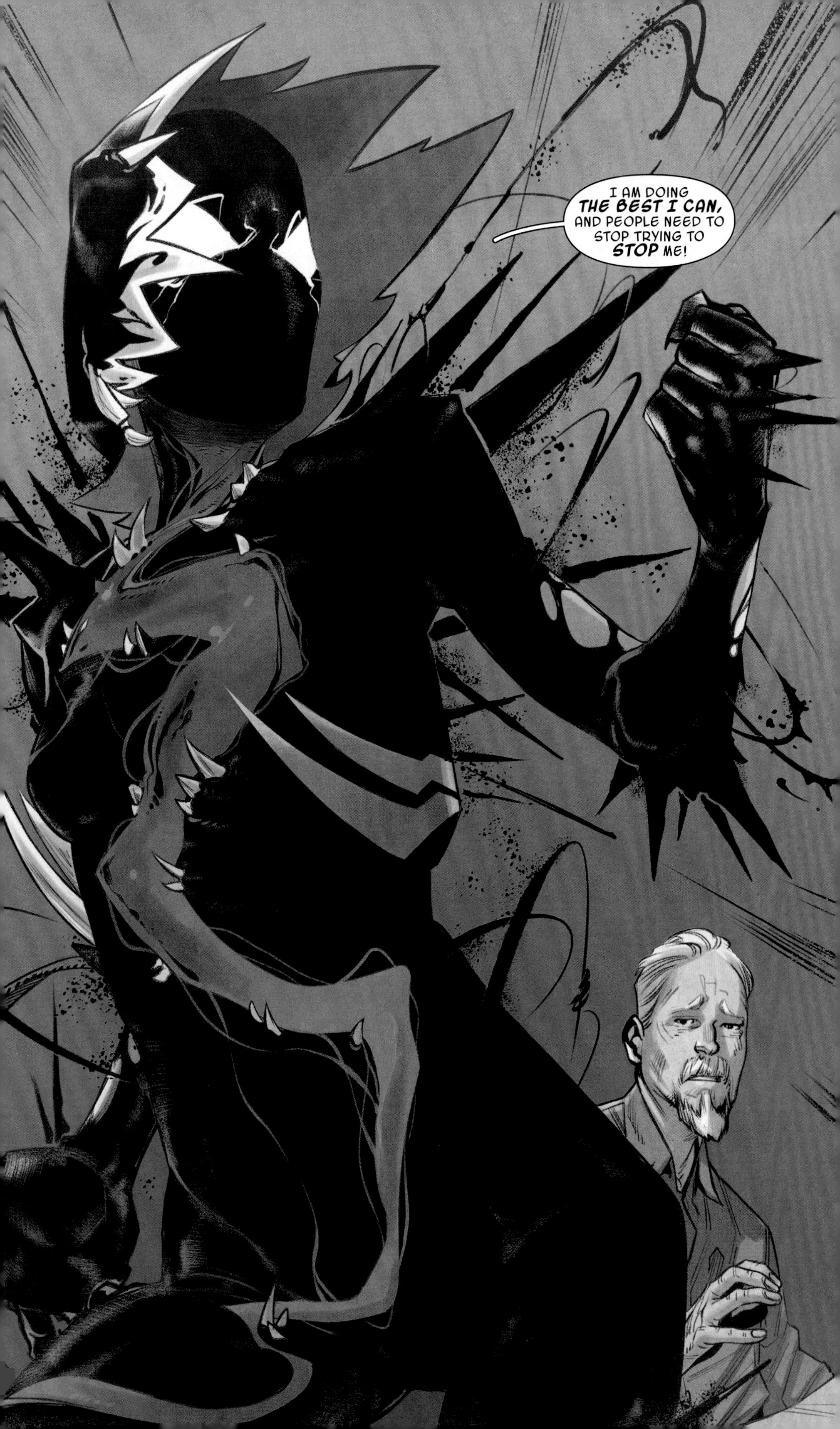
I AM DOING THE BEST I CAN, AND PEOPLE NEED TO STOP TRYING TO STOP ME!

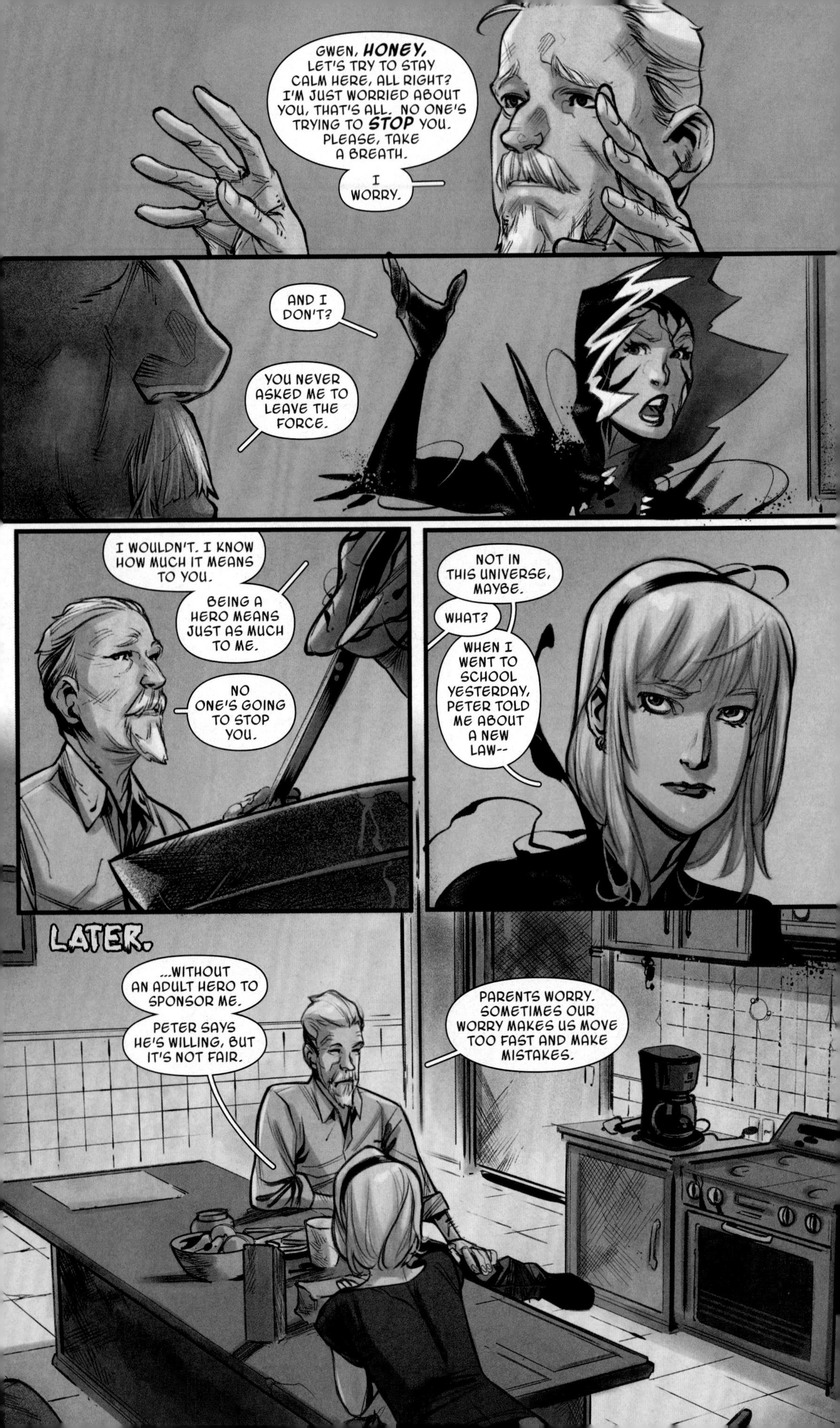
GWEN, HONEY, LET'S TRY TO STAY CALM HERE, ALL RIGHT? I'M JUST WORRIED ABOUT YOU, THAT'S ALL. NO ONE'S TRYING TO STOP YOU. PLEASE, TAKE A BREATH.
I WORRY.
AND I DON'T?
YOU NEVER ASKED ME TO LEAVE THE FORCE.
I WOULDN'T. I KNOW HOW MUCH IT MEANS TO YOU.
BEING A HERO MEANS JUST AS MUCH TO ME.
NO ONE'S GOING TO STOP YOU.
NOT IN THIS UNIVERSE, MAYBE.
WHAT?
WHEN I WENT TO SCHOOL YESTERDAY, PETER TOLD ME ABOUT A NEW LAW--
LATER.
...WITHOUT AN ADULT HERO TO SPONSOR ME.
PETER SAYS HE'S WILLING, BUT IT'S NOT FAIR.
PARENTS WORRY. SOMETIMES OUR WORRY MAKES US MOVE TOO FAST AND MAKE MISTAKES.

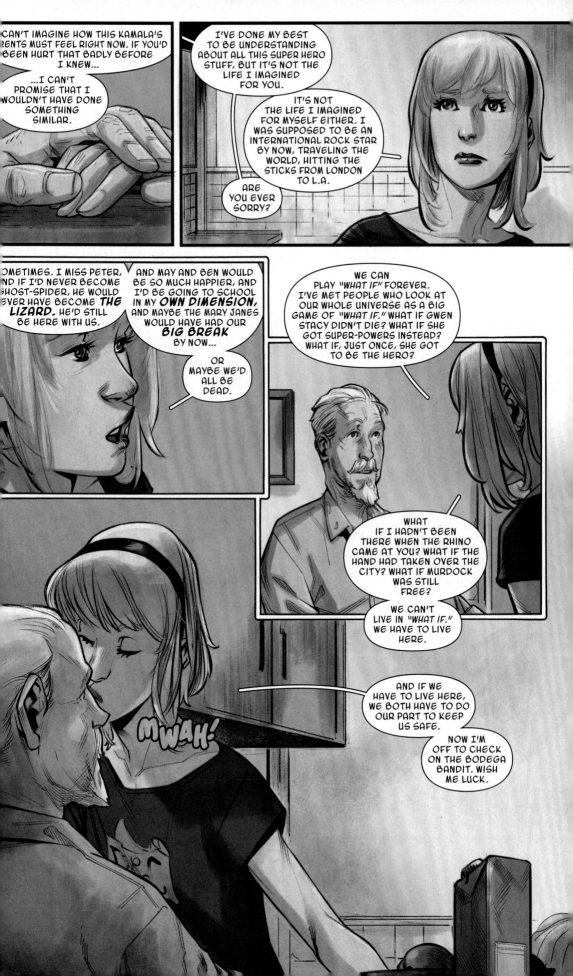

CAN'T IMAGINE HOW THIS KAMALA'S
RENTS MUST FEEL RIGHT NOW. IF YOU'D
BEEN HURT THAT BADLY BEFORE
I KNEW...

...I CAN'T
PROMISE THAT I
WOULDN'T HAVE DONE
SOMETHING
SIMILAR.

I'VE DONE MY BEST
TO BE UNDERSTANDING
ABOUT ALL THIS SUPER HERO
STUFF, BUT IT'S NOT THE
LIFE I IMAGINED
FOR YOU.

IT'S NOT
THE LIFE I IMAGINED
FOR MYSELF EITHER. I
WAS SUPPOSED TO BE AN
INTERNATIONAL ROCK STAR
BY NOW, TRAVELING THE
WORLD, HITTING THE
STICKS FROM LONDON
TO L.A.

ARE
YOU EVER
SORRY?

OMETIMES. I MISS PETER,
ND IF I'D NEVER BECOME
HOST-SPIDER, HE WOULD
EVER HAVE BECOME *THE
LIZARD.* HE'D STILL
BE HERE WITH US.

AND MAY AND BEN WOULD
BE SO MUCH HAPPIER, AND
I'D BE GOING TO SCHOOL
IN MY *OWN DIMENSION,*
AND MAYBE THE MARY JANES
WOULD HAVE HAD OUR
BIG BREAK
BY NOW...

OR
MAYBE WE'D
ALL BE
DEAD.

WE CAN
PLAY *"WHAT IF"* FOREVER.
I'VE MET PEOPLE WHO LOOK AT
OUR WHOLE UNIVERSE AS A BIG
GAME OF *"WHAT IF."* WHAT IF GWEN
STACY DIDN'T DIE? WHAT IF SHE
GOT SUPER-POWERS INSTEAD?
WHAT IF, JUST ONCE, SHE GOT
TO BE THE HERO?

WHAT
IF I HADN'T BEEN
THERE WHEN THE RHINO
CAME AT YOU? WHAT IF THE
HAND HAD TAKEN OVER THE
CITY? WHAT IF MURDOCK
WAS STILL
FREE?

WE CAN'T
LIVE IN *"WHAT IF."*
WE HAVE TO LIVE
HERE.

AND IF WE
HAVE TO LIVE HERE,
WE BOTH HAVE TO DO
OUR PART TO KEEP
US SAFE.

NOW I'M
OFF TO CHECK
ON THE BODEGA
BANDIT. WISH
ME LUCK.

MWAH!

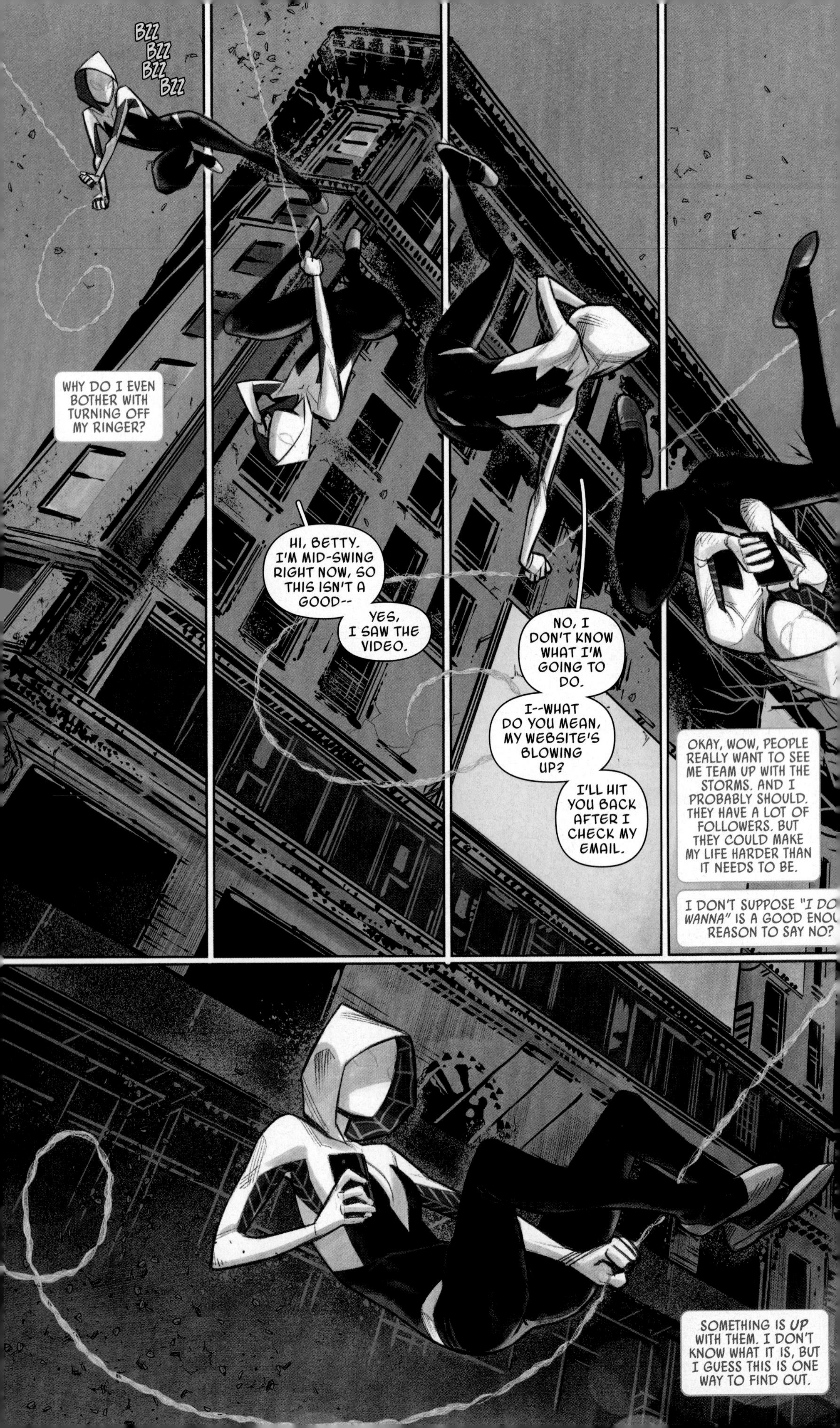
BZZ BZZ BZZ BZZ
WHY DO I EVEN BOTHER WITH TURNING OFF MY RINGER?
HI, BETTY. I'M MID-SWING RIGHT NOW, SO THIS ISN'T A GOOD--
YES, I SAW THE VIDEO.
NO, I DON'T KNOW WHAT I'M GOING TO DO.
I--WHAT DO YOU MEAN, MY WEBSITE'S BLOWING UP?
I'LL HIT YOU BACK AFTER I CHECK MY EMAIL.
OKAY, WOW, PEOPLE REALLY WANT TO SEE ME TEAM UP WITH THE STORMS. AND I PROBABLY SHOULD. THEY HAVE A LOT OF FOLLOWERS. BUT THEY COULD MAKE MY LIFE HARDER THAN IT NEEDS TO BE.
SOMETHING IS *UP* WITH THEM. I DON'T KNOW WHAT IT IS, BUT I GUESS THIS IS ONE WAY TO FIND OUT.

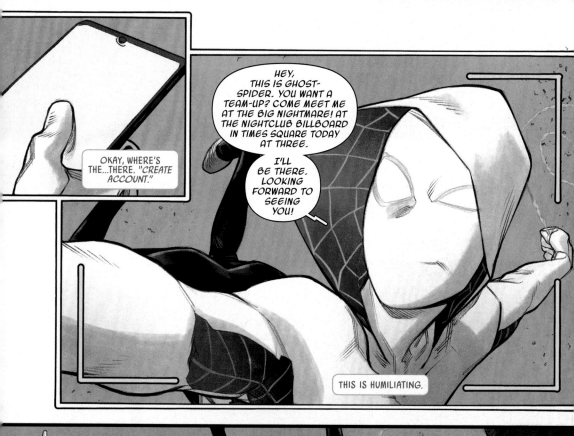

OKAY, WHERE'S THE...THERE. "CREATE ACCOUNT."

HEY, THIS IS GHOST-SPIDER. YOU WANT A TEAM-UP? COME MEET ME AT THE BIG NIGHTMARE! AT THE NIGHTCLUB BILLBOARD IN TIMES SQUARE TODAY AT THREE.

I'LL BE THERE. LOOKING FORWARD TO SEEING YOU!

THIS IS HUMILIATING.

THWWP

THERE. THAT'S DONE, AND I PROBABLY NEEDED AN ACCOUNT ANYWAY.

BETTY WILL BE THRILLED. IT RAISES VISIBILITY IN A WAY THAT'LL BENEFIT MY WEB TRAFFIC. MJ WILL SAY I'M BEING FULL OF MYSELF.

AND MAYBE SHE'S RIGHT.

MAYBE THEY'RE ALL RIGHT AND I'M TRYING TO DO TOO MUCH BECAUSE I FEEL LIKE I'M THE ONLY ONE WHO CAN.

BUT THAT MEANS I HAVE TO KEEP TRYING.

FOR THE SAKE OF THE PEOPLE WHO NEED ME, I HAVE TO KEEP TRYING.

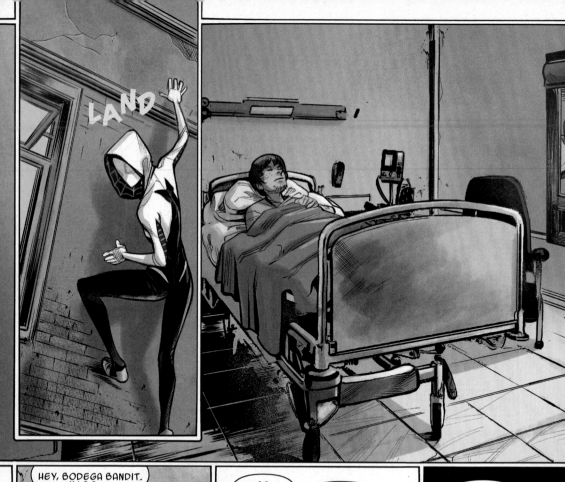

HEY, BODEGA BANDIT. *MISS* ME?

GHOST-SPIDER! I KNEW YOU'D COME.

I'M NOT FAMILY, SO YOU CAN'T TELL ANYONE I'M HERE.

HEH. BREAKING THE LAW FOR ME, HUH?

YEAH, WELL. YOU HAVE A WAY ABOUT YOU.

SO HAVE THEY FOUND...?

I STOPPED THE MEN WHO SHOT YOU. THEY'RE IN PRISON. THEY'LL BE THERE FOR A WHILE.

THAT'S NOT WHO I MEANT.

...OH. NOT YET. THE POLICE ARE STILL LOOKING.

I BET THEY'RE NOT LOOKING VERY HARD, ARE THEY? HE'S JUST A HAMSTER.

BUT HE'S LITTLE AND HE'S ALONE, AND THERE ARE SO MANY CATS...

I'M STILL LOOKING. WE'LL FIND HIM. DON'T WORRY. FOCUS ON GETTING BETTER.

I'M DOING MY BEST.

I'LL BE BACK TO THWARTING YOU BEFORE YOU KNOW IT.

YEAH, YOU WILL. BECAUSE YOU'RE MY NEMESIS.

THAT'S RIGHT. I'M YOUR *NEMESIS.*

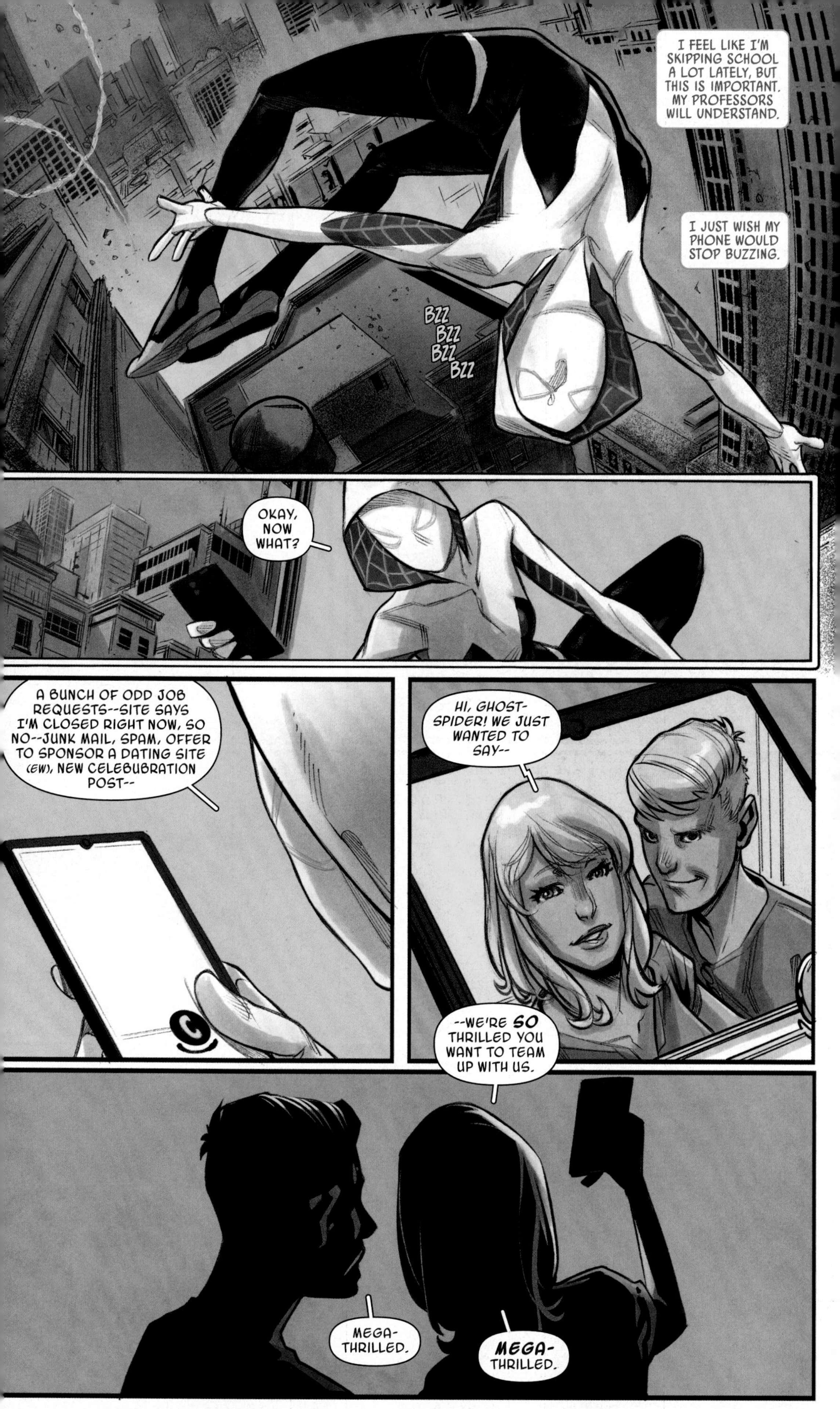
I FEEL LIKE I'M SKIPPING SCHOOL A LOT LATELY, BUT THIS IS IMPORTANT. MY PROFESSORS WILL UNDERSTAND.
I JUST WISH MY PHONE WOULD STOP BUZZING.
BZZ BZZ BZZ BZZ
OKAY, NOW WHAT?
A BUNCH OF ODD JOB REQUESTS--SITE SAYS I'M CLOSED RIGHT NOW, SO NO--JUNK MAIL, SPAM, OFFER TO SPONSOR A DATING SITE (EW), NEW CELEBUBRATION POST--
HI, GHOST-SPIDER! WE JUST WANTED TO SAY--
--WE'RE SO THRILLED YOU WANT TO TEAM UP WITH US.
MEGA-THRILLED.
MEGA-THRILLED.

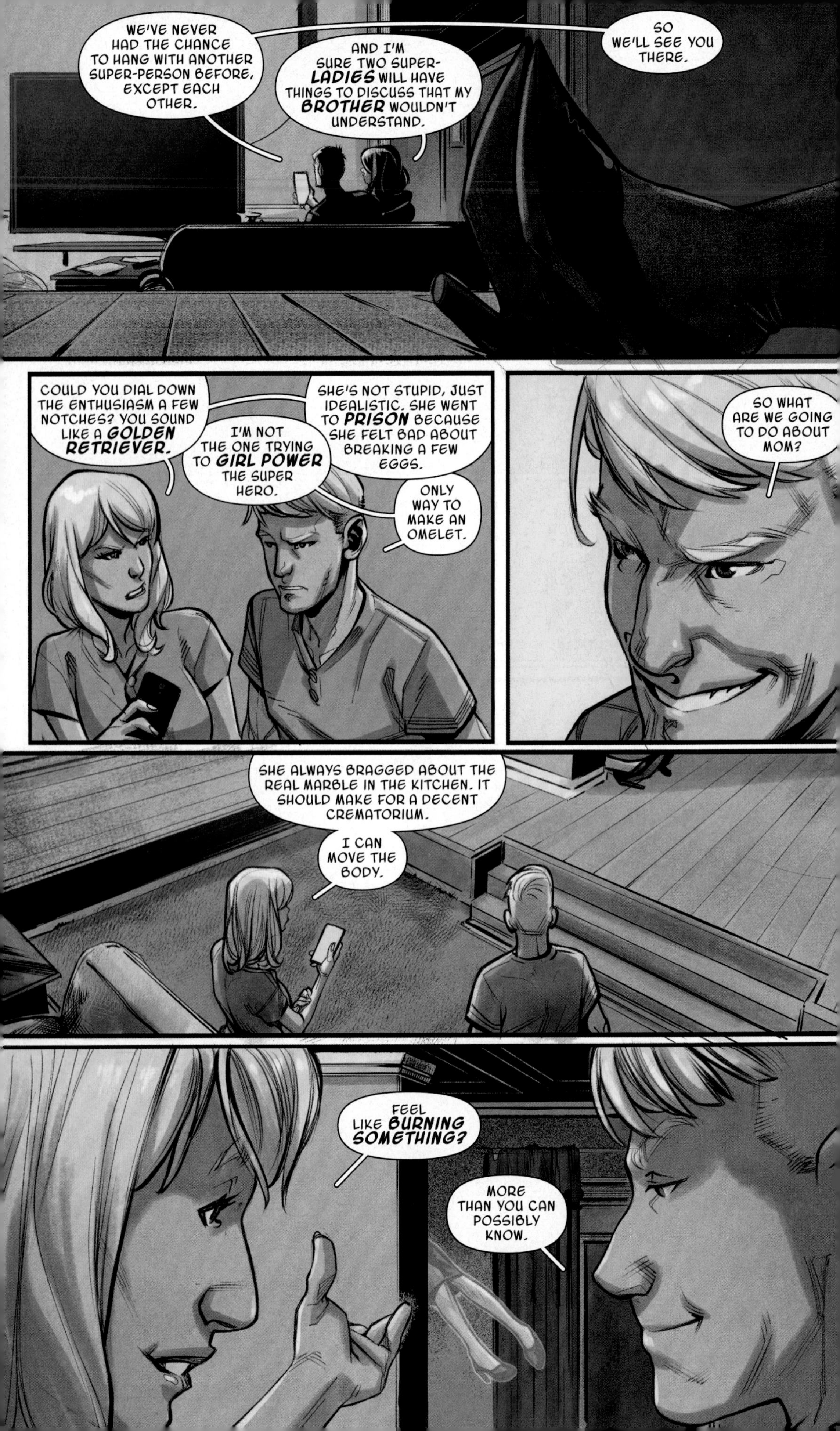
WE'VE NEVER HAD THE CHANCE TO HANG WITH ANOTHER SUPER-PERSON BEFORE, EXCEPT EACH OTHER.
AND I'M SURE TWO SUPER-LADIES WILL HAVE THINGS TO DISCUSS THAT MY BROTHER WOULDN'T UNDERSTAND.
SO WE'LL SEE YOU THERE.
COULD YOU DIAL DOWN THE ENTHUSIASM A FEW NOTCHES? YOU SOUND LIKE A GOLDEN RETRIEVER.
I'M NOT THE ONE TRYING TO GIRL POWER THE SUPER HERO.
SHE'S NOT STUPID, JUST IDEALISTIC. SHE WENT TO PRISON BECAUSE SHE FELT BAD ABOUT BREAKING A FEW EGGS.
ONLY WAY TO MAKE AN OMELET.
SO WHAT ARE WE GOING TO DO ABOUT MOM?
SHE ALWAYS BRAGGED ABOUT THE REAL MARBLE IN THE KITCHEN. IT SHOULD MAKE FOR A DECENT CREMATORIUM.
I CAN MOVE THE BODY.
FEEL LIKE BURNING SOMETHING?
MORE THAN YOU CAN POSSIBLY KNOW.

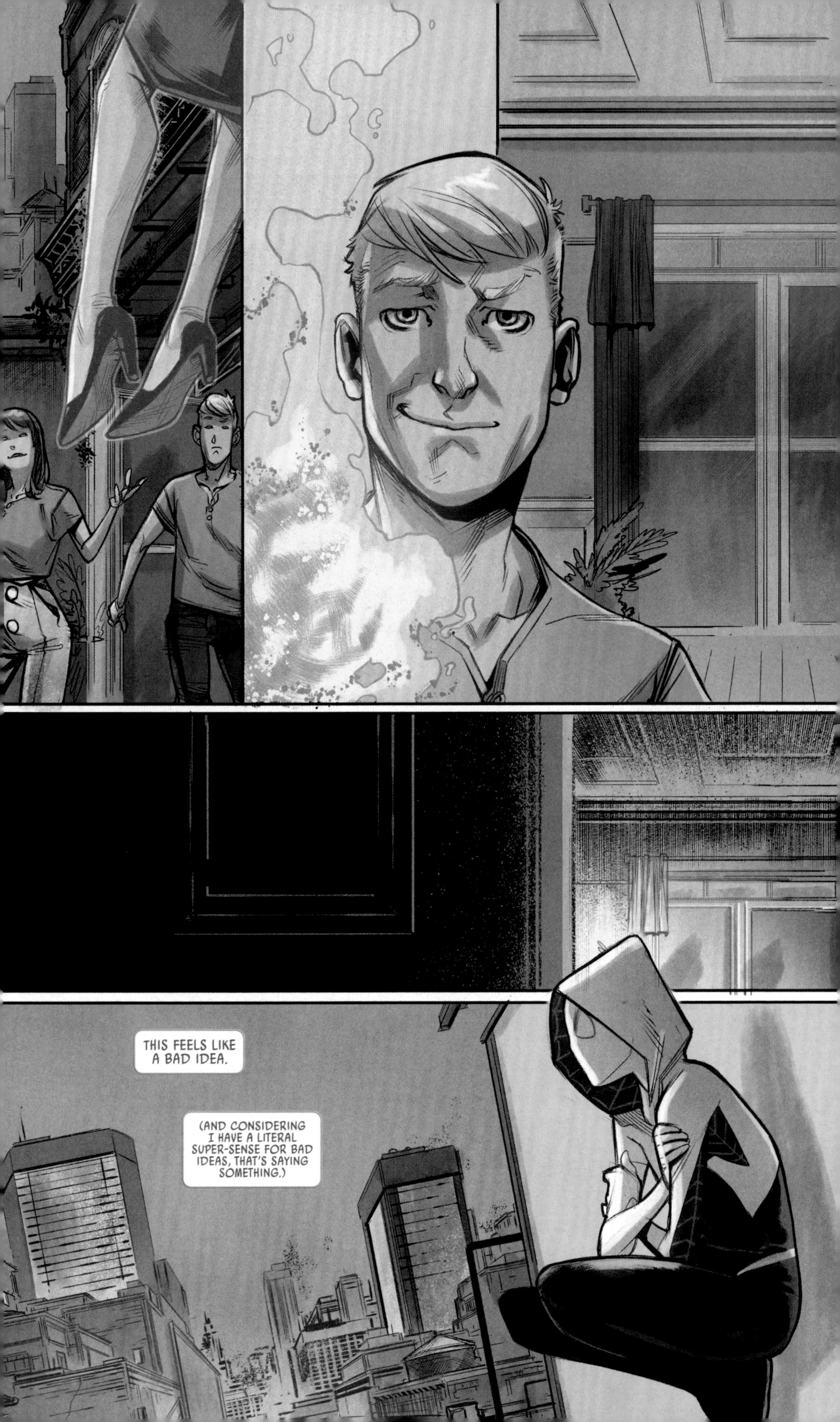
THIS FEELS LIKE A BAD IDEA.
(AND CONSIDERING I HAVE A LITERAL SUPER-SENSE FOR BAD IDEAS, THAT'S SAYING SOMETHING.)

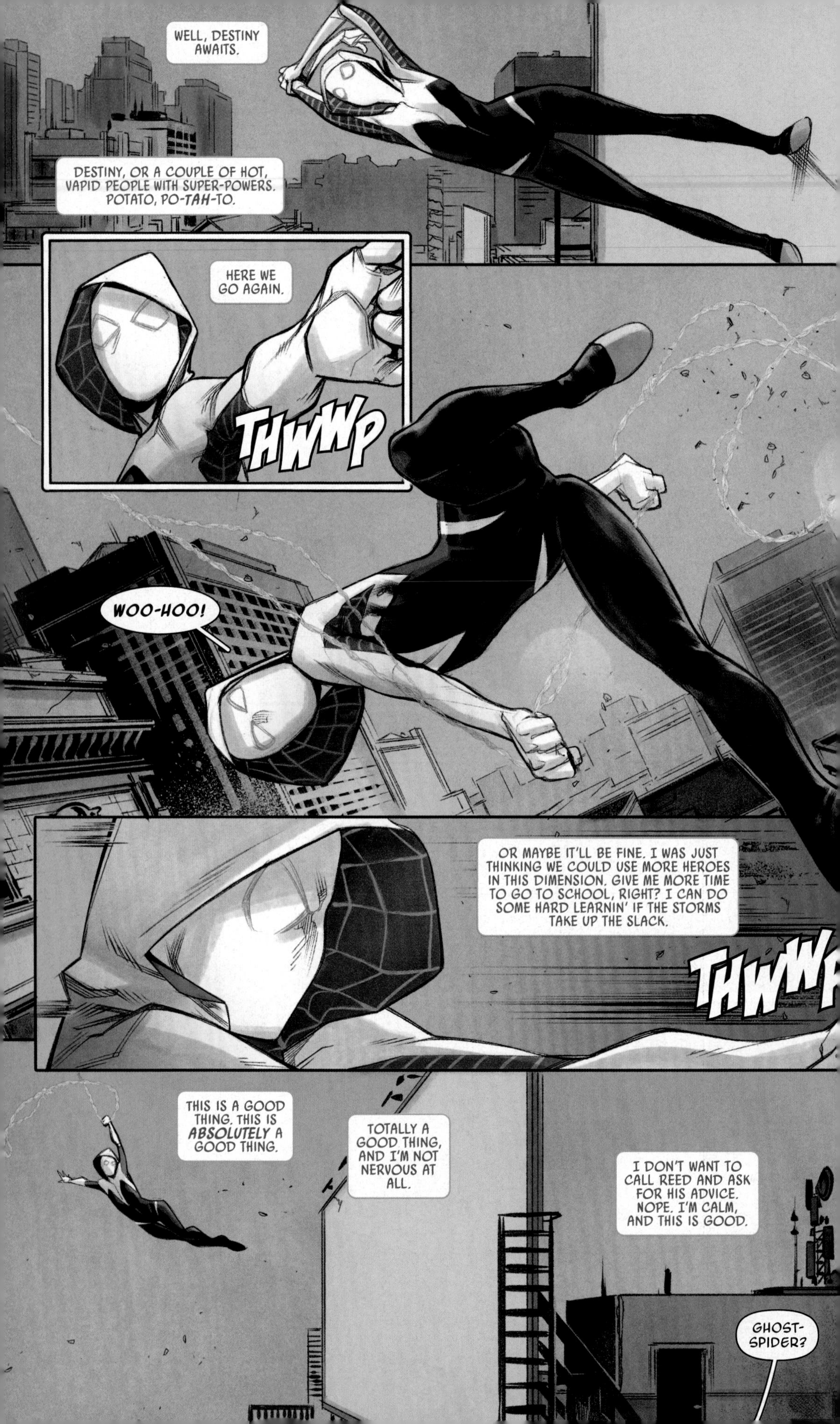
WELL, DESTINY AWAITS.
DESTINY, OR A COUPLE OF HOT, VAPID PEOPLE WITH SUPER-POWERS. POTATO, PO-*TAH*-TO.
HERE WE GO AGAIN.
THWWP
WOO-HOO!
OR MAYBE IT'LL BE FINE. I WAS JUST THINKING WE COULD USE MORE HEROES IN THIS DIMENSION. GIVE ME MORE TIME TO GO TO SCHOOL, RIGHT? I CAN DO SOME HARD LEARNIN' IF THE STORMS TAKE UP THE SLACK.
THWWP
THIS IS A GOOD THING. THIS IS ***ABSOLUTELY*** A GOOD THING.
TOTALLY A GOOD THING, AND I'M NOT NERVOUS AT ALL.
I DON'T WANT TO CALL REED AND ASK FOR HIS ADVICE. NOPE. I'M CALM, AND THIS IS GOOD.
GHOST-SPIDER?

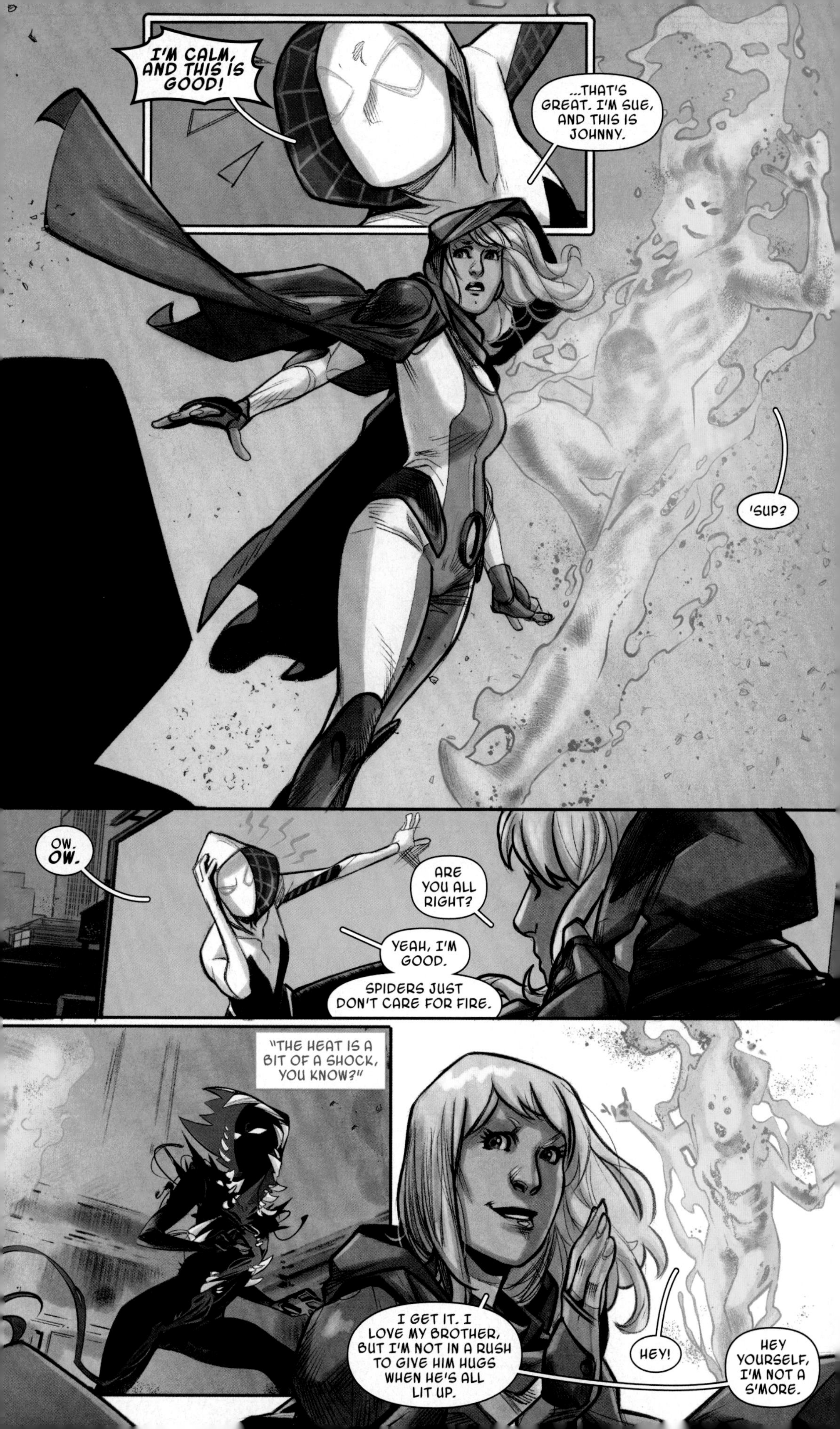
I'M CALM, AND THIS IS GOOD!
...THAT'S GREAT. I'M SUE, AND THIS IS JOHNNY.
'SUP?
OW. OW.
ARE YOU ALL RIGHT?
YEAH, I'M GOOD.
SPIDERS JUST DON'T CARE FOR FIRE.
"THE HEAT IS A BIT OF A SHOCK, YOU KNOW?"
I GET IT. I LOVE MY BROTHER, BUT I'M NOT IN A RUSH TO GIVE HIM HUGS WHEN HE'S ALL LIT UP.
HEY!
HEY YOURSELF, I'M NOT A S'MORE.

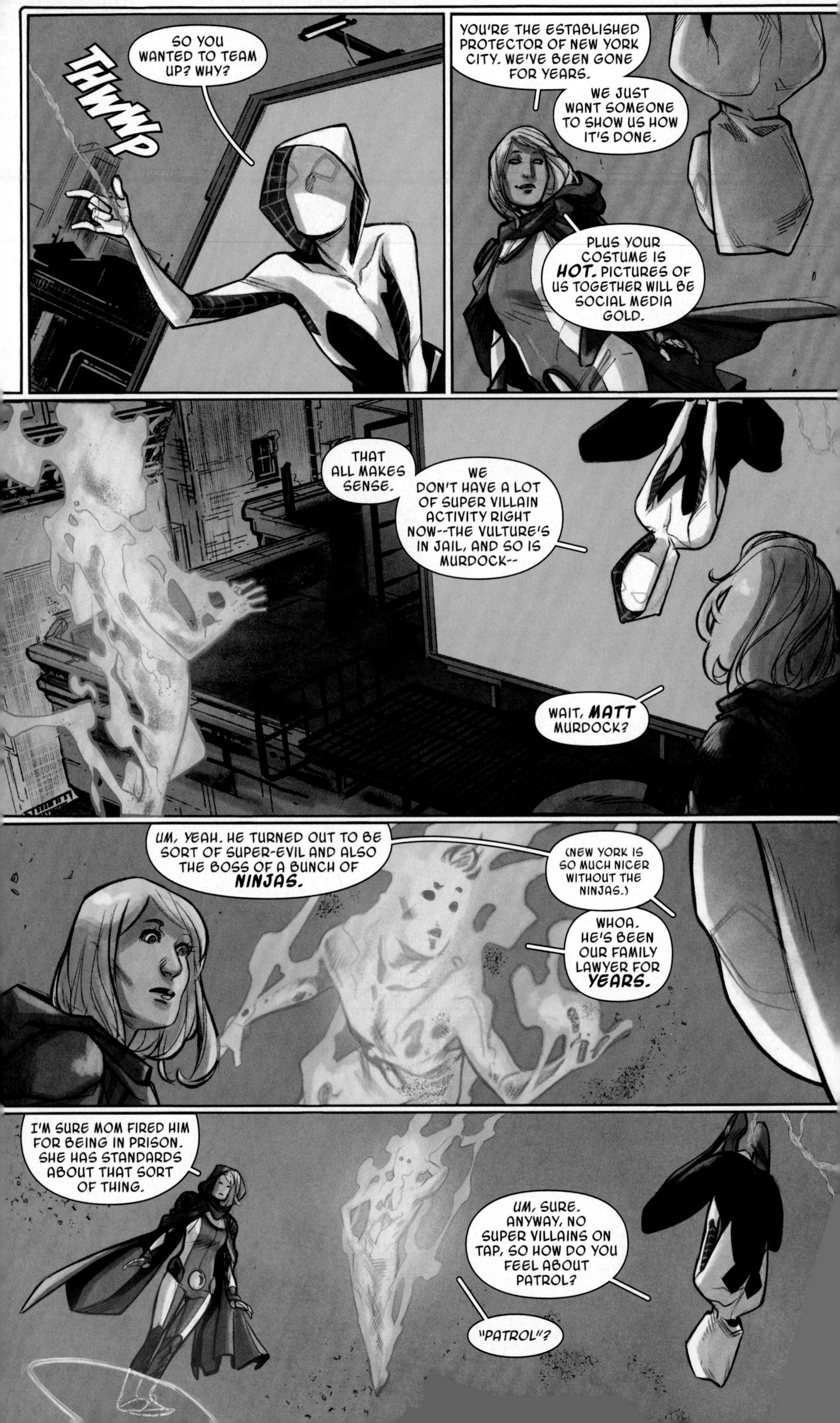
THWIP
SO YOU WANTED TO TEAM UP? WHY?
YOU'RE THE ESTABLISHED PROTECTOR OF NEW YORK CITY. WE'VE BEEN GONE FOR YEARS.
WE JUST WANT SOMEONE TO SHOW US HOW IT'S DONE.
PLUS YOUR COSTUME IS HOT. PICTURES OF US TOGETHER WILL BE SOCIAL MEDIA GOLD.
THAT ALL MAKES SENSE.
WE DON'T HAVE A LOT OF SUPER VILLAIN ACTIVITY RIGHT NOW--THE VULTURE'S IN JAIL, AND SO IS MURDOCK--
WAIT, MATT MURDOCK?
UM, YEAH. HE TURNED OUT TO BE SORT OF SUPER-EVIL AND ALSO THE BOSS OF A BUNCH OF NINJAS.
(NEW YORK IS SO MUCH NICER WITHOUT THE NINJAS.)
WHOA. HE'S BEEN OUR FAMILY LAWYER FOR YEARS.
I'M SURE MOM FIRED HIM FOR BEING IN PRISON. SHE HAS STANDARDS ABOUT THAT SORT OF THING.
UM, SURE. ANYWAY, NO SUPER VILLAINS ON TAP, SO HOW DO YOU FEEL ABOUT PATROL?
"PATROL"?

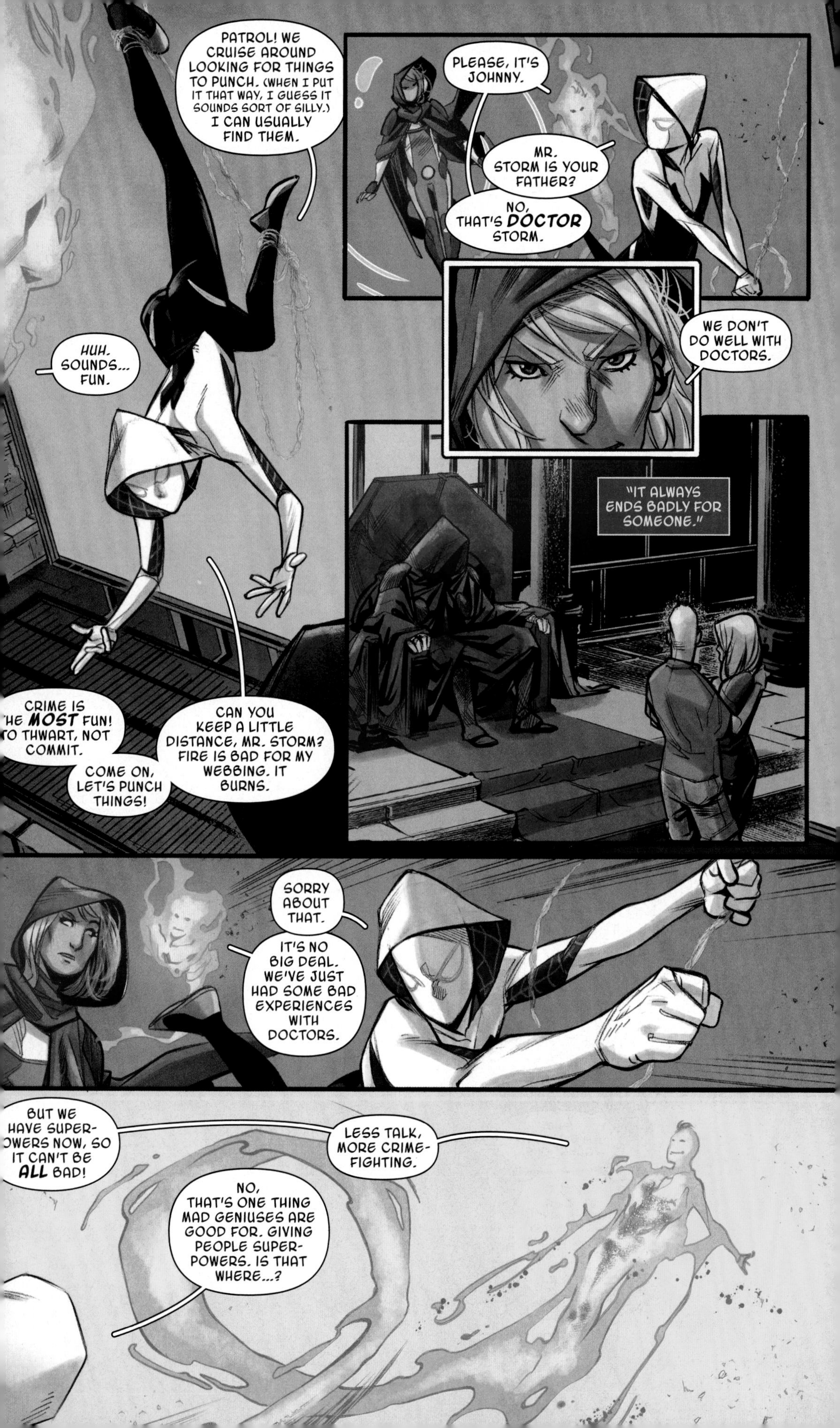
PATROL! WE CRUISE AROUND LOOKING FOR THINGS TO PUNCH. (WHEN I PUT IT THAT WAY, I GUESS IT SOUNDS SORT OF SILLY.) I CAN USUALLY FIND THEM.
HUH. SOUNDS... FUN.
CRIME IS THE MOST FUN! TO THWART, NOT COMMIT.
COME ON, LET'S PUNCH THINGS!
CAN YOU KEEP A LITTLE DISTANCE, MR. STORM? FIRE IS BAD FOR MY WEBBING. IT BURNS.
PLEASE, IT'S JOHNNY.
MR. STORM IS YOUR FATHER?
NO, THAT'S DOCTOR STORM.
WE DON'T DO WELL WITH DOCTORS.
"IT ALWAYS ENDS BADLY FOR SOMEONE."
SORRY ABOUT THAT.
IT'S NO BIG DEAL. WE'VE JUST HAD SOME BAD EXPERIENCES WITH DOCTORS.
BUT WE HAVE SUPER-POWERS NOW, SO IT CAN'T BE ALL BAD!
LESS TALK, MORE CRIME-FIGHTING.
NO, THAT'S ONE THING MAD GENIUSES ARE GOOD FOR. GIVING PEOPLE SUPER-POWERS. IS THAT WHERE...?

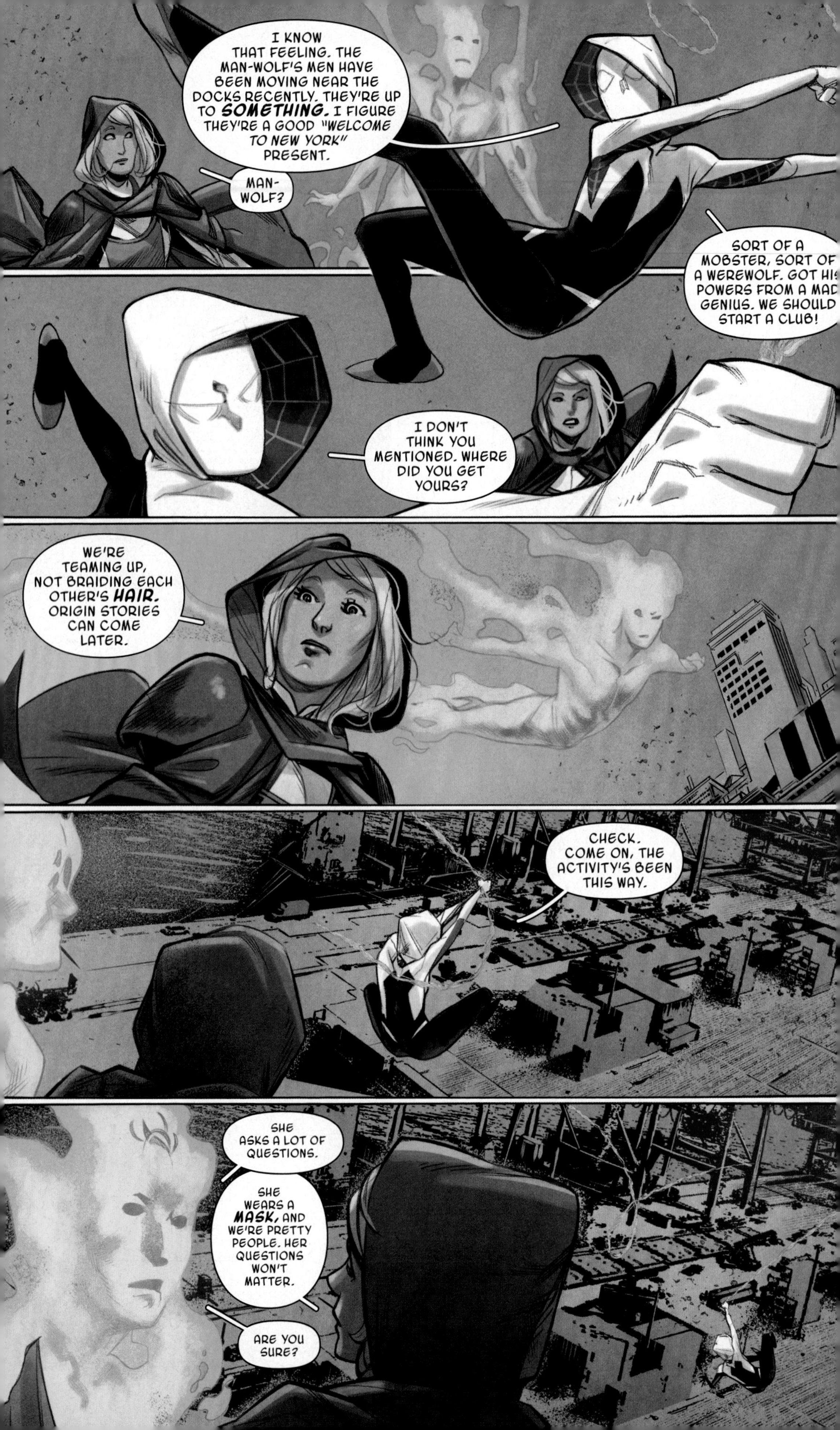
I KNOW THAT FEELING. THE MAN-WOLF'S MEN HAVE BEEN MOVING NEAR THE DOCKS RECENTLY. THEY'RE UP TO **SOMETHING.** I FIGURE THEY'RE A GOOD "WELCOME TO NEW YORK" PRESENT.
MAN-WOLF?
SORT OF A MOBSTER, SORT OF A WEREWOLF. GOT HIS POWERS FROM A MAD GENIUS. WE SHOULD START A CLUB!
I DON'T THINK YOU MENTIONED. WHERE DID YOU GET YOURS?
WE'RE TEAMING UP, NOT BRAIDING EACH OTHER'S **HAIR.** ORIGIN STORIES CAN COME LATER.
CHECK. COME ON, THE ACTIVITY'S BEEN THIS WAY.
SHE ASKS A LOT OF QUESTIONS.
SHE WEARS A **MASK,** AND WE'RE PRETTY PEOPLE. HER QUESTIONS WON'T MATTER.
ARE YOU SURE?

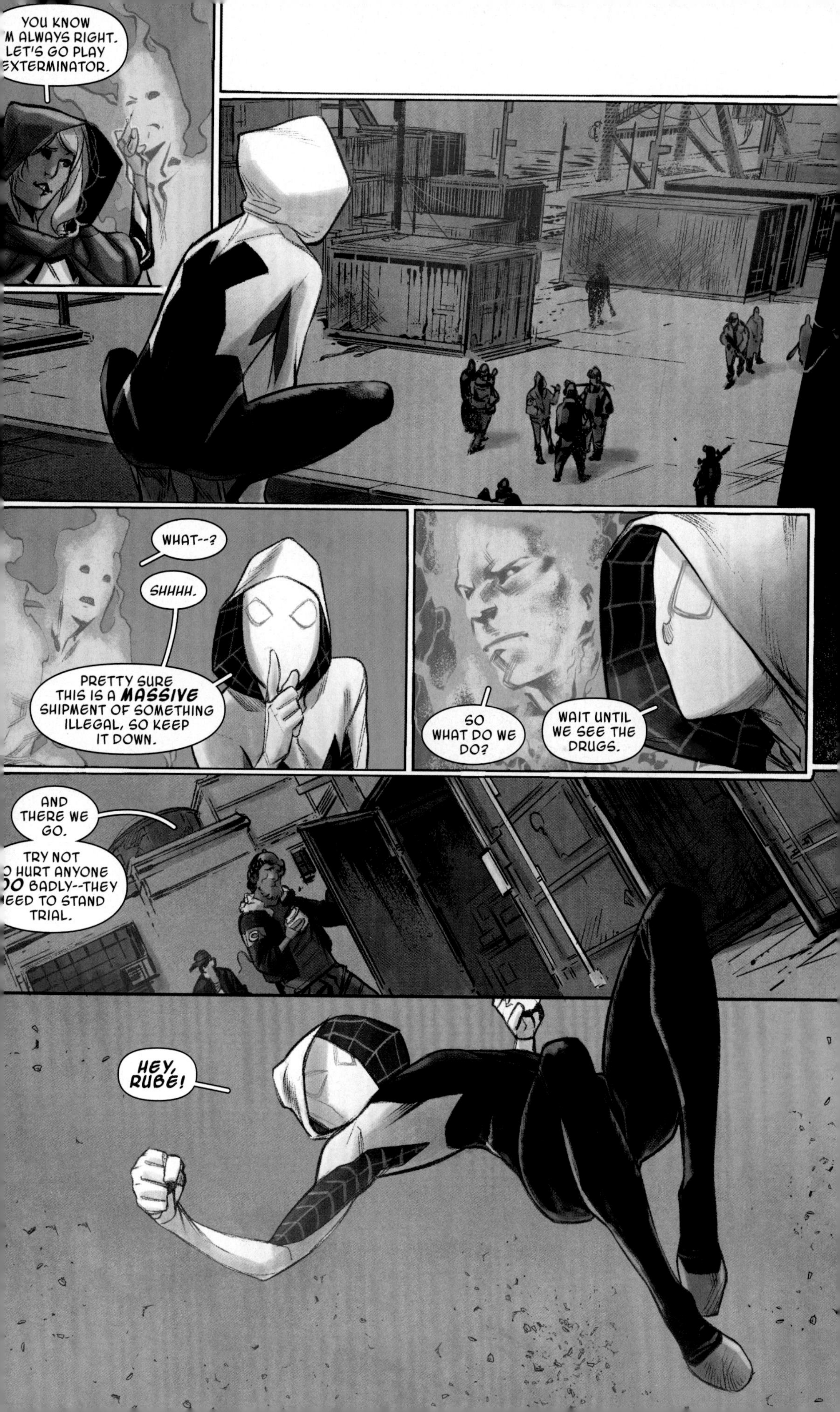
YOU KNOW
M ALWAYS RIGHT. LET'S GO PLAY EXTERMINATOR.
WHAT--?
SHHHH.
PRETTY SURE THIS IS A **MASSIVE** SHIPMENT OF SOMETHING ILLEGAL, SO KEEP IT DOWN.
SO WHAT DO WE DO?
WAIT UNTIL WE SEE THE DRUGS.
AND THERE WE GO.
TRY NOT O HURT ANYONE OO BADLY--THEY EED TO STAND TRIAL.
HEY, RUBE!

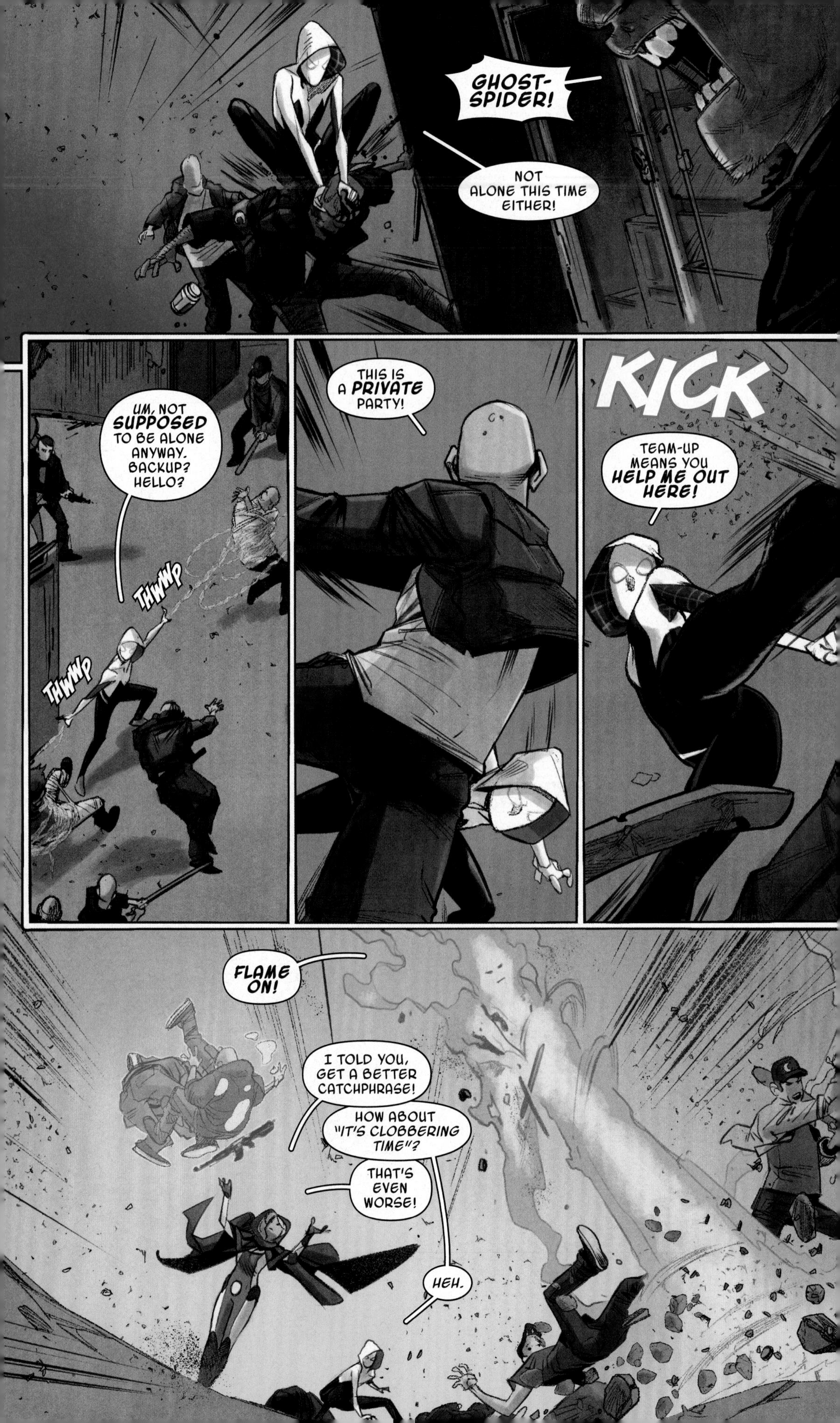
GHOST-SPIDER!
NOT ALONE THIS TIME EITHER!
UM, NOT SUPPOSED TO BE ALONE ANYWAY. BACKUP? HELLO?
THWWP
THWWP
THIS IS A PRIVATE PARTY!
KICK
TEAM-UP MEANS YOU HELP ME OUT HERE!
FLAME ON!
I TOLD YOU, GET A BETTER CATCHPHRASE!
HOW ABOUT "IT'S CLOBBERING TIME"?
THAT'S EVEN WORSE!
HEH.

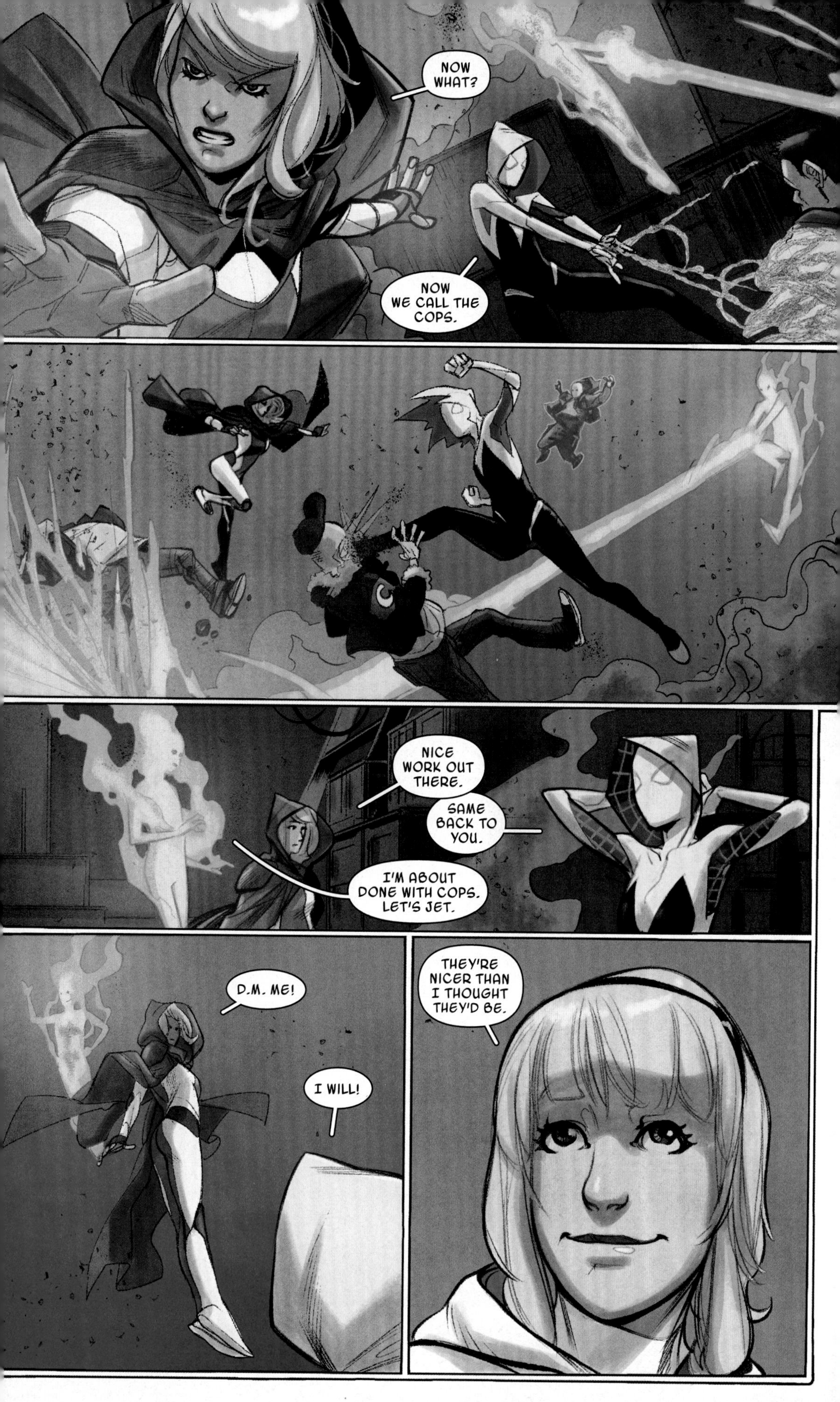
NOW WHAT?
NOW WE CALL THE COPS.
NICE WORK OUT THERE.
SAME BACK TO YOU.
I'M ABOUT DONE WITH COPS. LET'S JET.
D.M. ME!
I WILL!
THEY'RE NICER THAN I THOUGHT THEY'D BE.

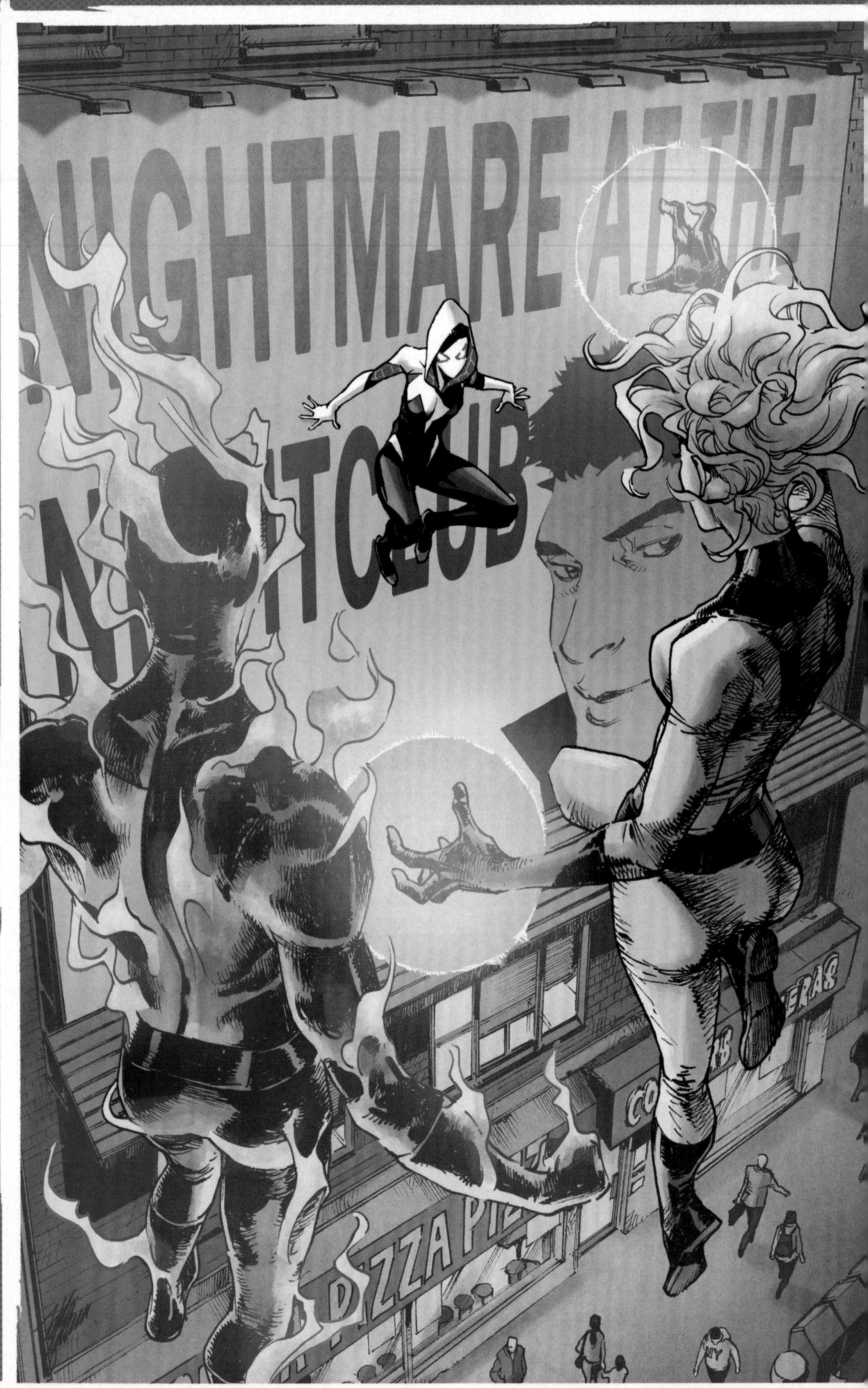

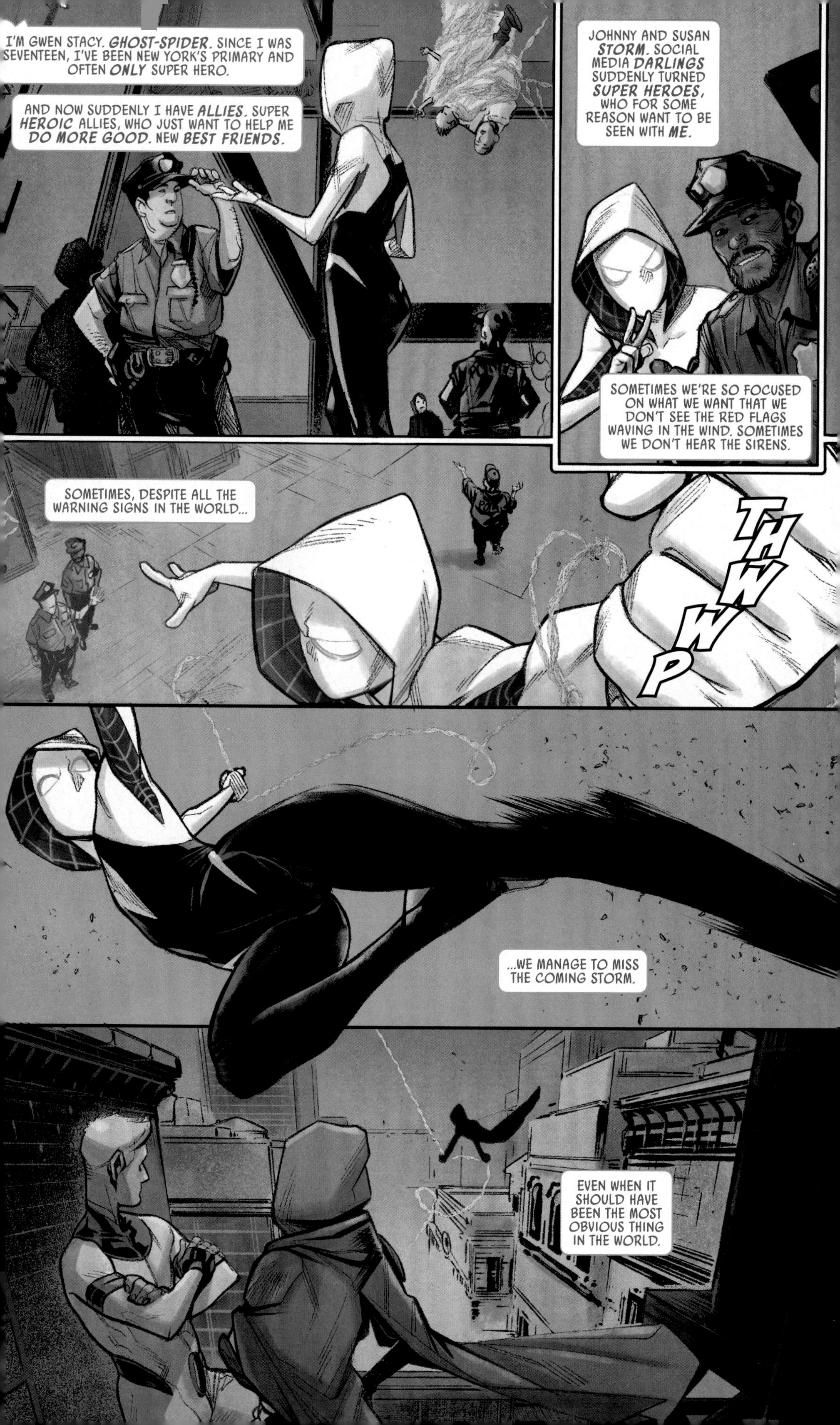
I'M GWEN STACY. GHOST-SPIDER. SINCE I WAS SEVENTEEN, I'VE BEEN NEW YORK'S PRIMARY AND OFTEN ONLY SUPER HERO.
AND NOW SUDDENLY I HAVE ALLIES. SUPER HEROIC ALLIES, WHO JUST WANT TO HELP ME DO MORE GOOD. NEW BEST FRIENDS.
JOHNNY AND SUSAN STORM. SOCIAL MEDIA DARLINGS SUDDENLY TURNED SUPER HEROES, WHO FOR SOME REASON WANT TO BE SEEN WITH ME.
SOMETIMES WE'RE SO FOCUSED ON WHAT WE WANT THAT WE DON'T SEE THE RED FLAGS WAVING IN THE WIND. SOMETIMES WE DON'T HEAR THE SIRENS.
SOMETIMES, DESPITE ALL THE WARNING SIGNS IN THE WORLD...
THWWP
...WE MANAGE TO MISS THE COMING STORM.
EVEN WHEN IT SHOULD HAVE BEEN THE MOST OBVIOUS THING IN THE WORLD.

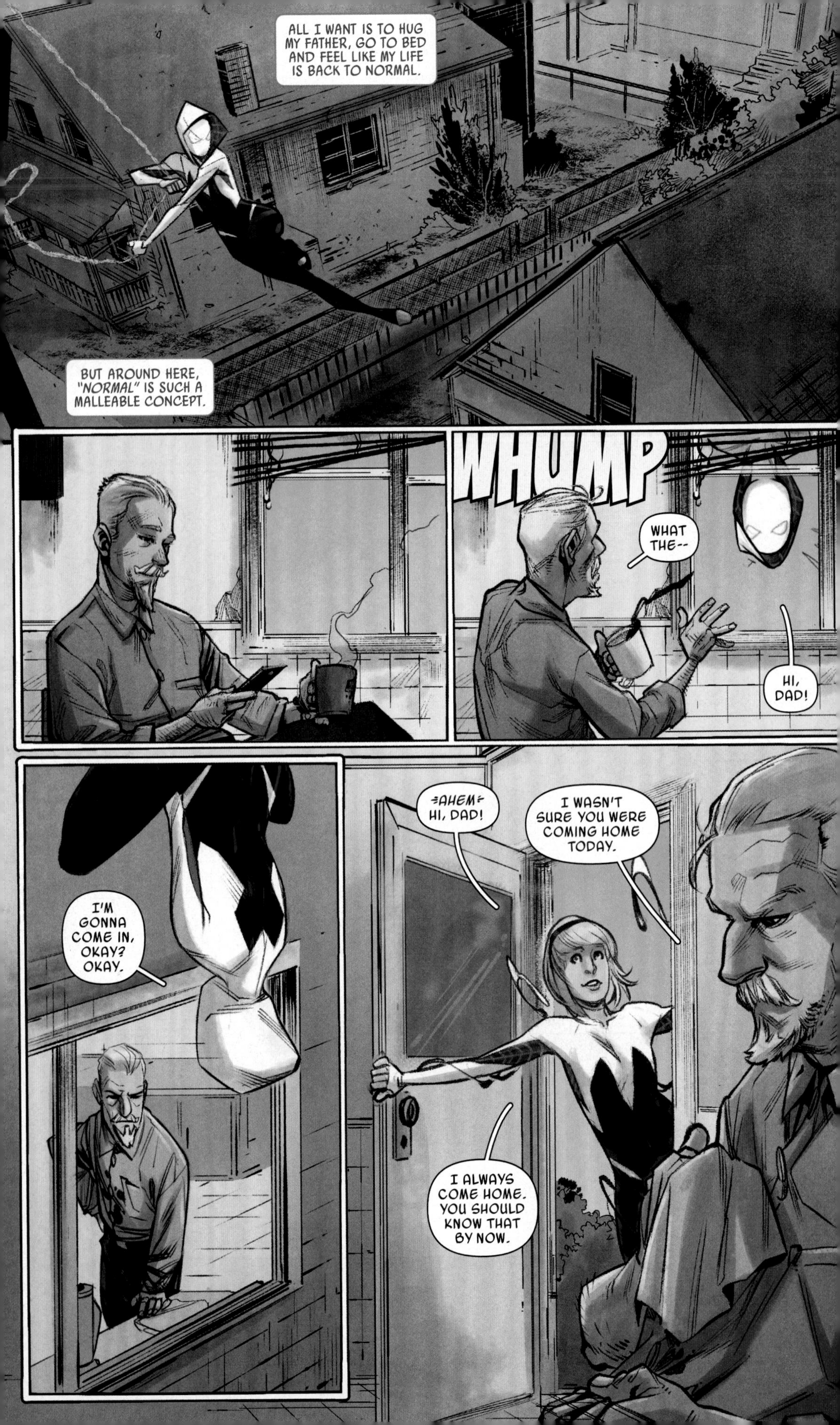
ALL I WANT IS TO HUG MY FATHER, GO TO BED AND FEEL LIKE MY LIFE IS BACK TO NORMAL.
BUT AROUND HERE, "NORMAL" IS SUCH A MALLEABLE CONCEPT.
WHUMP
WHAT THE--
HI, DAD!
I'M GONNA COME IN, OKAY? OKAY.
AHEM HI, DAD!
I WASN'T SURE YOU WERE COMING HOME TODAY.
I ALWAYS COME HOME. YOU SHOULD KNOW THAT BY NOW.

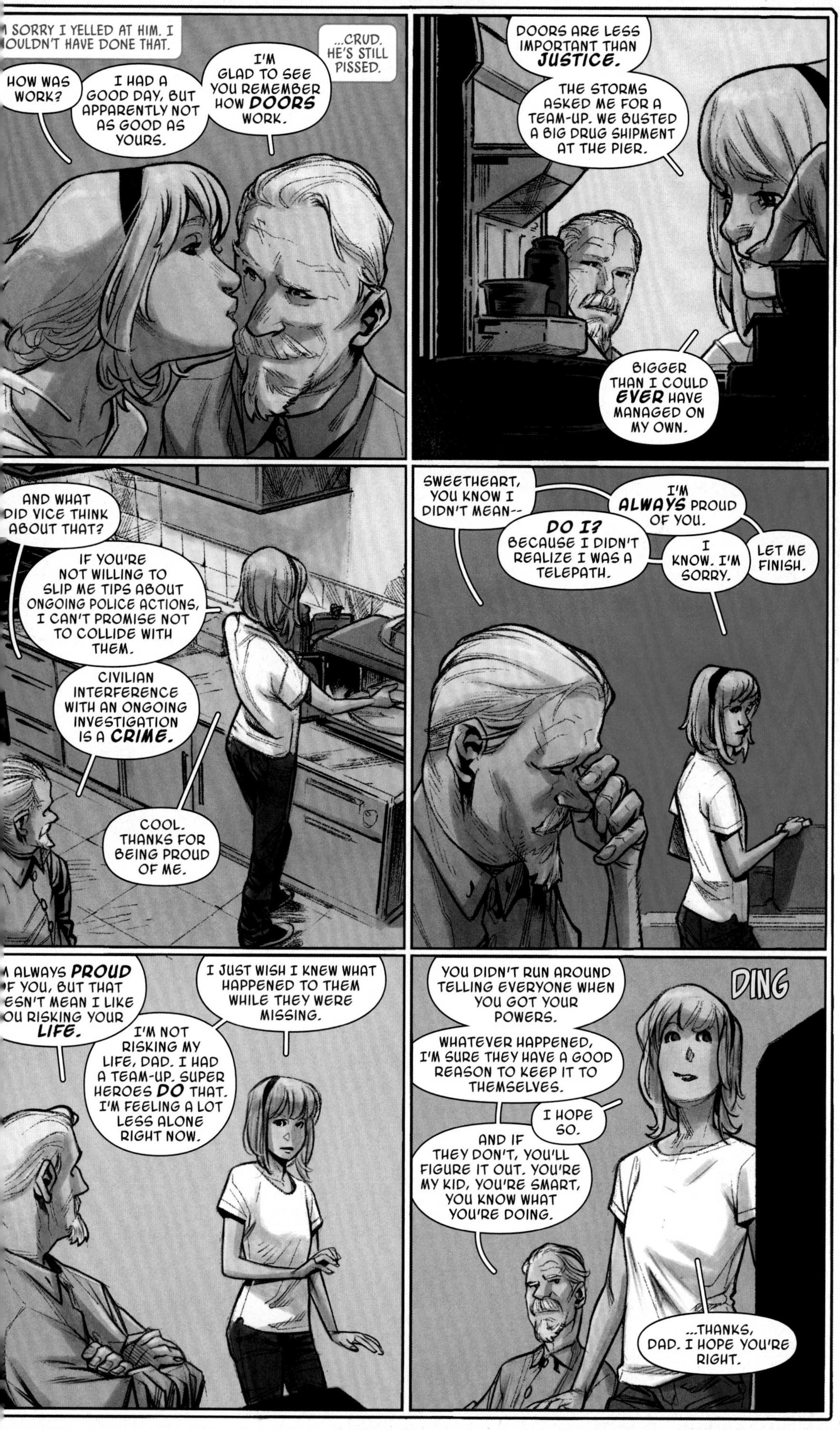

…M SORRY I YELLED AT HIM. I …OULDN'T HAVE DONE THAT.
HOW WAS WORK?
I HAD A GOOD DAY, BUT APPARENTLY NOT AS GOOD AS YOURS.
I'M GLAD TO SEE YOU REMEMBER HOW DOORS WORK.
...CRUD. HE'S STILL PISSED.
DOORS ARE LESS IMPORTANT THAN JUSTICE.
THE STORMS ASKED ME FOR A TEAM-UP. WE BUSTED A BIG DRUG SHIPMENT AT THE PIER.
BIGGER THAN I COULD EVER HAVE MANAGED ON MY OWN.
AND WHAT DID VICE THINK ABOUT THAT?
IF YOU'RE NOT WILLING TO SLIP ME TIPS ABOUT ONGOING POLICE ACTIONS, I CAN'T PROMISE NOT TO COLLIDE WITH THEM.
CIVILIAN INTERFERENCE WITH AN ONGOING INVESTIGATION IS A CRIME.
COOL. THANKS FOR BEING PROUD OF ME.
SWEETHEART, YOU KNOW I DIDN'T MEAN--
DO I? BECAUSE I DIDN'T REALIZE I WAS A TELEPATH.
I'M ALWAYS PROUD OF YOU.
I KNOW. I'M SORRY.
LET ME FINISH.
…M ALWAYS PROUD …F YOU, BUT THAT …ESN'T MEAN I LIKE …OU RISKING YOUR LIFE.
I'M NOT RISKING MY LIFE, DAD. I HAD A TEAM-UP. SUPER HEROES DO THAT. I'M FEELING A LOT LESS ALONE RIGHT NOW.
I JUST WISH I KNEW WHAT HAPPENED TO THEM WHILE THEY WERE MISSING.
YOU DIDN'T RUN AROUND TELLING EVERYONE WHEN YOU GOT YOUR POWERS.
WHATEVER HAPPENED, I'M SURE THEY HAVE A GOOD REASON TO KEEP IT TO THEMSELVES.
I HOPE SO.
AND IF THEY DON'T, YOU'LL FIGURE IT OUT. YOU'RE MY KID, YOU'RE SMART, YOU KNOW WHAT YOU'RE DOING.
DING
...THANKS, DAD. I HOPE YOU'RE RIGHT.

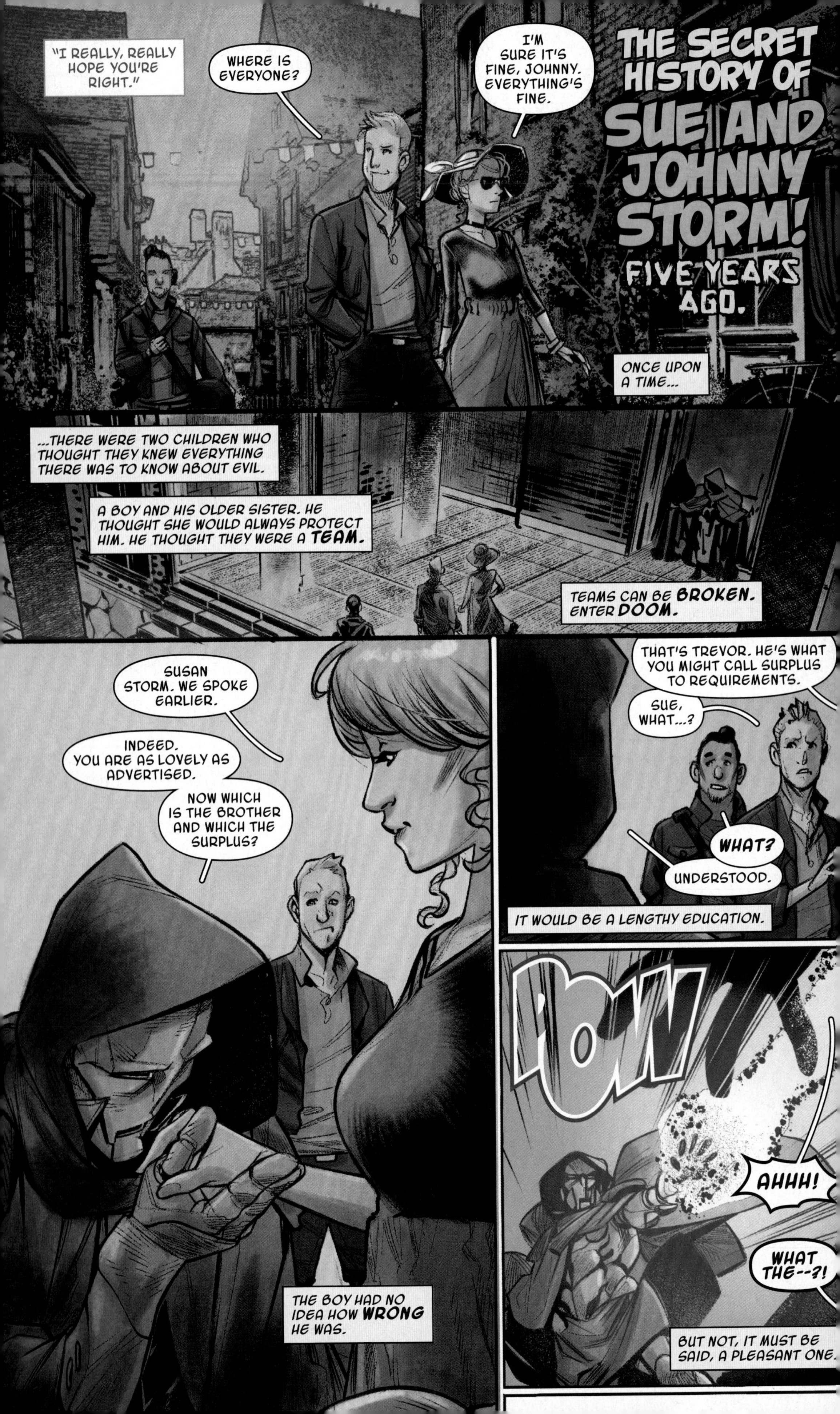

"I REALLY, REALLY HOPE YOU'RE RIGHT."
WHERE IS EVERYONE?
I'M SURE IT'S FINE, JOHNNY. EVERYTHING'S FINE.
THE SECRET HISTORY OF SUE AND JOHNNY STORM!
FIVE YEARS AGO.
ONCE UPON A TIME...
...THERE WERE TWO CHILDREN WHO THOUGHT THEY KNEW EVERYTHING THERE WAS TO KNOW ABOUT EVIL.
A BOY AND HIS OLDER SISTER. HE THOUGHT SHE WOULD ALWAYS PROTECT HIM. HE THOUGHT THEY WERE A **TEAM.**
TEAMS CAN BE **BROKEN.** ENTER **DOOM.**
SUSAN STORM. WE SPOKE EARLIER.
INDEED. YOU ARE AS LOVELY AS ADVERTISED.
NOW WHICH IS THE BROTHER AND WHICH THE SURPLUS?
THE BOY HAD NO IDEA HOW **WRONG** HE WAS.
THAT'S TREVOR. HE'S WHAT YOU MIGHT CALL SURPLUS TO REQUIREMENTS.
SUE, WHAT...?
WHAT?
UNDERSTOOD.
IT WOULD BE A LENGTHY EDUCATION.
POW
AHHH!
WHAT THE--?!
BUT NOT, IT MUST BE SAID, A PLEASANT ONE.

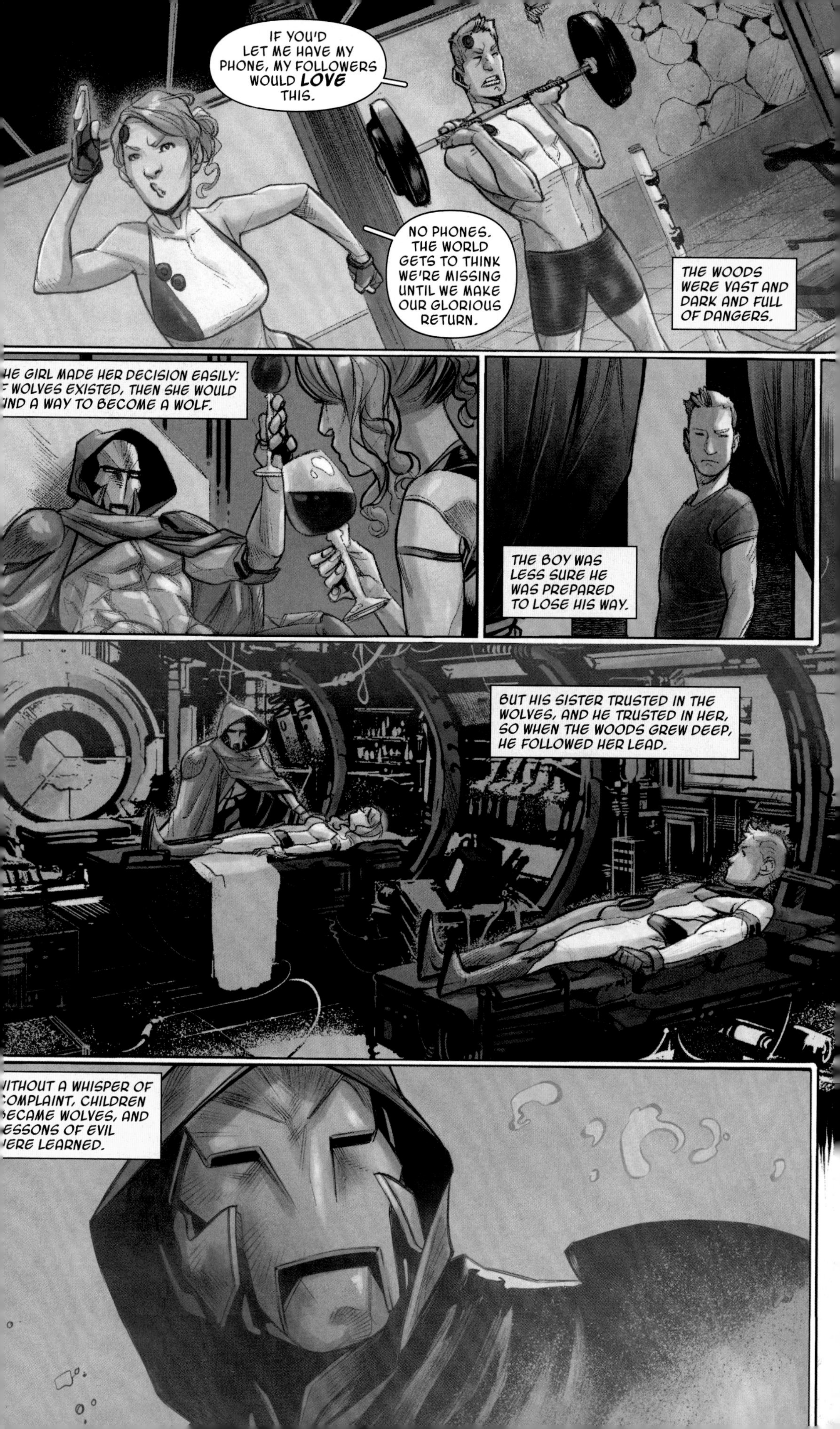

IF YOU'D LET ME HAVE MY PHONE, MY FOLLOWERS WOULD **LOVE** THIS.
NO PHONES. THE WORLD GETS TO THINK WE'RE MISSING UNTIL WE MAKE OUR GLORIOUS RETURN.
THE WOODS WERE VAST AND DARK AND FULL OF DANGERS.
HE GIRL MADE HER DECISION EASILY: F WOLVES EXISTED, THEN SHE WOULD IND A WAY TO BECOME A WOLF.
THE BOY WAS LESS SURE HE WAS PREPARED TO LOSE HIS WAY.
BUT HIS SISTER TRUSTED IN THE WOLVES, AND HE TRUSTED IN HER, SO WHEN THE WOODS GREW DEEP, HE FOLLOWED HER LEAD.
ITHOUT A WHISPER OF OMPLAINT, CHILDREN ECAME WOLVES, AND ESSONS OF EVIL ERE LEARNED.

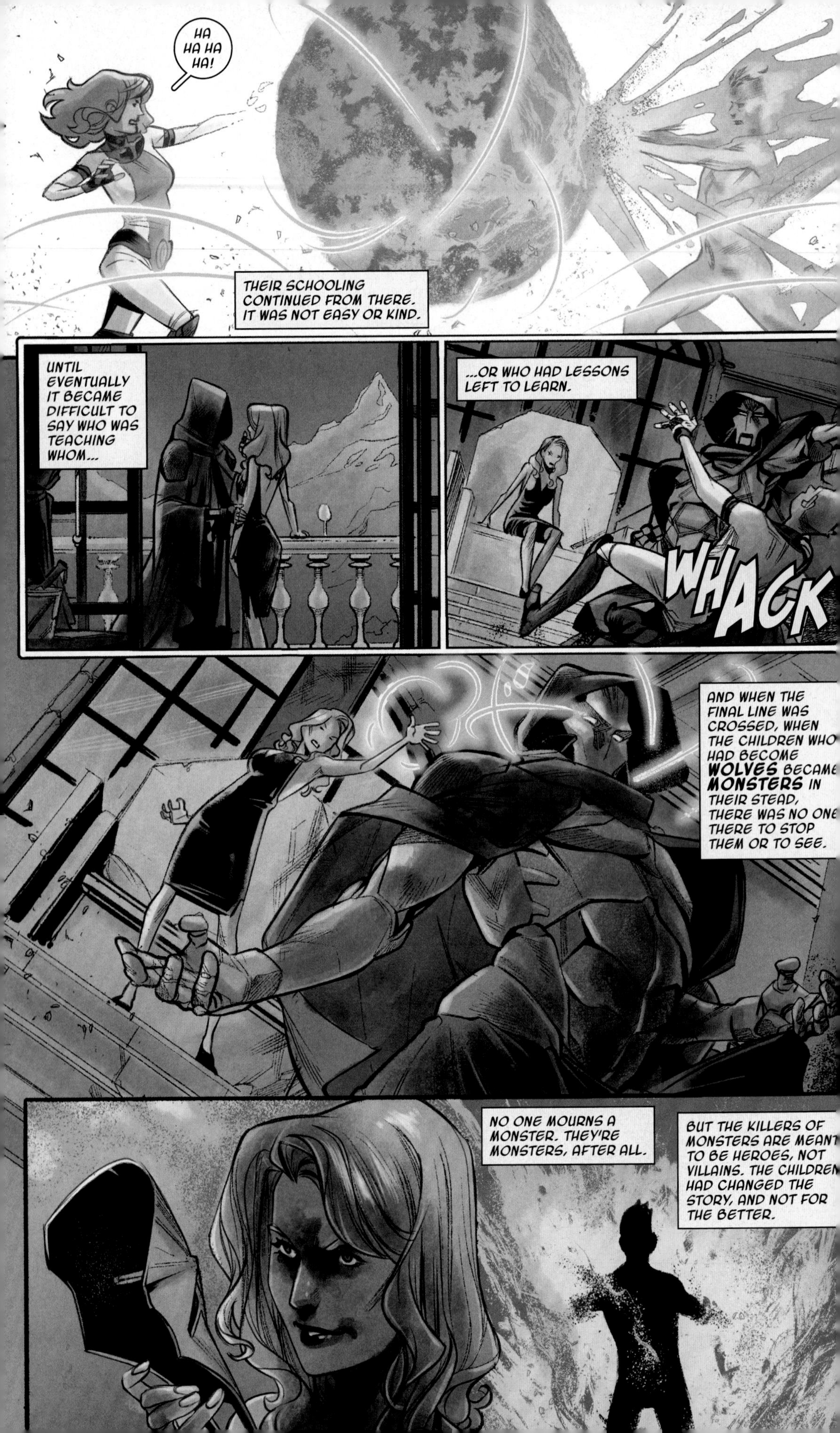
HA HA HA HA!
THEIR SCHOOLING CONTINUED FROM THERE. IT WAS NOT EASY OR KIND.
UNTIL EVENTUALLY IT BECAME DIFFICULT TO SAY WHO WAS TEACHING WHOM...
...OR WHO HAD LESSONS LEFT TO LEARN.
WHACK
AND WHEN THE FINAL LINE WAS CROSSED, WHEN THE CHILDREN WHO HAD BECOME WOLVES BECAME MONSTERS IN THEIR STEAD, THERE WAS NO ONE THERE TO STOP THEM OR TO SEE.
NO ONE MOURNS A MONSTER. THEY'RE MONSTERS, AFTER ALL.
BUT THE KILLERS OF MONSTERS ARE MEANT TO BE HEROES, NOT VILLAINS. THE CHILDREN HAD CHANGED THE STORY, AND NOT FOR THE BETTER.

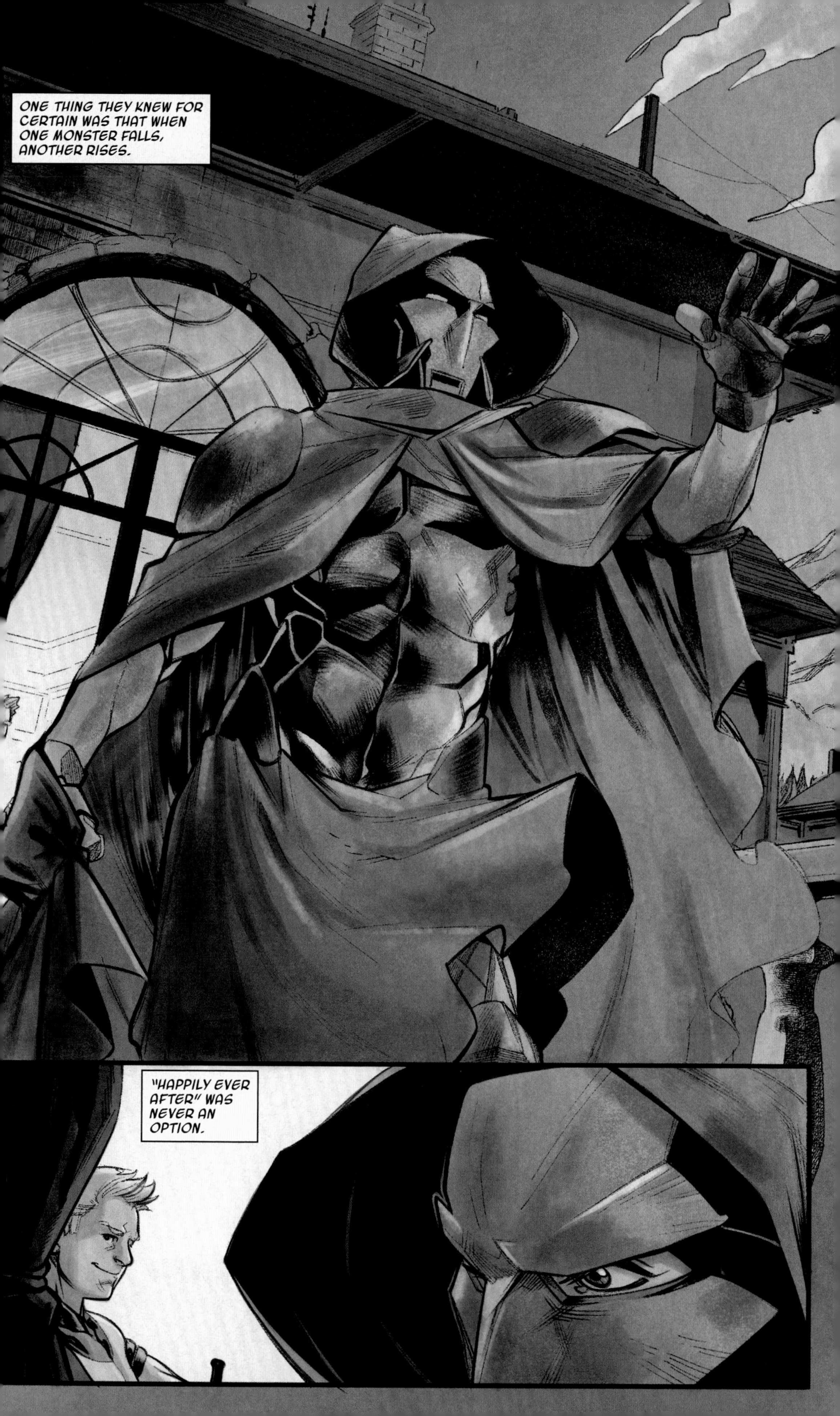
ONE THING THEY KNEW FOR CERTAIN WAS THAT WHEN ONE MONSTER FALLS, ANOTHER RISES.
"HAPPILY EVER AFTER" WAS NEVER AN OPTION.

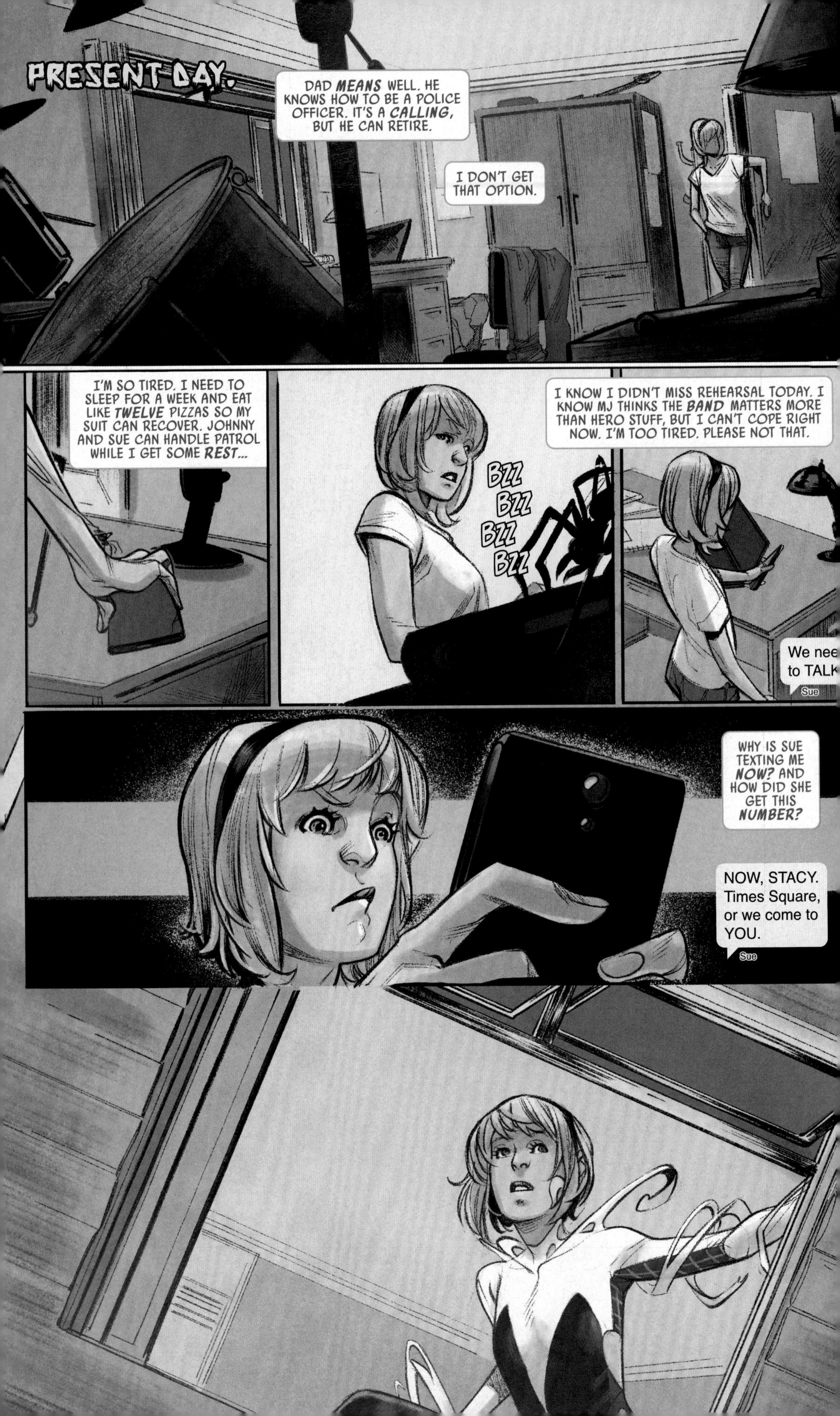
PRESENT DAY.
DAD MEANS WELL. HE KNOWS HOW TO BE A POLICE OFFICER. IT'S A CALLING, BUT HE CAN RETIRE.
I DON'T GET THAT OPTION.
I'M SO TIRED. I NEED TO SLEEP FOR A WEEK AND EAT LIKE TWELVE PIZZAS SO MY SUIT CAN RECOVER. JOHNNY AND SUE CAN HANDLE PATROL WHILE I GET SOME REST...
BZZ BZZ BZZ BZZ
I KNOW I DIDN'T MISS REHEARSAL TODAY. I KNOW MJ THINKS THE BAND MATTERS MORE THAN HERO STUFF, BUT I CAN'T COPE RIGHT NOW. I'M TOO TIRED. PLEASE NOT THAT.
Sue
WHY IS SUE TEXTING ME NOW? AND HOW DID SHE GET THIS NUMBER?
NOW, STACY. Times Square, or we come to YOU.
Sue

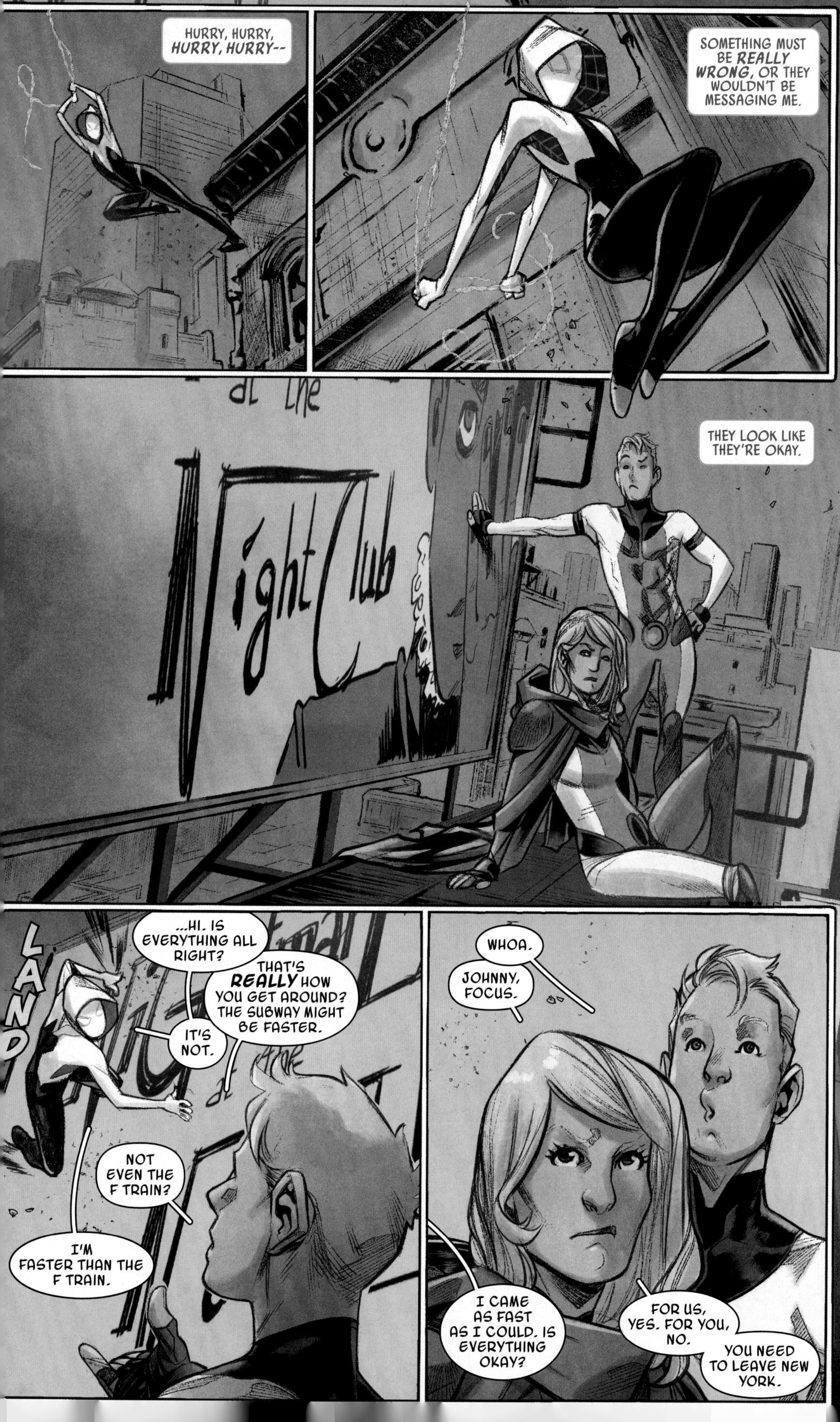

HURRY, HURRY, HURRY, HURRY--
SOMETHING MUST BE REALLY WRONG, OR THEY WOULDN'T BE MESSAGING ME.
THEY LOOK LIKE THEY'RE OKAY.
LAND
...HI. IS EVERYTHING ALL RIGHT?
THAT'S REALLY HOW YOU GET AROUND? THE SUBWAY MIGHT BE FASTER.
IT'S NOT.
NOT EVEN THE F TRAIN?
I'M FASTER THAN THE F TRAIN.
WHOA.
JOHNNY, FOCUS.
I CAME AS FAST AS I COULD. IS EVERYTHING OKAY?
FOR US, YES. FOR YOU, NO.
YOU NEED TO LEAVE NEW YORK.

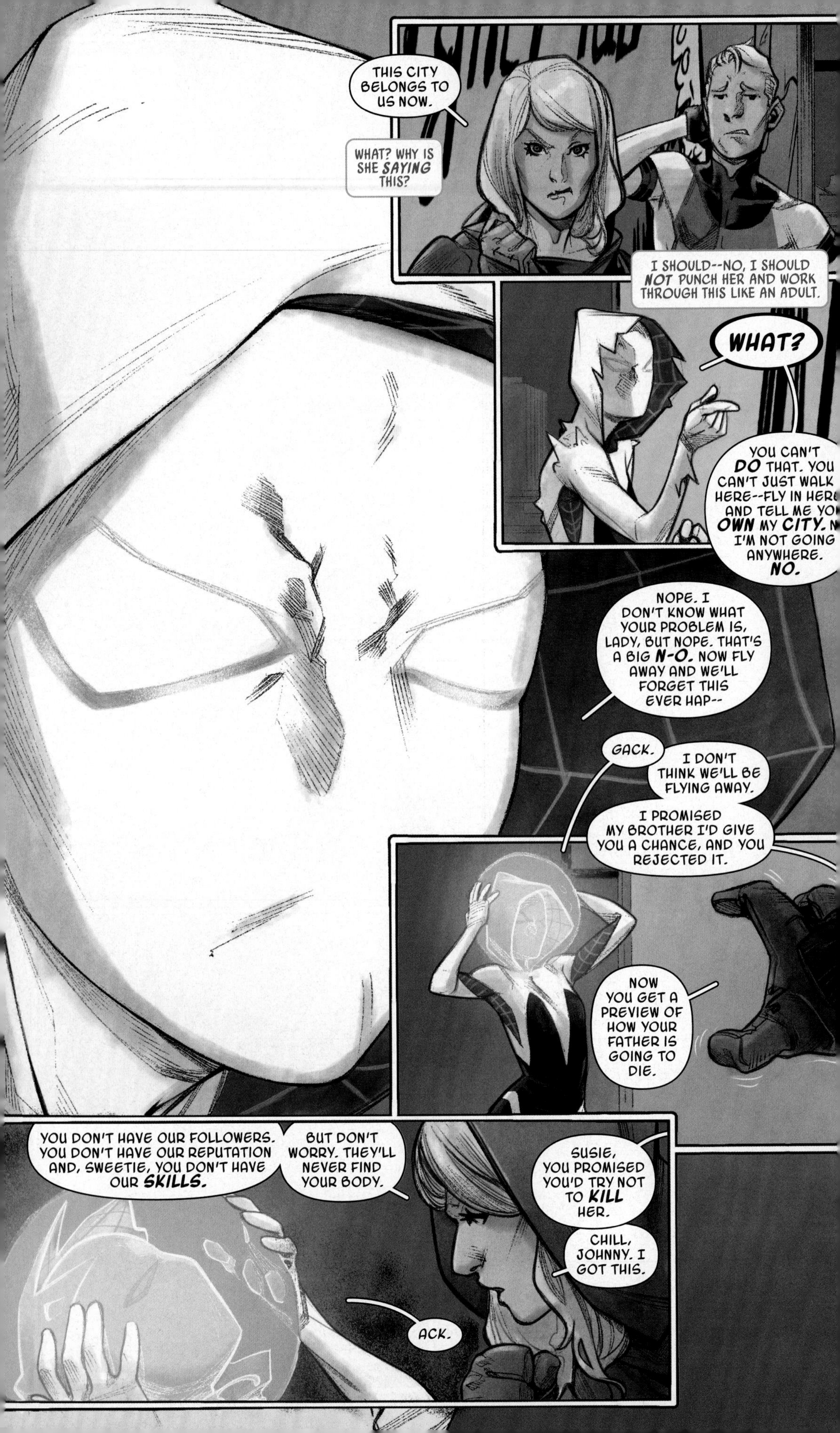
THIS CITY BELONGS TO US NOW.
WHAT? WHY IS SHE *SAYING* THIS?
I SHOULD--NO, I SHOULD *NOT* PUNCH HER AND WORK THROUGH THIS LIKE AN ADULT.
WHAT?
YOU CAN'T *DO* THAT. YOU CAN'T JUST WALK HERE--FLY IN HER AND TELL ME YO *OWN* MY *CITY.* I'M NOT GOING ANYWHERE. *NO.*
NOPE. I DON'T KNOW WHAT YOUR PROBLEM IS, LADY, BUT NOPE. THAT'S A BIG *N-O.* NOW FLY AWAY AND WE'LL FORGET THIS EVER HAP--
GACK.
I DON'T THINK WE'LL BE FLYING AWAY.
I PROMISED MY BROTHER I'D GIVE YOU A CHANCE, AND YOU REJECTED IT.
NOW YOU GET A PREVIEW OF HOW YOUR FATHER IS GOING TO DIE.
YOU DON'T HAVE OUR FOLLOWERS. YOU DON'T HAVE OUR REPUTATION AND, SWEETIE, YOU DON'T HAVE OUR *SKILLS.*
BUT DON'T WORRY. THEY'LL NEVER FIND YOUR BODY.
SUSIE, YOU PROMISED YOU'D TRY NOT TO *KILL* HER.
CHILL, JOHNNY. I GOT THIS.
ACK.

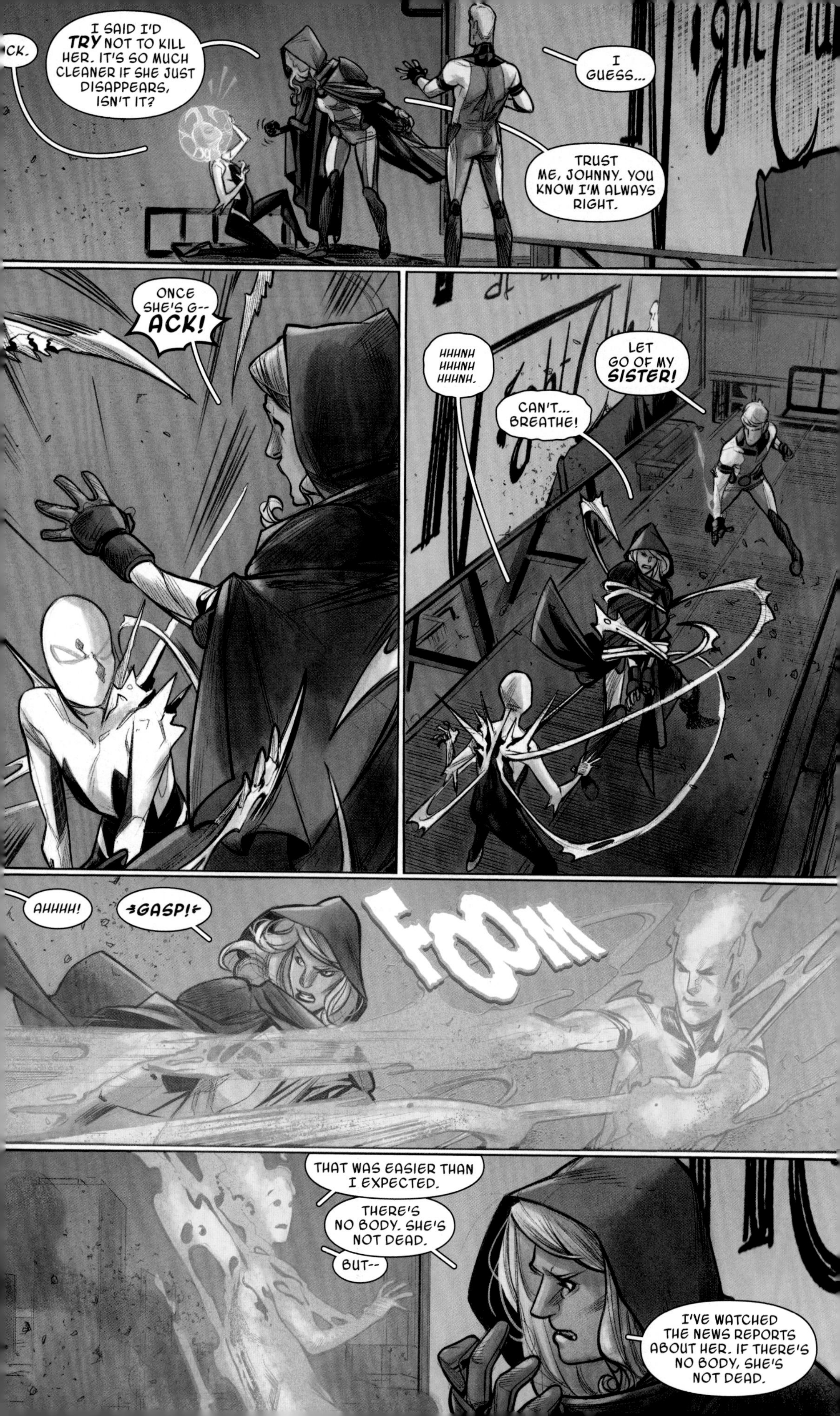
CK.
I SAID I'D TRY NOT TO KILL HER. IT'S SO MUCH CLEANER IF SHE JUST DISAPPEARS, ISN'T IT?
I GUESS...
TRUST ME, JOHNNY. YOU KNOW I'M ALWAYS RIGHT.
ONCE SHE'S G-- ACK!
HHHNH HHHNH HHHNH.
LET GO OF MY SISTER!
CAN'T... BREATHE!
AHHHH!
GASP!
FOOM
THAT WAS EASIER THAN I EXPECTED.
THERE'S NO BODY. SHE'S NOT DEAD.
BUT--
I'VE WATCHED THE NEWS REPORTS ABOUT HER. IF THERE'S NO BODY, SHE'S NOT DEAD.

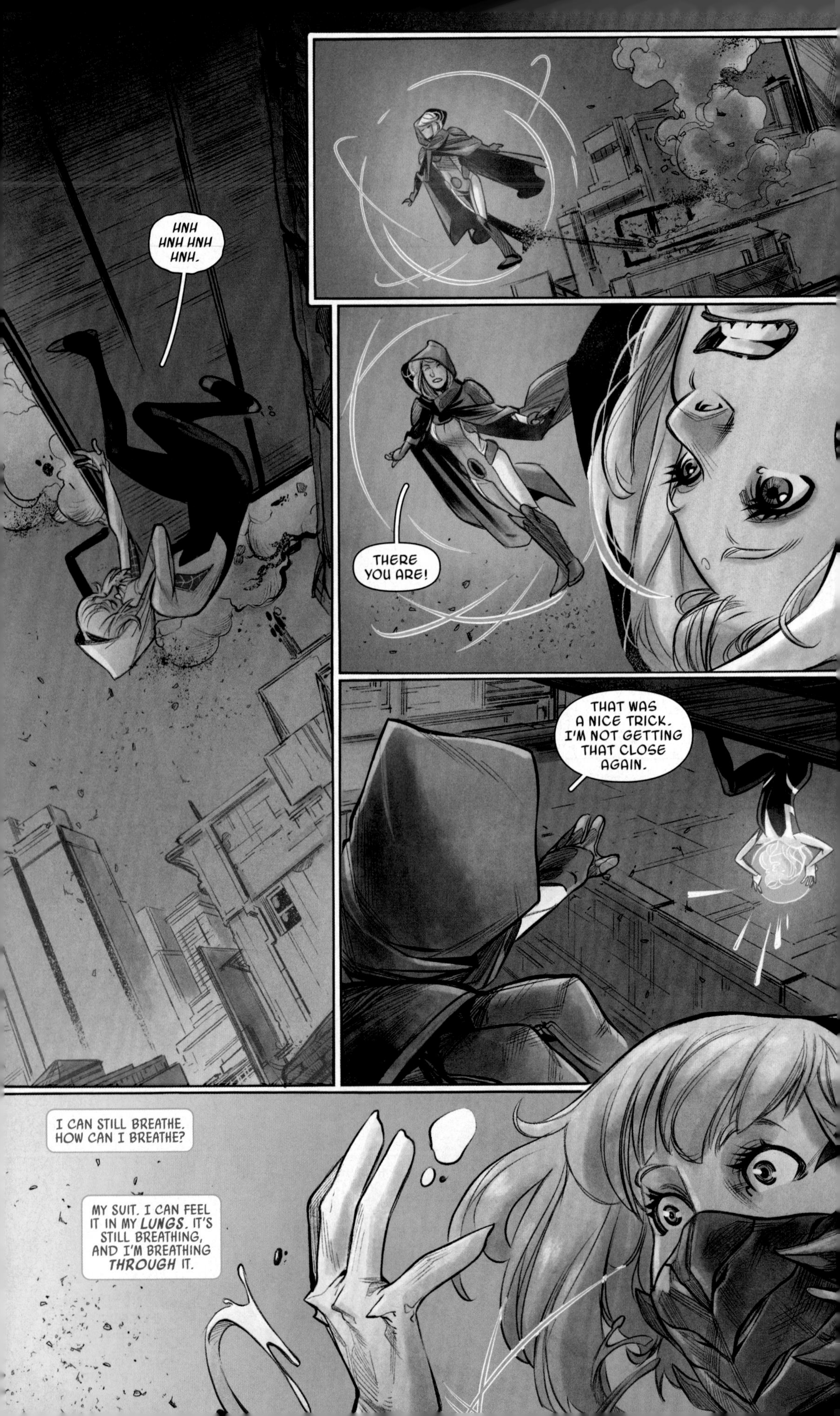
HNH HNH HNH HNH.
THERE YOU ARE!
THAT WAS A NICE TRICK. I'M NOT GETTING THAT CLOSE AGAIN.
I CAN STILL BREATHE. HOW CAN I BREATHE?
MY SUIT. I CAN FEEL IT IN MY LUNGS. IT'S STILL BREATHING, AND I'M BREATHING THROUGH IT.

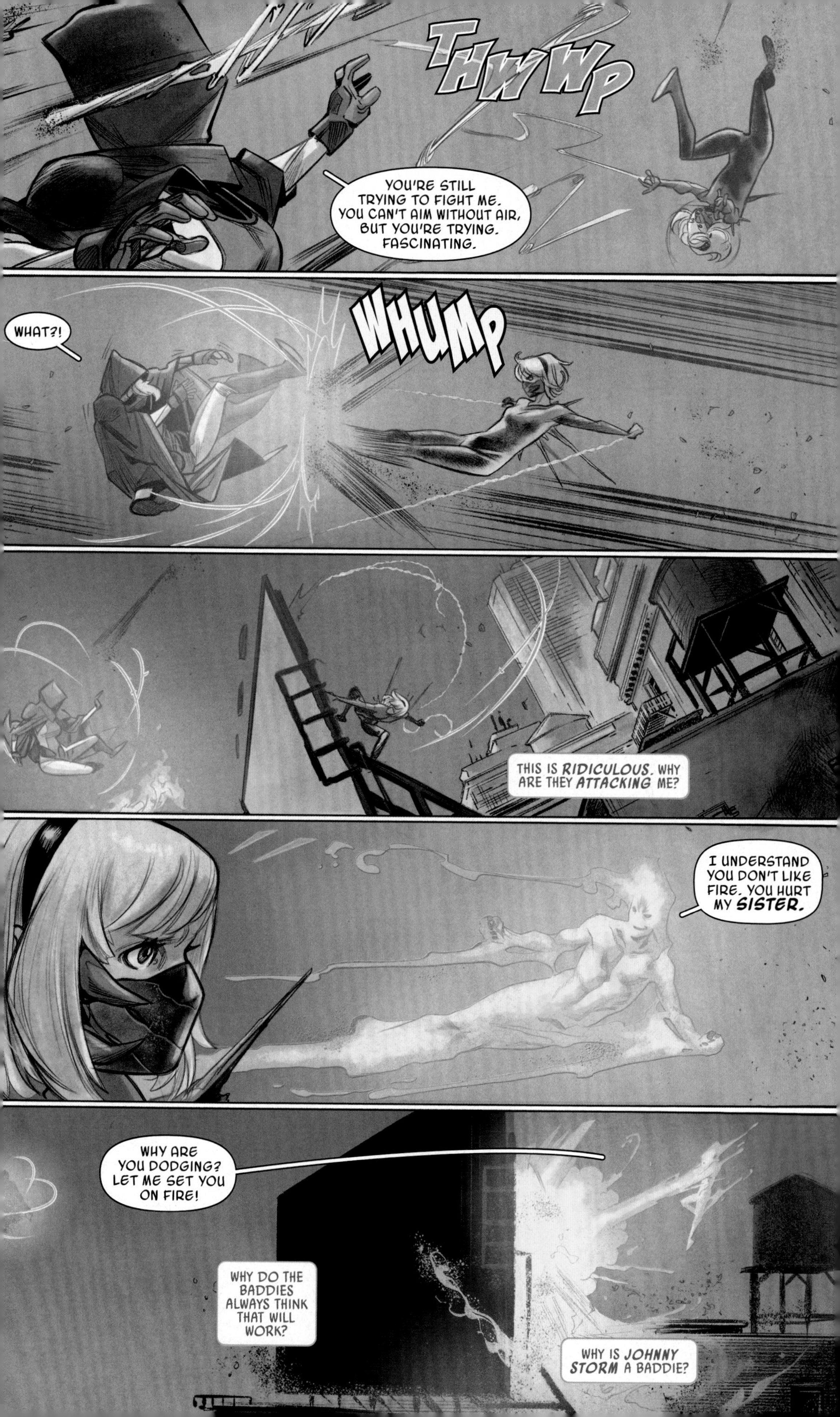
THWWP
YOU'RE STILL TRYING TO FIGHT ME. YOU CAN'T AIM WITHOUT AIR, BUT YOU'RE TRYING. FASCINATING.
WHAT?!
WHUMP
THIS IS RIDICULOUS. WHY ARE THEY ATTACKING ME?
I UNDERSTAND YOU DON'T LIKE FIRE. YOU HURT MY SISTER.
WHY ARE YOU DODGING? LET ME SET YOU ON FIRE!
WHY DO THE BADDIES ALWAYS THINK THAT WILL WORK?
WHY IS JOHNNY STORM A BADDIE?

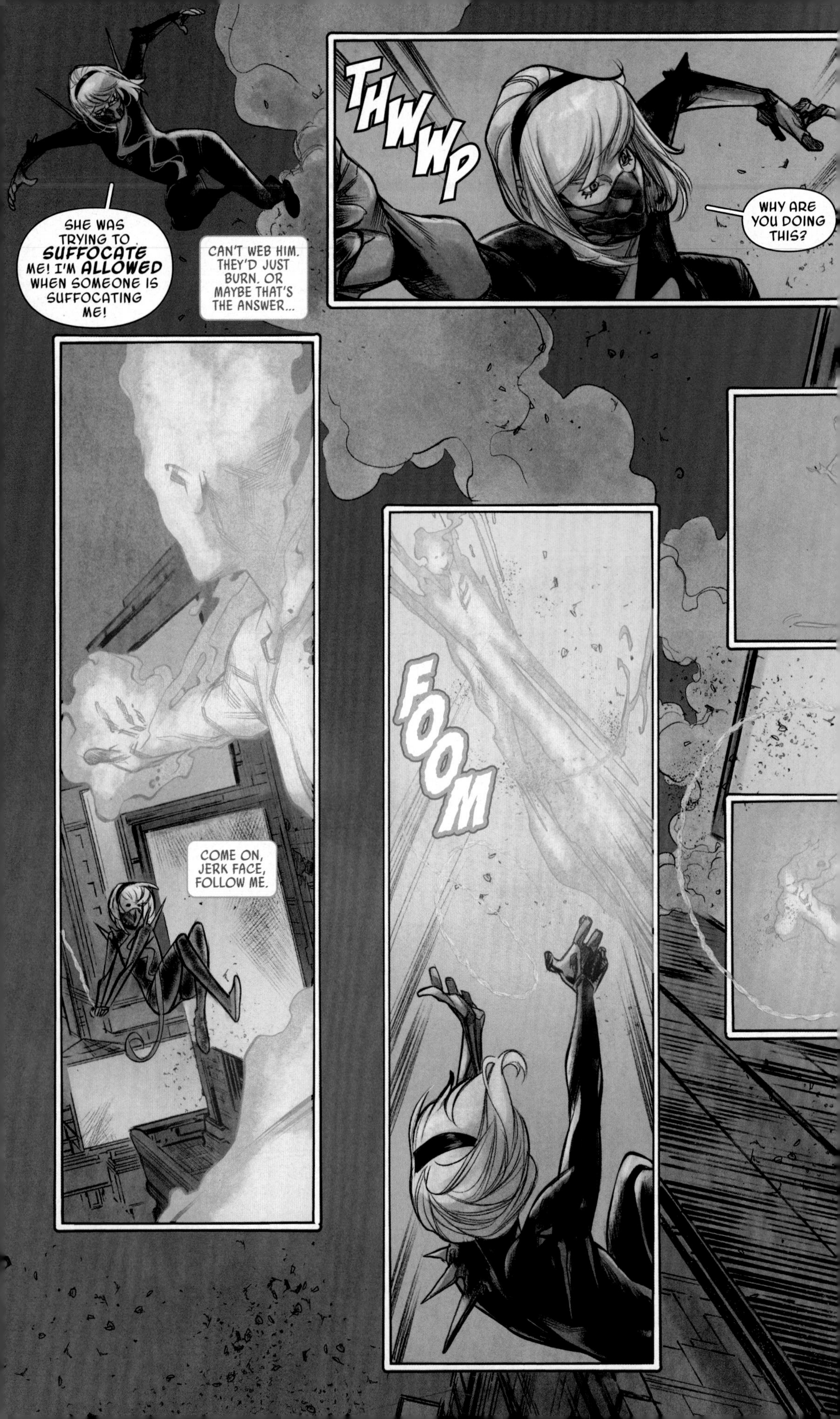

SHE WAS TRYING TO SUFFOCATE ME! I'M ALLOWED WHEN SOMEONE IS SUFFOCATING ME!
CAN'T WEB HIM. THEY'D JUST BURN. OR MAYBE THAT'S THE ANSWER...
THWWP
WHY ARE YOU DOING THIS?
COME ON, JERK FACE, FOLLOW ME.
FOOM

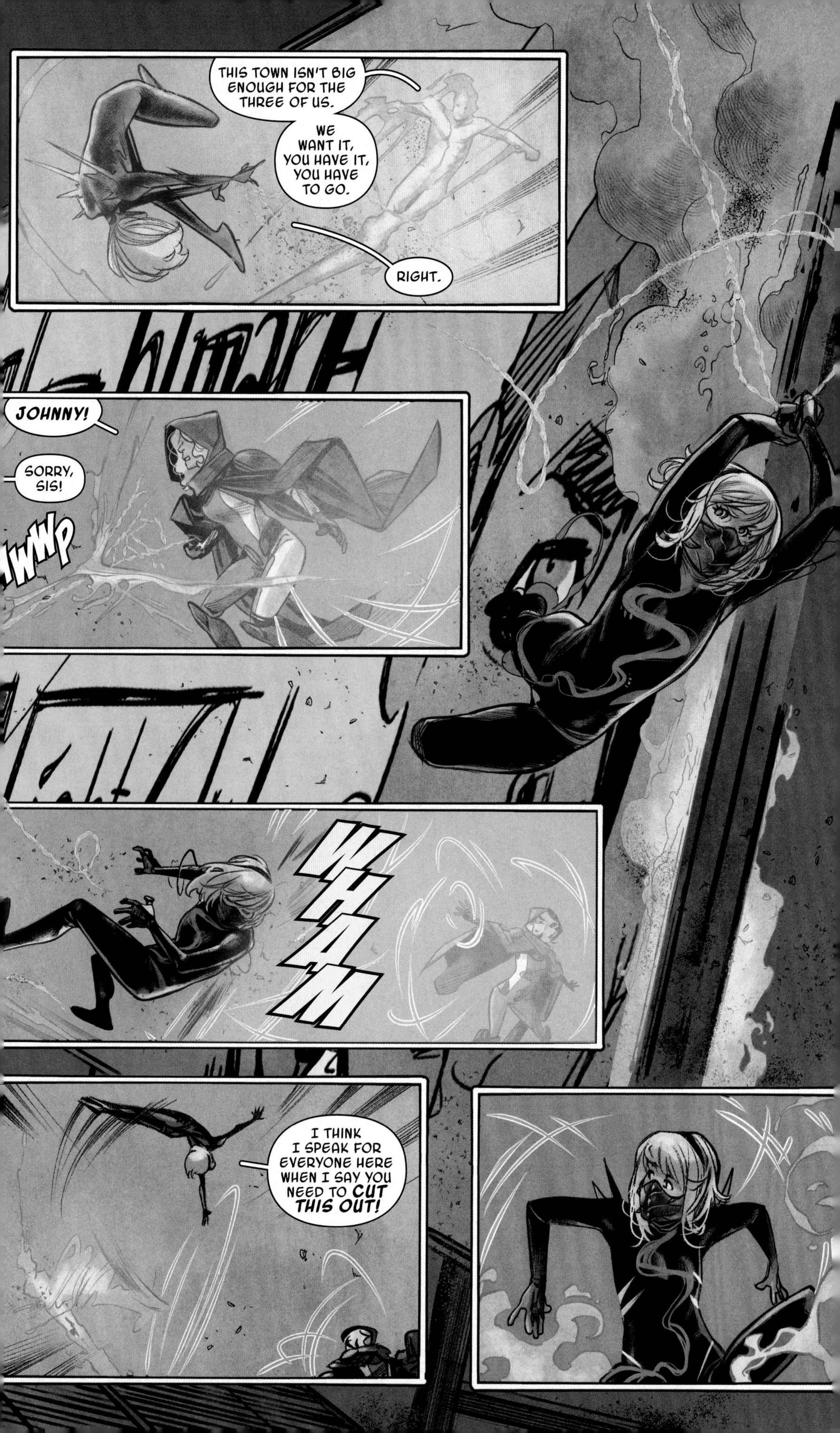
THIS TOWN ISN'T BIG ENOUGH FOR THE THREE OF US.
WE WANT IT, YOU HAVE IT, YOU HAVE TO GO.
RIGHT.
JOHNNY!
SORRY, SIS!
WHAM
I THINK I SPEAK FOR EVERYONE HERE WHEN I SAY YOU NEED TO **CUT THIS OUT!**

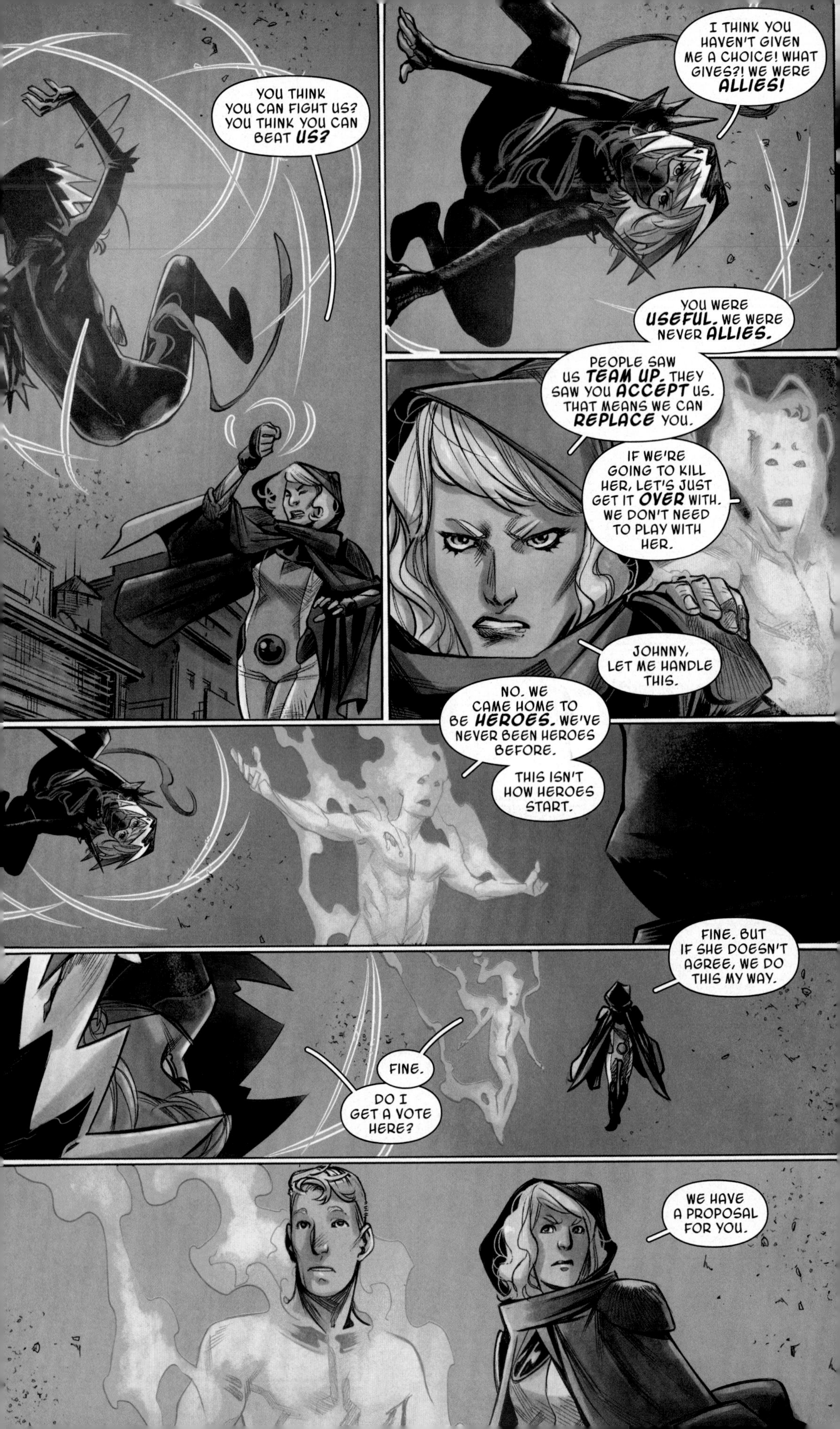

YOU THINK YOU CAN FIGHT US? YOU THINK YOU CAN BEAT US?
I THINK YOU HAVEN'T GIVEN ME A CHOICE! WHAT GIVES?! WE WERE ALLIES!
YOU WERE USEFUL. WE WERE NEVER ALLIES.
PEOPLE SAW US TEAM UP. THEY SAW YOU ACCEPT US. THAT MEANS WE CAN REPLACE YOU.
IF WE'RE GOING TO KILL HER, LET'S JUST GET IT OVER WITH. WE DON'T NEED TO PLAY WITH HER.
JOHNNY, LET ME HANDLE THIS.
NO. WE CAME HOME TO BE HEROES. WE'VE NEVER BEEN HEROES BEFORE.
THIS ISN'T HOW HEROES START.
FINE. BUT IF SHE DOESN'T AGREE, WE DO THIS MY WAY.
FINE.
DO I GET A VOTE HERE?
WE HAVE A PROPOSAL FOR YOU.

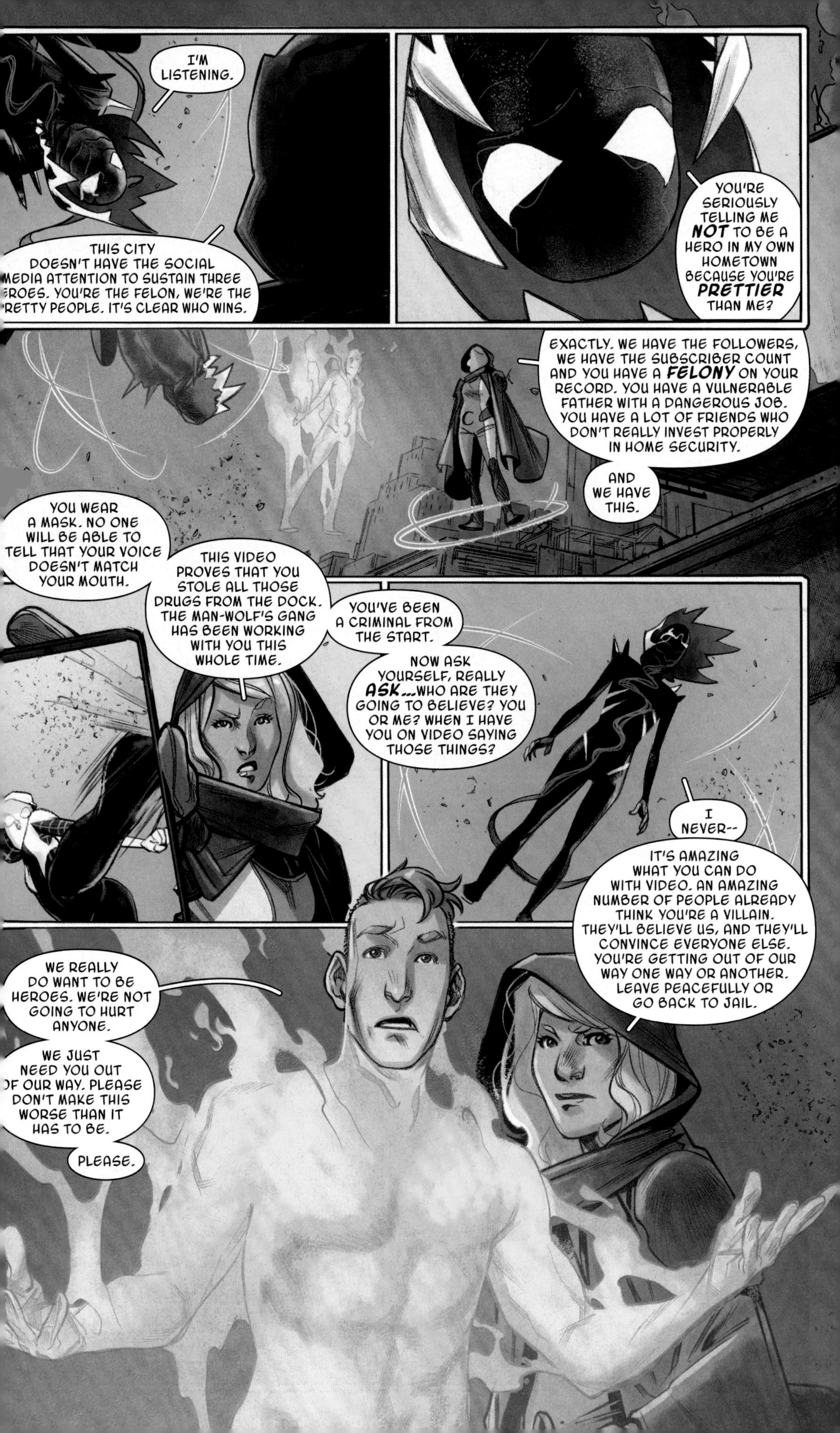
I'M LISTENING.
THIS CITY DOESN'T HAVE THE SOCIAL MEDIA ATTENTION TO SUSTAIN THREE HEROES. YOU'RE THE FELON, WE'RE THE PRETTY PEOPLE. IT'S CLEAR WHO WINS.
YOU'RE SERIOUSLY TELLING ME NOT TO BE A HERO IN MY OWN HOMETOWN BECAUSE YOU'RE PRETTIER THAN ME?
EXACTLY. WE HAVE THE FOLLOWERS, WE HAVE THE SUBSCRIBER COUNT AND YOU HAVE A FELONY ON YOUR RECORD. YOU HAVE A VULNERABLE FATHER WITH A DANGEROUS JOB. YOU HAVE A LOT OF FRIENDS WHO DON'T REALLY INVEST PROPERLY IN HOME SECURITY.
AND WE HAVE THIS.
YOU WEAR A MASK. NO ONE WILL BE ABLE TO TELL THAT YOUR VOICE DOESN'T MATCH YOUR MOUTH.
THIS VIDEO PROVES THAT YOU STOLE ALL THOSE DRUGS FROM THE DOCK. THE MAN-WOLF'S GANG HAS BEEN WORKING WITH YOU THIS WHOLE TIME.
YOU'VE BEEN A CRIMINAL FROM THE START.
NOW ASK YOURSELF, REALLY ASK...WHO ARE THEY GOING TO BELIEVE? YOU OR ME? WHEN I HAVE YOU ON VIDEO SAYING THOSE THINGS?
I NEVER--
IT'S AMAZING WHAT YOU CAN DO WITH VIDEO. AN AMAZING NUMBER OF PEOPLE ALREADY THINK YOU'RE A VILLAIN. THEY'LL BELIEVE US, AND THEY'LL CONVINCE EVERYONE ELSE. YOU'RE GETTING OUT OF OUR WAY ONE WAY OR ANOTHER. LEAVE PEACEFULLY OR GO BACK TO JAIL.
WE REALLY DO WANT TO BE HEROES. WE'RE NOT GOING TO HURT ANYONE.
WE JUST NEED YOU OUT OF OUR WAY. PLEASE DON'T MAKE THIS WORSE THAN IT HAS TO BE.
PLEASE.

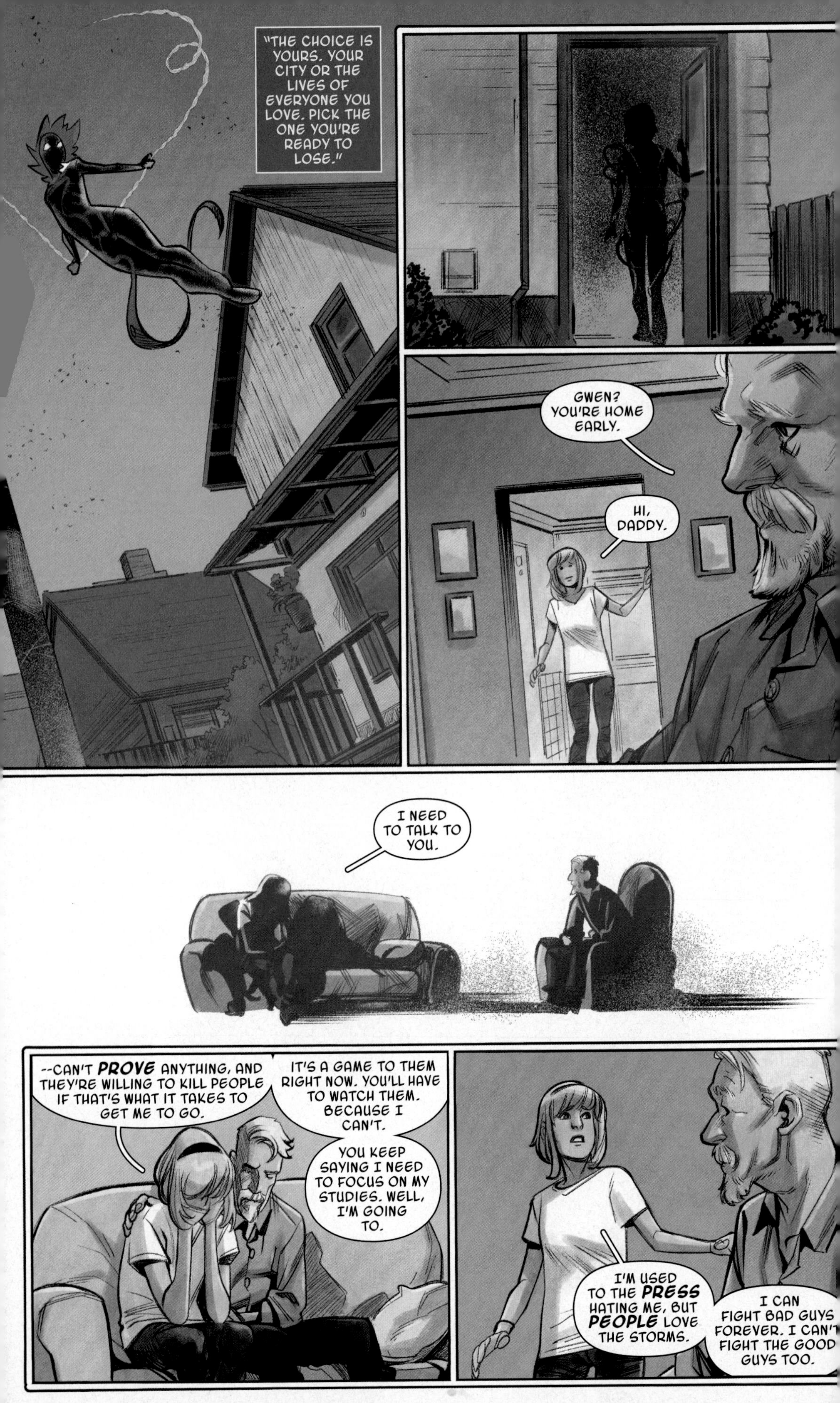
"THE CHOICE IS YOURS. YOUR CITY OR THE LIVES OF EVERYONE YOU LOVE. PICK THE ONE YOU'RE READY TO LOSE."
GWEN? YOU'RE HOME EARLY.
HI, DADDY.
I NEED TO TALK TO YOU.
--CAN'T PROVE ANYTHING, AND THEY'RE WILLING TO KILL PEOPLE IF THAT'S WHAT IT TAKES TO GET ME TO GO.
IT'S A GAME TO THEM RIGHT NOW. YOU'LL HAVE TO WATCH THEM. BECAUSE I CAN'T.
YOU KEEP SAYING I NEED TO FOCUS ON MY STUDIES. WELL, I'M GOING TO.
I'M USED TO THE PRESS HATING ME, BUT PEOPLE LOVE THE STORMS.
I CAN FIGHT BAD GUYS FOREVER. I CAN'T FIGHT THE GOOD GUYS TOO.

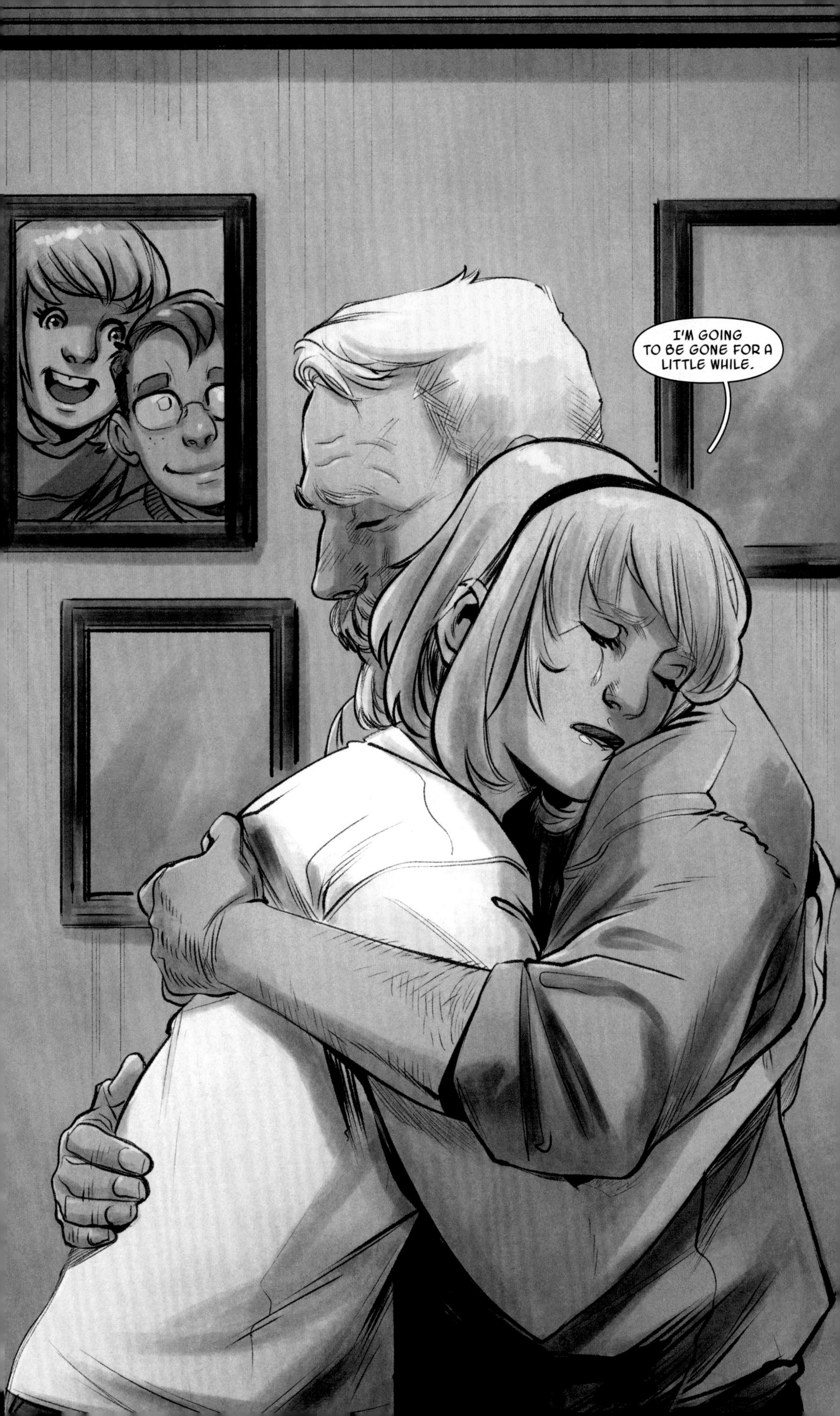
I'M GOING TO BE GONE FOR A LITTLE WHILE.

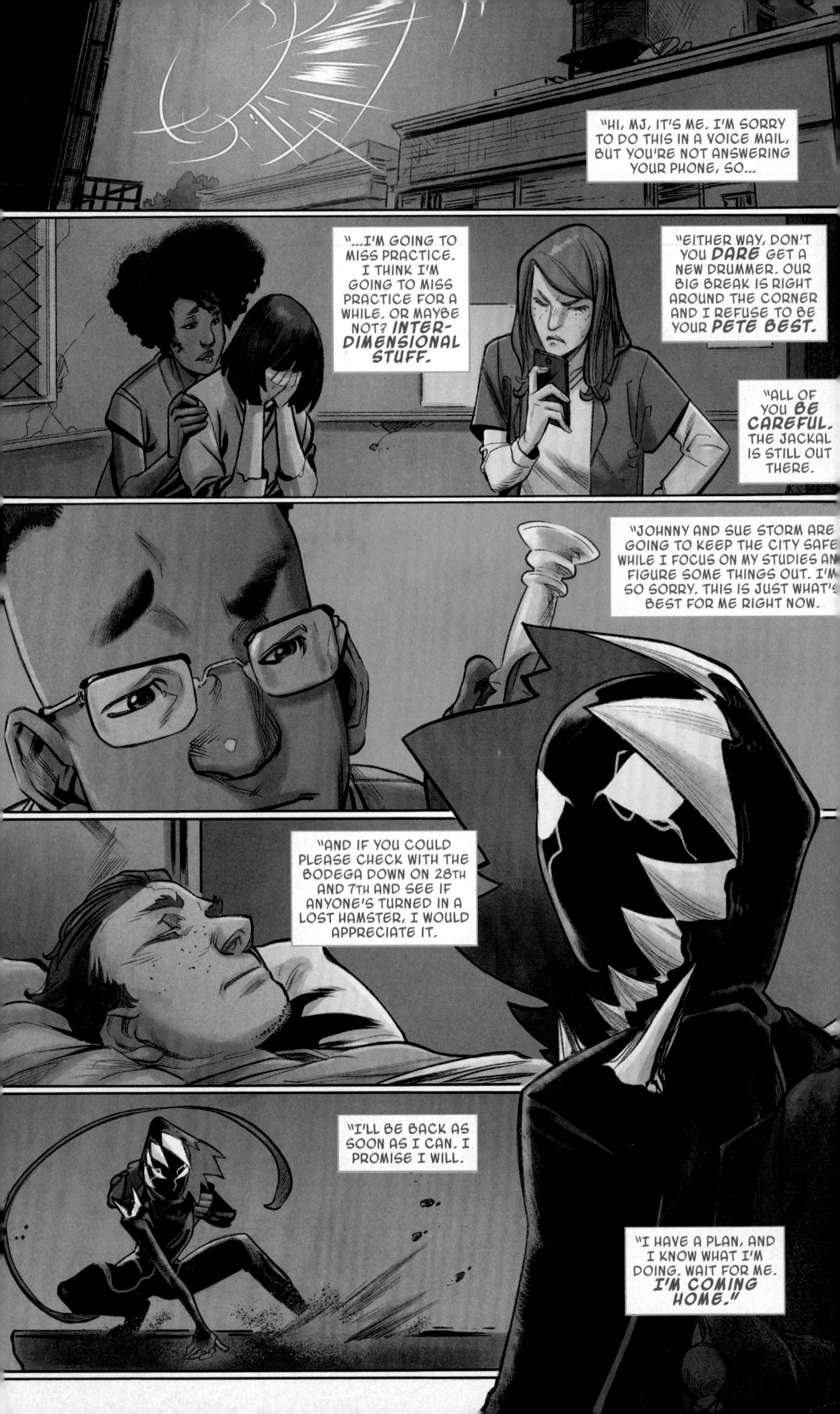
"HI, MJ, IT'S ME. I'M SORRY TO DO THIS IN A VOICE MAIL, BUT YOU'RE NOT ANSWERING YOUR PHONE, SO...
"...I'M GOING TO MISS PRACTICE. I THINK I'M GOING TO MISS PRACTICE FOR A WHILE. OR MAYBE NOT? INTER-DIMENSIONAL STUFF.
"EITHER WAY, DON'T YOU DARE GET A NEW DRUMMER. OUR BIG BREAK IS RIGHT AROUND THE CORNER AND I REFUSE TO BE YOUR PETE BEST.
"ALL OF YOU BE CAREFUL. THE JACKAL IS STILL OUT THERE.
"JOHNNY AND SUE STORM ARE GOING TO KEEP THE CITY SAFE WHILE I FOCUS ON MY STUDIES AN FIGURE SOME THINGS OUT. I'M SO SORRY. THIS IS JUST WHAT'S BEST FOR ME RIGHT NOW.
"AND IF YOU COULD PLEASE CHECK WITH THE BODEGA DOWN ON 28TH AND 7TH AND SEE IF ANYONE'S TURNED IN A LOST HAMSTER, I WOULD APPRECIATE IT.
"I'LL BE BACK AS SOON AS I CAN. I PROMISE I WILL.
"I HAVE A PLAN, AND I KNOW WHAT I'M DOING. WAIT FOR ME. I'M COMING HOME."

GWENCILS DOWN

o in here, out there, around the world and aboard all the
s at sea! Gweditor Devin Lewis reporting to you live and in
ls from the heart of the Multiverse—and in whichever corner
eality you're occupying presently, we hope you're doing so
ly and happily.

issue that you're reading right now is, of course, no ordinary
e of GHOST-SPIDER—if there ever was one. Because this
e of GHOST-SPIDER is the last of this arc and this particular
er-starring series.

as nearly two years ago that Seanan first pitched her take
Ghost-Spider—a raucous and rebellious romp through the
vel Multiverse with Gwen and her supporting cast at its core.
Seanan herself can say it best:

king on Ghost-Spider has been a literal dream come
e for me. As someone who grew up on Marvel Comics
whose first comic-related trauma was reading an old
k issue featuring the death of the original Gwen Stacy,
was a character I had always wanted to work with but
er expected to have the opportunity. And doing it, not
in ongoing canon, but also with this incredible team of
sts, colorists, letterers and editorial support was more
I could ever have expected.

as talking to a friend who writes for Marvel several
rs ago about my desire to write for them, and he said,
n't do it. Once you see how the sausage is made, you'll
them less." I was so afraid that he was right, but he
ldn't have been more wrong. Knowing how the sausage
nade just makes me want to stay in the factory forever.

n so proud of our team and the work we have done and
way we've been able to adapt to pressures both internal
external. (Learning to write around universe-spanning
nts is an adventure!) And I promise...you can't keep a
d ghost down.

n we kicked this volume off, it was a huge stroke of luck that we
able to enlist the artistic talents of none other than Takeshi
azawa, a comics superstar who illustrated the AWESOME series
DER-MAN LOVES MARY JANE and recently had a tremendous
on MS. MARVEL. Takeshi is one of the best in the biz and
ght such a sense of life and wonder into Gwen's world—and
such an air of menace to Miles Warren, A.K.A. the Jackal!

ting the chance to draw Gwen with this wonderfully
nted team was an amazing experience. Thank you to
nan for the exciting stories month after month, Ian for
impeccable color work, Rosi for saving my butt many
es over and the editorial team for their continued guidance
direction throughout. I will miss Gwen and hope to have
chance to continue with her adventures in the future.
nk you all for reading and supporting the book!

we were even luckier when Ig Guara's schedule opened up right
e were preparing to start work on the second arc of this series.

Ig's got such a great sense of style, drama and passion—he took
the story Seanan, Takeshi and Ian (more on him in a moment!)
had crafted and RAN with it! Ig is a master of edge-of-your-seat
adventure, and he knocked the entire second arc out of the park.
But why hear it from me? Here's Ig himself!

I had fallen in love with Gwen ever since I saw her. (The
powers of an amazing design!) Together with Miles Morales,
they have been my favorite characters for years! So when
the invite to work on the book came, I was literally jumping
and hugging my wife with happiness!

It has been a crazy, delightful ride. I have learned a lot
about storytelling and my own craft as I worked with this
incredibly talented team. If it were up to me, this book
would be going forever, as Gwen still has a lot to show us!

Thank you for reading this, and hope to see you all again!

But GHOST-SPIDER isn't a series printed in black and white!
No, sir (or madam), GHOST-SPIDER is printed in glorious CMYK
color, and who better to imbue Gwen and her world with those
colors than Ian Herring?! Another MS. MARVEL mainstay, Ian is
one of the most talented color artists in the industry today and
has such a unique approach to his work that asking him to join
us on GHOST-SPIDER was an easy call. From Ian:

These past twenty issues have been a thrill to be part of.
Thank you to Takeshi, who had brought me on along before
Gwen had fully transitioned into Ghost-Spider. I was lucky to
be able to have this journey with Seanan, Rosi, Ig, Clayton,
Devin, Danny & Lauren! The vibrant world of Earth-65
and Gwen's dimension-hopping antics kept me on my toes,
color-wise, but I'll always remember the touching scenes
between Gwen and her father the most. Thanks for reading,
and I hope we all get to see Ghost-Spider again soon!

So that's that, Gwen-thusiasts! Another arc and volume of your
favorite interdimensional adventure comes to a close.

You may well be asking yourself: What's next for Gwen Stacy? Is she
really going to leave her reality to the Storm siblings? And what
about the Jackal? She's still got to get him back to his home reality!

Well, keep your eyes peeled, True Believers, because we're already
hard at work on Gwen's next adventure—and the clues are in the
pages of our last few issues! We've got big plans for her, and she'll
be playing a part in some of our biggest stories in the coming
year—and it'll all have to do with what's unfolded in this very issue!

BUT I'VE ALREADY SAID TOO MUCH! I better close out this column
before I spoil [REDACTED].

Stay safe!
Devin
5.20.20

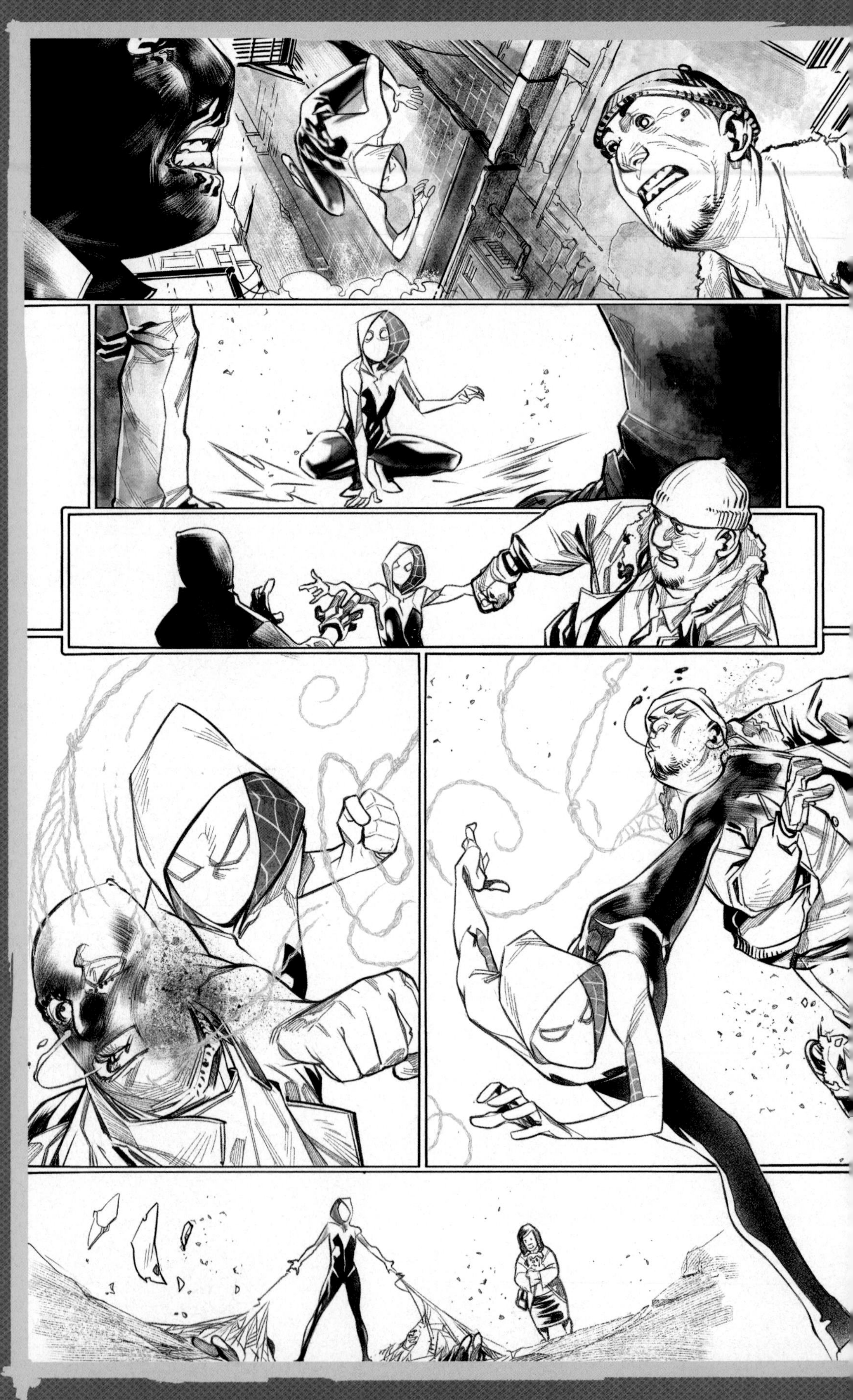

#7, page 17 art by **Ig Guara**

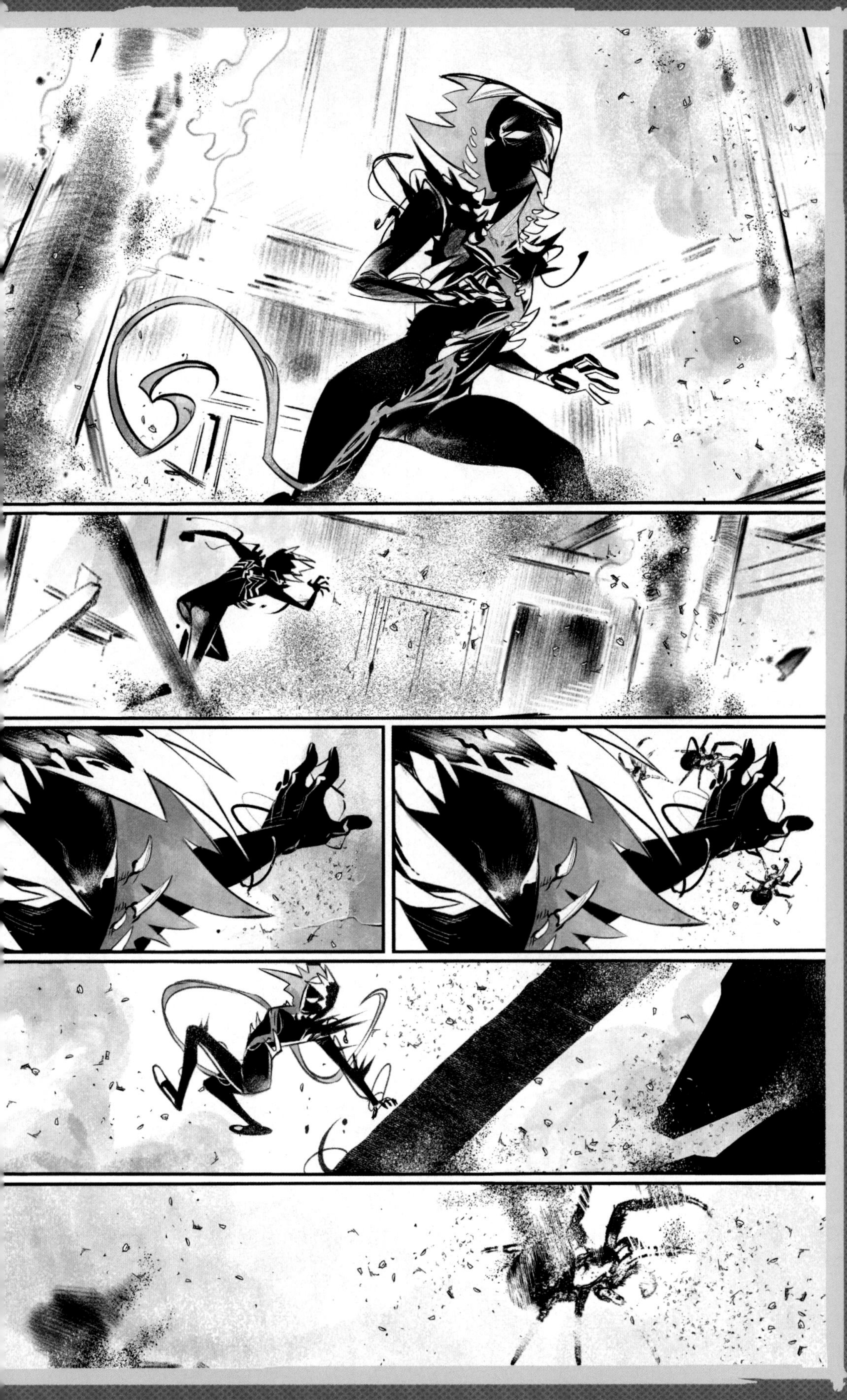

#8, page 15 art by Ig Guara

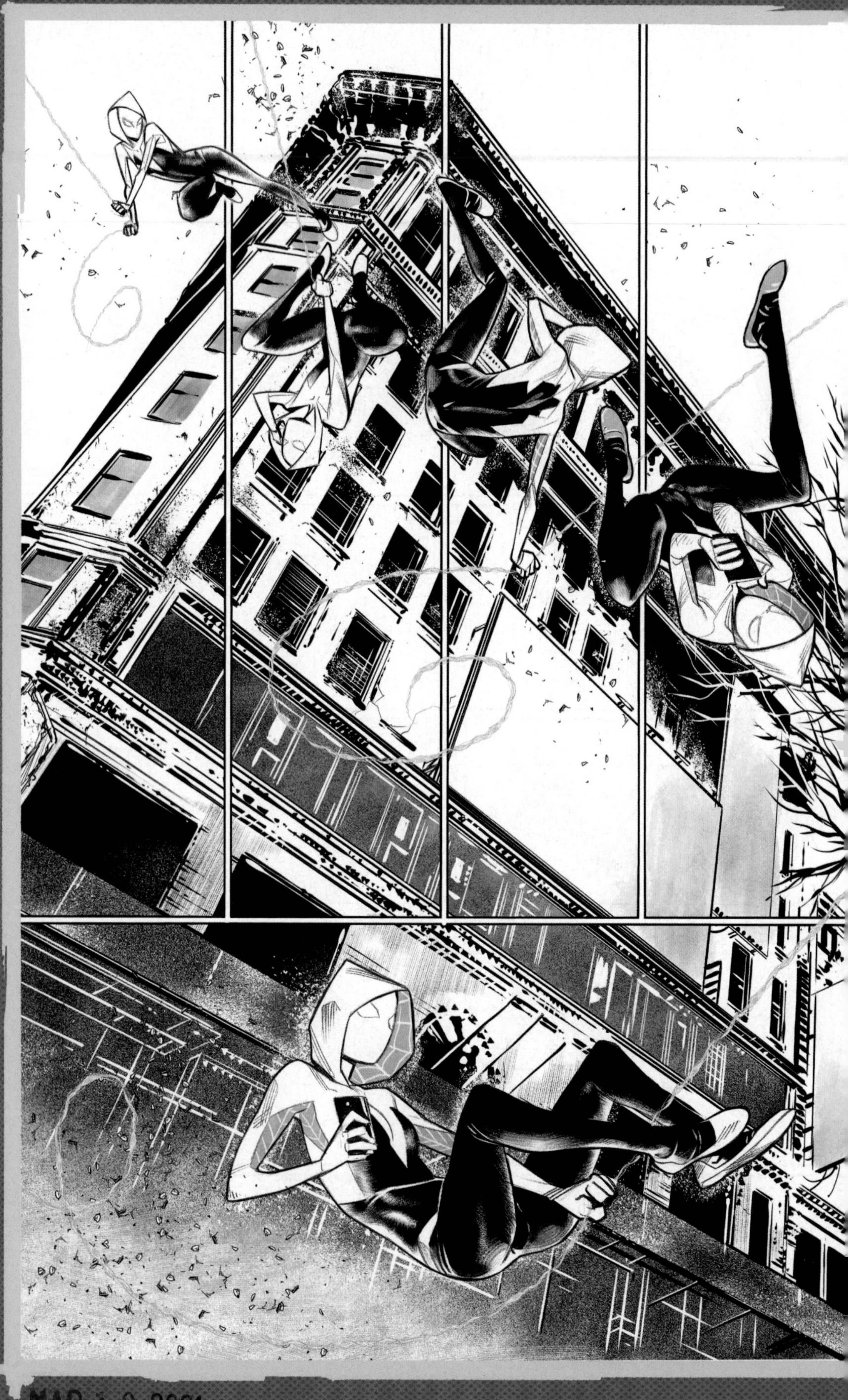

#9, page 7 art by **Ig Guara**